INTERNET 2020

The Twelfth International Conference on Evolving Internet

October 18 – 22, 2020

INTERNET 2020 Editors

Lin Han, Future Networks, Futurewei, USA

Printed from e-media with permission by:

Curran Associates, Inc.
57 Morehouse Lane
Red Hook, NY 12571

Some format issues inherent in the e-media version may also appear in this print version.

International Academy, Research, and Industry Association (IARIA)
412 Derby Way
Wilmington, DE 19810

Phone: (408) 893-6407
Fax: (408) 527-6351

petre@iaria.org

Additional copies of this publication are available from:

Curran Associates, Inc.
57 Morehouse Lane
Red Hook, NY 12571 USA
Phone: 845-758-0400
Fax: 845-758-2633
Email: curran@proceedings.com
Web: www.proceedings.com

Table of Contents

INTERNET 2020

Foreword

The Twelfth International Conference on Evolving Internet (INTERNET 2020), held between October 18–22, 2020, dealt with challenges raised by evolving Internet making use of the progress in different advanced mechanisms and theoretical foundations. The gap analysis aimed at mechanisms and features concerning the Internet itself, as well as special applications for software defined radio networks, wireless networks, sensor networks, or Internet data streaming and mining.

Originally designed in the spirit of interchange between scientists, the Internet reached a status where large-scale technical limitations impose rethinking its fundamentals. This refers to design aspects (flexibility, scalability, etc.), technical aspects (networking, routing, traffic, address limitation, etc), as well as economics (new business models, cost sharing, ownership, etc.). Evolving Internet poses architectural, design, and deployment challenges in terms of performance prediction, monitoring and control, admission control, extendibility, stability, resilience, delay-tolerance, and interworking with the existing infrastructures or with specialized networks.

We take here the opportunity to warmly thank all the members of the INTERNET 2020 Technical Program Committee, as well as the numerous reviewers. The creation of such a high quality conference program would not have been possible without their involvement. We also kindly thank all the authors who dedicated much of their time and efforts to contribute to INTERNET 2020. We truly believe that, thanks to all these efforts, the final conference program consisted of top quality contributions.

Also, this event could not have been a reality without the support of many individuals, organizations, and sponsors. We are grateful to the members of the INTERNET 2020 organizing committee for their help in handling the logistics and for their work to make this professional meeting a success.

We hope that INTERNET 2020 was a successful international forum for the exchange of ideas and results between academia and industry and for the promotion of progress in the field of the evolving internet.

INTERNET 2020 Chairs

INTERNET 2020 Steering Committee

Eugen Borcoci, University "Politehnica" of Bucharest (UPB), Romania
Dirceu Cavendish, Kyushu Institute of Technology, Japan
Przemyslaw (Przemek) Pochec, University of New Brunswick, Canada
Terje Jensen, Telenor, Norway
Parimala Thulasiraman, University of Manitoba - Winnipeg, Canada
Renwei (Richard) Li, Future Networks, Futurewei, USA

INTERNET 2020 Publicity Chair

Jose M. Jimenez, Universitat Politecnica de Valencia, Spain
Jose Luis García, Universitat Politecnica de Valencia, Spain

INTERNET 2020 Industry/Research Advisory Committee

Michael Bahr, Siemens AG Corporate Technology, Munich, Germany
Hanmin Jung, KISTI, Korea
Yung Ryn (Elisha) Choe, Sandia National Laboratories, Livermore, USA
Dirceu Cavendish, Kyushu Institute of Technology, Japan
Steffen Fries, Siemens AG, Germany
Terje Jensen, Telenor, Norway

INTERNET 2020

Committee

INTERNET 2020 Steering Committee

Eugen Borcoci, University "Politehnica" of Bucharest (UPB), Romania
Dirceu Cavendish, Kyushu Institute of Technology, Japan
Terje Jensen, Telenor, Norway
Parimala Thulasiraman, University of Manitoba - Winnipeg, Canada
Renwei (Richard) Li, Future Networks, Futurewei, USA
Przemyslaw (Przemek) Pochec, University of New Brunswick, Canada

INTERNET 2020 Publicity Chair

Jose M. Jimenez, Universitat Politecnica de Valencia, Spain
Jose Luis García, Universitat Politecnica de Valencia, Spain

INTERNET 2020 Industry/Research Advisory Committee

Michael Bahr, Siemens AG Corporate Technology, Munich, Germany
Hanmin Jung, KISTI, Korea
Yung Ryn (Elisha) Choe, Sandia National Laboratories, Livermore, USA
Dirceu Cavendish, Kyushu Institute of Technology, Japan
Steffen Fries, Siemens AG, Germany
Terje Jensen, Telenor, Norway

INTERNET 2020 Technical Program Committee

Majed Alowaidi, Majmaah University, Saudi Arabia
Mário Antunes, Polytechnic of Leiria & INESC-TEC, Portugal
Damian Arellanes Molina, UniversityofManchester, UK
Marcin Bajer, ABB Corporate Research Center Krakow, Poland
Driss Benhaddou, University of Houston, USA
Nik Bessis, Edge Hill University, UK
Maumita Bhattacharya, Charles Sturt University, Australia
Filippo Bianchini, Studio Legale Bianchini, Perugia, Italy
Eugen Borcoci, University "Politehnica" of Bucharest (UPB), Romania
Fernando Boronat Seguí, Universidad Politécnica De Valencia-Campus De Gandia, Spain
Christos Bouras, University of Patras, Greece
Matthew Butler, Bournemouth University, UK
Alina Buzachis, University of Messina, Italy
Lianjie Cao, Hewlett Packard Labs, USA
Dirceu Cavendish, Kyushu Institute of Technology, Japan
Hao Che, University of Texas at Arlington, USA

Mudasser F. Wyne, National University, USA
Zhicheng Yang, PingAn Tech - US Research Lab, USA
Ali Yavari, Swinburne University of Technology, Australia
Habib Zaidi, Geneva University Hospital, Switzerland
Huanle Zhang, University of California, Davis, USA

Copyright Information

For your reference, this is the text governing the copyright release for material published by IARIA.

The copyright release is a transfer of publication rights, which allows IARIA and its partners to drive the dissemination of the published material. This allows IARIA to give articles increased visibility via distribution, inclusion in libraries, and arrangements for submission to indexes.

I, the undersigned, declare that the article is original, and that I represent the authors of this article in the copyright release matters. If this work has been done as work-for-hire, I have obtained all necessary clearances to execute a copyright release. I hereby irrevocably transfer exclusive copyright for this material to IARIA. I give IARIA permission or reproduce the work in any media format such as, but not limited to, print, digital, or electronic. I give IARIA permission to distribute the materials without restriction to any institutions or individuals. I give IARIA permission to submit the work for inclusion in article repositories as IARIA sees fit.

I, the undersigned, declare that to the best of my knowledge, the article is does not contain libelous or otherwise unlawful contents or invading the right of privacy or infringing on a proprietary right.

Following the copyright release, any circulated version of the article must bear the copyright notice and any header and footer information that IARIA applies to the published article.

IARIA grants royalty-free permission to the authors to disseminate the work, under the above provisions, for any academic, commercial, or industrial use. IARIA grants royalty-free permission to any individuals or institutions to make the article available electronically, online, or in print.

IARIA acknowledges that rights to any algorithm, process, procedure, apparatus, or articles of manufacture remain with the authors and their employers.

I, the undersigned, understand that IARIA will not be liable, in contract, tort (including, without limitation, negligence), pre-contract or other representations (other than fraudulent misrepresentations) or otherwise in connection with the publication of my work.

Exception to the above is made for work-for-hire performed while employed by the government. In that case, copyright to the material remains with the said government. The rightful owners (authors and government entity) grant unlimited and unrestricted permission to IARIA, IARIA's contractors, and IARIA's partners to further distribute the work.

IoTSEAR: A System for Enforcing Access Control Rules with the IoT

Andreas Put

imec-DistriNet, KU Leuven
Leuven, Belgium
andreas.put@kuleuven.be

Bart De Decker

imec-DistriNet, KU Leuven
Leuven, Belgium
bart.dedecker@kuleuven.be

***Abstract*—Internet of Things (IoT) environments are composed of heterogeneous sensors and devices that collect and share contextual information. This data can improve the accuracy and usability of access control systems, as authentication and authorization requirements can be specified more precisely. However, certain security requirements need to be enforced in order to use such data in access control decision processes. In short, the data must be authentic, recent, and unforgeable. In this paper, we present a generic model for context, which takes *data-security* into account along with properties about the device, or context-source. Security-objects, such as message signatures, are modeled as *proofs*, which are verifiable, while information about the context-source, communication channel, and the data itself is captured as *meta-data*. This model allows an access control system to verify the authenticity and trustworthiness of context-data by (1) checking the presence of a specific proof and verifying it, and (2) analyzing the associated meta-data. It covers not only data from IoT sources, but also authorization and identity tokens. In addition, we present IoTSEAR, a middleware for trustworthy context-aware access control, which uses this model internally. Finally, we show performance results of our IoTSEAR prototype, which show that the overhead is low and that the system is usable even on commodity hardware.**

Keywords–Access Control, Security, Internet of Things

I. Introduction

The rapid advancement of computing technologies has led to the paradigm shift from static device configurations to dynamic ubiquitous environments. Such a shift brings with it opportunities and challenges. On the one hand, users demand access to software services or information resources in an anytime, anywhere fashion. On the other hand, access to such services or resources needs to be carefully controlled, due to the additional security challenges and threats coming with dynamically changing environments. Consider a home-care setting in which IoT technologies enable the elderly and patients recovering from invasive treatments to stay in their own home instead of a healthcare facility. In such an environment, automation capabilities can facilitate the homeowner's day-to-day activities, while caregivers provide routine care to the inhabitant. The home is equipped with a smart lock, which automatically opens to the caregiver if (1) the patient is present in the home, (2) the health care provider authenticates the caregiver when she scans her NFC badge, and (3) the visit was scheduled. The home is equipped with an access control server, which accesses patient's presence status through a presence detector. Furthermore, the healthcare facility operates a federated access control service through which an (authenticated) identity is obtained using the output from an NFC terminal, which is integrated in the smart lock. Finally this identity is used to verify whether the visit is scheduled.

The access controller is required to combine different types of contextual information, whose properties and origin are completely different. The calendar service could authenticate itself with an SSL certificate, and the information it provides can be signed, while the presence detector sends its information over a Bluetooth channel without additional security controls.

Using context information empowers access control systems with extra capabilities and flexibility. However, it also opens up new attack vectors. Therefore, the following issues have to be addressed: (1) identifying the context information and associated context sources that satisfy a set of security requirements for it to be used in the access control decision process; (2) defining policies to specify context-aware access permissions; (3) enforcing these access control policies.

In order to address the first issue, we have developed a generic model for context, taking into account the device, or context-source, that produces the context information and the environment it was collected in. In addition, abstractions in this model encapsulate both context generated from IoT environments, and by (third party) access control systems, such as authorization tokens and identity assertions. System designers are able to translate security requirements to a set of conditions on properties of this model. Examples of such requirements are: the context must originate from a trusted device (authenticity + integrity), the connection must be end-to-end secured, or the context must be explicitly linked to a specific person.

The second issue defines the requirement for a context-aware access-control policy language. IoTSEAR supports the PACCo policy language [1] by default. However, it can be extended so support other policy languages as well.

To address the third issue, we propose IoTSEAR, a context-aware access control middleware designed for IoT applications. The IoTSEAR middleware framework is designed with the same design principles in mind as the Priman framework [2]. Priman provides application developers with secure and privacy-friendly authentication mechanisms in a developer-friendly manner. It offers a generic, easy to use API with simple, intuitive concepts by isolating the security- and technology-specific details into configuration policies. This *separation of concerns* between application developers and security experts furthermore increases the manageability of systems, as service providers are able to modify authentication mechanisms at run-time, without requiring application code modifications. As IoTSEAR's design follows these principles, its implementation should result in a usable (from a developer's point of view), configurable (from a service provider's point of view), and extensible middleware. Moreover, while Priman is an authentication framework, IoTSEAR is a general access control middleware. It includes support for context-aware authorization, distributed authorization schemes and authentication schemes.

This work presents two main contributions:

- A generic model for context in an IoT-based access control setting. This model also encapsulates information related to data-security and data-origin, with which a third party is able to verify the authenticity and trustworthiness of the context information.
- The architecture, prototype implementation, and benchmarks of IoTSEAR, a system for enforcing access control rules in IoT environments.

This paper is structured as follows: Section II contains an overview of the related work, after which the generic model for context is explained in Section III. Furthermore, Section IV details the IoTSEAR middleware, which is discussed and evaluated in Section V.

II. Related Work

Automation is a central goal in many IoT ecosystems [3]. Several existing solutions [4] rely on cloud infrastructure to specify and enforce policies. Another cloud-based approach that defines intents and scopes on which these intents will have an effect is described in [5]. Besides academic initiatives, commercial solutions, like Google Cloud IoT [6], Home Assistant [7] and OpenRemote [8] offer intuitive cloud-based support to create automation rules. Similar to access control systems, a set of policy rules consisting of a set of conditions that must be fulfilled to trigger one or more actions are specified and enforced. However, the heterogeneity of IoT devices and the fact that many devices have low capabilities open new attack vectors [9]–[11]. An extensive access control framework to manage access to devices, however, is still missing [12].

Attribute-based access control (ABAC) [13] is a general purpose access control model which allows access rights to be constrained based on the attributes of subjects, objects, actions and the environment. In an ABAC policy, a logical expression consisting of attribute information is defined as a conditional rule. The applicability of such a policy to a request is determined by matching the attributes in the request and the environment to the attributes in the policy. The application of ABAC to the IoT has seen much interest in the last decade [14]. However, the potentially large amount of attributes required to establish dynamic policies is a challenge.

Capability-based access control (CapBAC) [15] defines a capability as a self contained key or token, that references a target object or resource along with an associated set of access rights. This allows for fine-grained, flexible access control, as holding such a token access to only those resources that are necessary for the holder's legitimate purpose. CapBAC has seen much interest in the IoT-sphere [16]–[19]. However, to our knowledge, no system exists that combines support for (1) attributes, capabilities and context in authorization, (2) dynamic verification controls for the used context, and (3) support for authentication into a complete access control middleware. IoTSEAR accomplishes this by building on previous work [1], [2], and with our context model (Section III), as all objects are internally handled as generic context structures.

PACCo [1] is a system that focuses on the secure and privacy-friendly collection of contextual information, after which capability tokens can be issued. Furthermore, a protocol is proposed in which *personal verifiable context* can be verified in a privacy-friendly, unlinkable, manner. This type of context allows a third party to cryptographically verify the authenticity and ownership of certain contextual information (i.e. the information is authentic and it belongs to the subject that makes the access request). The PACCo policy language, is a context-aware policy language which focuses on expressing rich context-based requirements and also considers the security requirements that appropriate context sources must adhere to. This policy language is used as the default policy language for the IoTSEAR implementation, in large part due to its capability to express such security constraints. However, the IoTSEAR architecture allows to support other policy languages as well.

III. A Generic Model for Contextual Information

In order to uniformly reason about different types of contextual information and their security properties, a generic model for context in access control is proposed in this section.

A. *Context in access control*

Abowd et al. [20] specifies a broad definition of *context*:

> "Any information that can be used to characterize the situation of an entity. This entity is a person, place, or object considered relevant to the interaction between a user and an application, including the user and applications themselves."

IoT environments produce a wide variety of information that is useful to take into account when making access control decisions. Some examples are: the current location of a subject, the proximity of a subject to a sensor or even to a specific person, the current time, etc. For access control systems, three context origins are clearly distinguishable:

a) IoT Device: The situation of an entity or environment is measured by, and accessible through IoT devices. For example, networked sensors and smart devices.

b) System state: The access controller's internal state is an important source of context, such as the current session information, connection type, internal database and clock.

c) Third party/Cloud Service: The information about a particular entity can be provided by a third party, such as a cloud service or a database. This information is often signed by the provider, and/or it is obtained through a secure, authenticated connection. Certificates, identity and authorization tokens are produced by these sources.

When access control systems consider not only *system state* information, but also information originating from *sensors* and *third party services*, they can enforce more context-rich policies. However, the context information that does not originate from the system itself should not be treated as trustworthy, but as *potentially faulty or even dangerous*. Indeed, the external context source (i.e. the sensor or third party) can

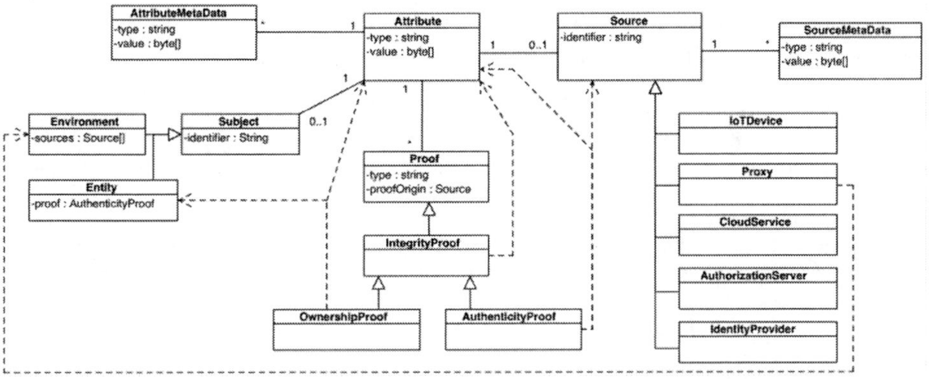

Figure 1. Model for context: the core element is *Attribute*, while *Source*, and *Proof* complete the set of the three most important elements.

be compromised, spoofed, or the context information could be forged or replayed. Therefore, it is essential that *context is validated before it is used in critical application functions*. Such validation strategies can range from simple input validation and error correction to integrity and authenticity validation, depending on the use case.

B. Context Model

In order to uniformly reason about different types of contextual information, their security requirements and the validation thereof, a generic model for contextual information is proposed. This model defines the concept of "contextual information" as an *Attribute*. This element has a variety of (optional) associated elements, that are dependent on the manner of context collection, or the environment in which the context is collected. Different validation strategies are possible depending on the availability of certain optional elements. The generic model for context is illustrated in Fig. 1.

Attribute: The core of the model is the *Attribute* element, which has a `value` and an `type` field. The *value* represents the raw output from the attribute's *Source*. This can range from a sensor-reading to an identity assertion or an authorization token. The *type* determines the actual type of the attribute, which also implies the encoding. The Attribute is the model's core, all other elements are optional. Attributes can have associated *AttributeMetaData* elements. This element also has a `type` and `value` fields. Examples of AttributeMetaData are: the time when the attribute is collected, the accuracy of a sensor reading, or other information related to the Attribute.

The Attribute is related to a *Subject*, which is either an *Entity*, or an *Environment*. Each distinct subject has a unique `identifier`. An *Environment* is characterized by the set of `sources` that are active in this particular environment. *Entities* represent people (or their personal device). An Entity contains a `proof` field, which is used to verify the authenticy of the Subject's identifier (see *Proof* paragraph below).

Source: A *Source* is either an *IoTDevice* (sensor, actuator, smart device), but it can also be a *Proxy*, *CloudService AuthorizationServer*, or an *IdentityProvider*. A *Proxy* acts similar to network proxy for a set of IoT devices (i.e. an *Environment*). Every source is uniquely identified by its `identifier` field. Similar to the Attribute element, the Source can have associated *SourceMetaData*. Examples are: the source's owner, operator, location, software version, device attestation status, etc.

Proof: The model supports three *Proof* kinds: *OwnershipProof*, *AuthenticityProof* and *IntegrityProof*. Each proof has a `type` field, which has a similar function to the attribute's type. A *Proof* has a `proofOrigin` field, which verifiably links it to its source. In addition, *Proxies* are able to add proofs and meta-data to the context structures that it relays. However, this depends on the scenario and system configuration.

Attributes that are used to establish an authenticated identity (e.g. [id='Alice', location='room123']) must contain an *OwnershipProof*, which links an *Attribute* to a specific *Entity* in a verifiable manner. For example, proving ownership of a certificate (and the attributes it contains) is done by proving knowledge of the certificate's private key, i.e. by signing a nonce. Note that a protocol for capable IoT devices (e.g., smartphone, proxy device) to create ownership proofs of contextual information is detailed in [1]. An *AuthenticityProof* allows to verify whether a specific source produced an attribute (e.g., a message signature). Finally, the *IntegrityProof* shows that the attribute value has not been modified or corrupted. Note that both Ownership- and AuthenticityProof are IntegrityProofs.

C. Instances of the context-model

To illustrate the flexibility of the generic model for context, it is applied to two distinct context types, which are extracted from the scenario illustrated in the introduction: (1) a simple Bluetooth beacon reading (presence context), and (2) a SAML [21] identity assertion (authenticated identity).

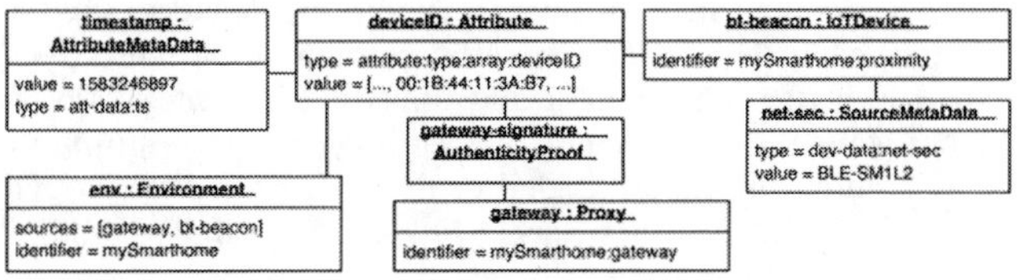

Figure 2. The context model applied to a proximity sensor reading

Fig. 2 shows the modeled context from a proximity sensor (e.g., a Bluetooth beacon). All types and identifiers, and their implications (value-encoding, device configuration, supported Attribute- and Source-MetaData types) are known to the system. In this example, the `deviceID` attribute has a `timestamp` as meta data, while the associated source (`bt-beacon`) has associated meta data detailing the wireless network security properties: *BLE-SM1L2*, or Bluetooth Low Energy, security mode 1 level 2, meaning 'unauthenticated pairing with encryption'. The environment in which the attribute is collected (`env`) is a room consisting of `bt-beacon` and `gateway`, a device which acts as a proxy to `bt-beacon`.

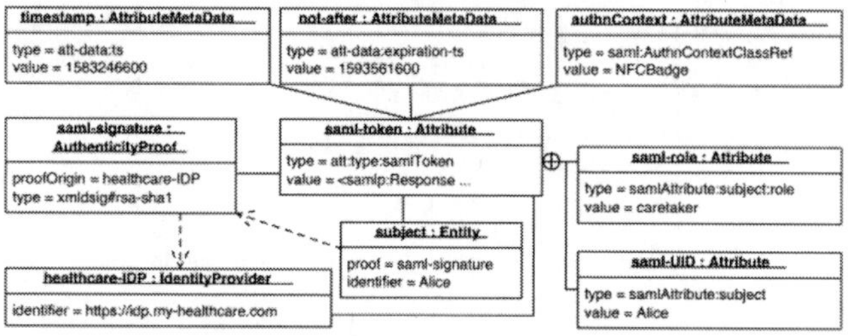

Figure 3. The context model applied to a SAML identity assertion

Fig. 3 shows the modeled context from a SAML response, received from a third party identity provider (`healthcare-IDP`). The value of the main attribute, `saml-token`, is the full content of the SAML response. This response asserts the values of two identity-attributes: 'subject=Alice' and 'role=caretaker'. The meta data attributes (`timestamp`, `not-after`, `authnContext`) are extracted from the raw SAML response, as is the `saml-signature`, which is modeled as an *AuthenticityProof*.

IV. IoTSEAR

The IoTSEAR middleware has two main responsibilities: managing contextual information and enforcing context aware access control rules.

A. Context management

Gathering context information is done by accessing IoT sensors, cloud services, and processing identity- and authorization-tokens. When IoTSEAR receives context data, it creates a *context structure* that conforms to the context model using the received data itself and known information about the environment, its devices and network properties. Fig. 4 illustrates three different ways of context collection. The middleware can process third party objects from a cloud service, identity provider (IDP) or authorization server (AS). Furthermore, part of the middleware can run on capable IoT devices, such as a smartphone. The IoTSEAR software running on these devices will read the sensor data and construct a context structure conforming to the model. Depending on the configuration, verification proofs are added to this structure. Proxy devices function similarly: they access the sensor readings, create the context structure, and (optionally) add a verification proof. Additionally, devices running the full middleware can act as a Proxy in addition to Identity Provider and Authorization Server.

Context DB is the database containing all context structures. Note that most types of contextual information have a limited lifetime. Hence, this database is regularly pruned of old context structures. The second database, *Environment DB*, contains information from which the SourceMetaData is constructed. Moreover, this database is initialized with all required verification objects: certificates, shared keys, and trust-relationships.

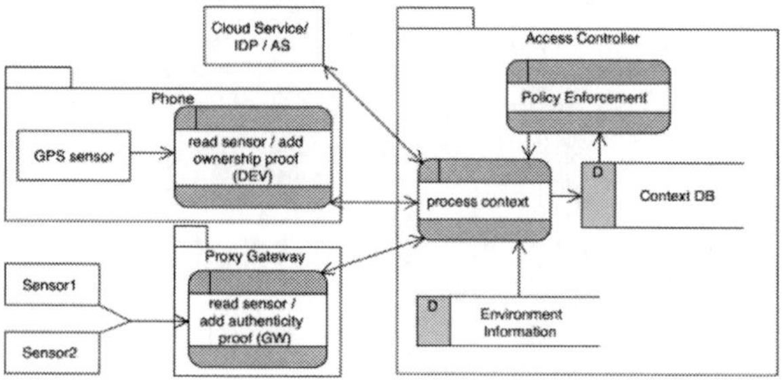

Figure 4. Context processing for three distinct sources.

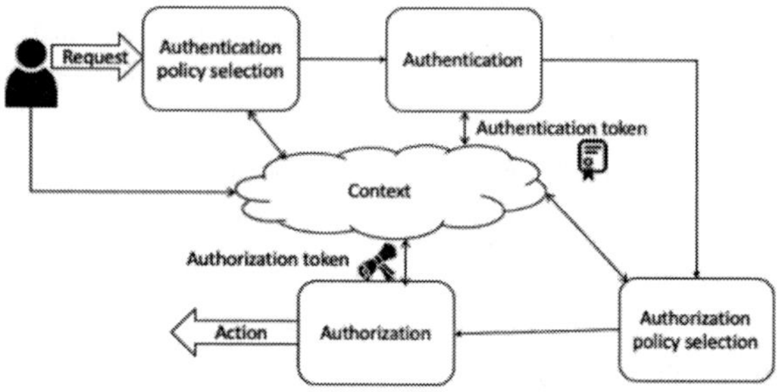

Figure 5. Context aware authentication and authorization

During *Policy Enforcement*, the middleware analyses the set of applicable policies. The necessary context structures are retrieved from *Context DB*. Absent context structures can be created at run-time by accessing the appropriate sources, after which all information is known to enforce the policies.

B. Context aware Authentication and Authorization

The typical IoTSEAR transaction is divided in four stages (see Fig. 5). The system has access to a set of context structures, represented in the figure by the 'context cloud'. The first stage starts when the system receives a request from a user. An appropriate authentication policy is selected based on the user's claimed identity. Here, the system can determine that stronger authentication is appropriate (e.g., two factor authentication), or that a more relaxed authentication is suitable, using predefined rules specified in policies. Note that the request itself also produces contextual information (i.e. session info), which can be used in the next steps, or subsequent transactions.

Biometric context and identity objects from third parties can be involved in the authentication phase. Afterwards, the system will produce a new *Authentication token*. These two steps can be skipped in case the user already authenticated, or authentication/identification is not necessary.

The authorization policy selection occurs analogous to the authentication policy selection. After the desired policies have been selected, their conditions are evaluated. The actions associated with those policies whose condition is satisfied are allowed or denied, according to the *policy effect*. Finally, when approved, an authorization token is created.

C. Architecture

The high-level architecture of the access control middleware is shown in Fig. 6. Applications interact with the middleware by inserting a *policy enforcement point* (PEP) in their code. This is a code block in which a a policy decision request is sent to the middleware, or more specifically, to a *policy decision point* (PDP). The PDP can be located on a different device or network. The request contains information, such as the type of event (e.g., an access request, an authentication request, etc.) and the (claimed) identity of the subject. The high-level architecture of IoTSEAR is divided in three main components:

a) Abstraction layer: In this layer, the abstractions and APIs used by developers are defined. In addition, the mechanisms with which the plugins are loaded, initialized and configured are implemented in this layer.

b) Plugin Layer: This layer encapsulates the plugins and extensions that are available. These plugins contain the actual functionality implementations of the IoTSEAR middleware.

c) Middleware Configuration: This component contains the environment-specific configurations, and the middleware configuration settings. Policy mappings enable the middleware to load the correct plug-ins with identifiers found in the policies.

The main APIs for application developers are located in the *abstraction layer*. This layer defines the interfaces to which each plugin must comply. The *Context Model* component is also located in this layer. Next, the API, abstractions and plug-in managers for a *PDP, Policy Engine and Policy Repository* are defined in this layer. These three components are responsible for policy selection and authorization. The *Authentication Engine*, on the other hand, is responsible for loading and executing the correct authentication plugin.

The *Plugin-layer* contains the plugins that are active in the system. The *Crypto primitives* component contains implementations for cryptographic operations, such as the different encryption, hashing and signature algorithms that are required to perform authentication, and to verify context structure. The *PDP implemenations* component contains, as the name suggests, implementations for different PDPs. Different PDPs (e.g., LocalPDP, TlsPDP, ...") support different communication methods (e.g., through a local or a TLS socket). The *Policy Rules* component contains the implementation of every condition and matching function in the policy language (see [1]). Hence, extending the policy language can be accomplished by defining a new plugin. Using the same strategy, it is also possible to support a completely different policy language. The *authentication protocols* component contains the extensions that execute a specific authentication protocol. This component, together with the *Authentication Engine* originates from the Priman Framework [2] (with minor adaptations).

V. Discussion and Practical Evaluation

This section entails a discussion on how contextual security requirements are enforced by IoTSEAR in addition to a performance analysis of the middleware.

A. Enforcing security requirements

In order to enforce security requirements on context used in access control decisions, the PACCo policy language [1] allows policy conditions to be labeled with a *security attribute*. This security attribute corresponds to a set of security requirements to which the used context must comply.

One possible security attribute configuration is inspired by the Eurosmart Security Assurance levels [22]:

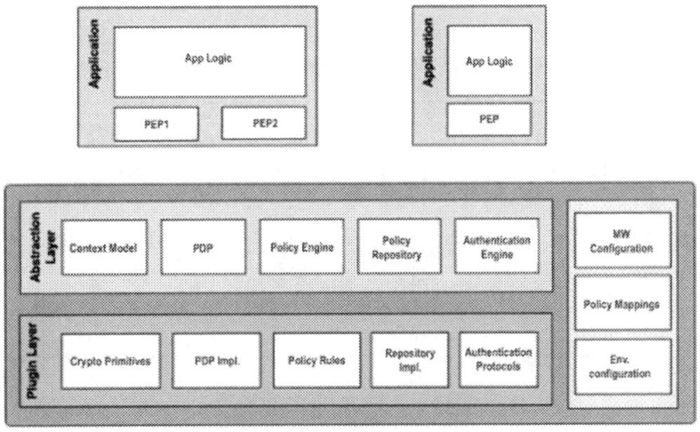

Figure 6. IoTSEAR Architecture

Basic: Minimize the basic risks of incidents.
Substantial: Minimize the known risks, and the risk of incidents carried out by actors with limited skills and resources.
High: Minimize the risk of state-of-the-art attacks carried out by actors with significant skills and resources.

These descriptions must be translated to a set of requirements on properties of a *context structure*. For example, *basic* can require that the context *Source* is trusted, i.e. the `Source identifier` is in a list of trusted sources

The level *substantial* can require the usage of a secure network, and an authenticity proof in addition to the *basic* requirements. Network information can be accessed through the *SourceMetaData*. A whitelist of allowed network types must be known, analogous to the list of trusted device identifiers. This is also the case for the whitelist of allowed proof types.

The level *high* can require that the software of the context source has no known bugs, that device attestation has been recently performed, in addition to the *substantial* requirements. The new requirements, however, require the used whitelists to be regularly updated.

The IoTSEAR middleware allows the definition and enforcement of custom security requirements. This requires a new plug-in to be created for each custom security attribute. Every plug-in implements a single method, which has one parameter, the *context structure*, and returns a boolean. Note that all elements in the model are accessible through the context structure. The security-attribute plugins are loaded based on the name of the security attribute in a policy, and checked by calling the single implemented method provided with the appropriate context structure as argument.

B. Practical evaluation

The IoTSEAR prototype is implemented in Java, and was tested on a machine with a 2,3 GHz Intel Core i5 processor and 16GB RAM. All test have been performed 100 times, and the (in memory) *ContextDB* contains 100 000 context structures. We show the average values in milliseconds (standard deviation is noted between parentheses).

The first test measures the processing of a context structure. Consider a worst case scenario, in which a SAML token is processed. Our test token contained 7KB of XML data, which is parsed and verified (SHA265 with RSA2048). Next, the context

TABLE I. PERFORMANCE RESULTS BASED ON THE AMOUNT OF POLICIES AND VERIFIED CONTEXT STRUCTURES (CS).

# policies / CS	Abs. Layer	CS Verif.	Evaluation	**Total**
10 / 1	1 (0)	16 (3)	4 (0)	**21**
40 / 1	1 (0)	67 (5)	7 (0)	**75**
100 / 1	2 (1)	180 (9)	11 (0)	**193**
10 / 10	2 (0)	198 (11)	16 (1)	**216**
40 / 10	4 (2)	760 (32)	54 (3)	**818**
100 / 10	7 (3)	1902 (93)	143 (9)	**2052**

structure is created and serialized using Google's protocol buffer [23]. This whole process takes 34 ms (6).

Table I shows the evaluation times for sets of simple and complex policies. The first policies that are evaluated are simple and pose two constraints: "subject=randomID" and "role=manager", which are evaluated using one SAML context structure. Next, complex policies are evaluated, which have additional constraints and require 10 context structures to evaluate. For both the simple and complex policies, the used context must adhere to the *high security level*. Using the example from Section V-A, this requires (for each CS) four SourceMetaData values to be matched to a whitelist, timestamp verification, and the verification of one AuthenticityProof (SHA265 with RSA2048 signature). The overhead introduced by the *Abstraction Layer* is minimal, while the verification of the *context structures (CS)* requires the most time. This is mainly due to the signature verification, which occurs 1000 times (100 x 10 structure) in the heaviest test. The amount of context structures to verify (and their verification requirements) have a large impact, but optimizations such as multi-threaded or ahead-of-time CS verification are possible.

Consider the scenario from the introduction, where a caregiver is given access to a patient's home if (1) the patient is present, (2) the health care provider authenticated the caregiver when she scans her badge, and (3) the visit was scheduled. Only one policy is evaluated, as it can be uniquely targeted by the access request (subject=*caregiver-id*, action=*door:open*). The healthcare-IDP is consulted at run-time, and has a response-time of 1 second. Taking this into account, it takes 1052 ms (4) to make this access control decision (of which 1021 is used to request and verify the context from the healthcare-IDP).

VI. CONCLUSIONS

This paper presented a generic model for context and described IoTSEAR, a middleware for context-aware access control. IoTSEAR uses the current context to select the most appropriate authentication and authorization policies. In doing so, the dynamic adaptation of the access control mechanism is facilitated. Furthermore, the security requirements of the used context can be precisely tailored to any given application, and are automatically enforced by the middleware. Finally, our performance tests showed that the overhead is limited, and that the middleware is suitable for commodity hardware.

REFERENCES

[1] A. Put and B. De Decker, "Attribute-based privacy-friendly access control with context," in International Conference on E-Business and Telecommunications. Springer, 2016, pp. 291–315.

[2] A. Put, I. Dacosta, M. Milutinovic, and B. De Decker, "Priman: facilitating the development of secure and privacy-preserving applications," in IFIP International Information Security Conference. Springer, 2014, pp. 403–416.

[3] C. Perera, A. Zaslavsky, P. Christen, and D. Georgakopoulos, "Context aware computing for the internet of things: A survey," IEEE communications surveys & tutorials, vol. 16, no. 1, 2013, pp. 414–454.

[4] H. Derhamy, J. Eliasson, J. Delsing, and P. Priller, "A survey of commercial frameworks for the internet of things," in 2015 IEEE 20th Conference on Emerging Technologies & Factory Automation (ETFA). IEEE, 2015, pp. 1–8.

[5] S. Nastic, S. Sehic, M. Vögler, H.-L. Truong, and S. Dustdar, "Patricia–a novel programming model for iot applications on cloud platforms," in 2013 IEEE 6th International Conference on Service-Oriented Computing and Applications. IEEE, 2013, pp. 53–60.

[6] Google cloud iot. Accessed on 06-10-2020. [Online]. Available: https://cloud.google.com/solutions/iot/

[7] Home assistant. Accessed on 06-10-2020. [Online]. Available: https://www.home-assistant.io/

[8] Openremote. Accessed on 06-10-2020. [Online]. Available: https://openremote.io/

[9] R. Roman, P. Najera, and J. Lopez, "Securing the internet of things," Computer, no. 9, 2011, pp. 51–58.

[10] Q. Jing, A. V. Vasilakos, J. Wan, J. Lu, and D. Qiu, "Security of the internet of things: perspectives and challenges," Wireless Networks, vol. 20, no. 8, 2014, pp. 2481–2501.

[11] G. Ho, D. Leung, P. Mishra, A. Hosseini, D. Song, and D. Wagner, "Smart locks: Lessons for securing commodity internet of things devices," in Proceedings of the 11th ACM on Asia conference on computer and communications security. ACM, 2016, pp. 461–472.

[12] M. Hossain, R. Hasan, and A. Skjellum, "Securing the internet of things: A meta-study of challenges, approaches, and open problems," in 2017 IEEE 37th International Conference on Distributed Computing Systems Workshops (ICDCSW). IEEE, 2017, pp. 220–225.

[13] E. Yuan and J. Tong, "Attributed based access control (abac) for web services," in IEEE International Conference on Web Services (ICWS'05). IEEE, 2005.

[14] A. Ouaddah, H. Mousannif, A. A. Elkalam, and A. A. Ouahman, "Access control in the internet of things: Big challenges and new opportunities," Computer Networks, vol. 112, 2017, pp. 237–262.

[15] L. Gong et al., "A secure identity-based capability system." in IEEE symposium on security and privacy, 1989, pp. 56–63.

[16] F. Malamateniou, M. Themistocleous, A. Prentza, D. Papakonstantinou, and G. Vassilacopoulos, "A context-aware, capability-based, role-centric access control model for iomt," in International Conference on Wireless Mobile Communication and Healthcare. Springer, 2016, pp. 125–131.

[17] D. Hussein, E. Bertin, and V. Frey, "A community-driven access control approach in distributed iot environments," IEEE Communications Magazine, vol. 55, no. 3, 2017, pp. 146–153.

[18] D. Hussein, E. Bertin, and V. Frey, "A community-driven access control approach in distributed iot environments," IEEE Communications Magazine, vol. 55, no. 3, 2017, pp. 146–153.

[19] S. Pal, M. Hitchens, V. Varadharajan, and T. Rabehaja, "Policy-based access control for constrained healthcare resources in the context of the internet of things," Journal of Network and Computer Applications, vol. 139, 2019, pp. 57–74.

[20] G. D. Abowd, A. K. Dey, P. J. Brown, N. Davies, M. Smith, and P. Steggles, "Towards a better understanding of context and context-awareness," in International symposium on handheld and ubiquitous computing. Springer, 1999, pp. 304–307.

[21] S. Cantor, J. Kemp, N. R. Philpott, and E. Maler, "Assertions and protocols for the oasis security assertion markup language," OASIS Standard (March 2005), 2005, pp. 1–86.

[22] Eurosmart iot certification scheme. Accessed on 06-10-2020. [Online]. Available: https://www.eurosmart.com/eurosmart-iot-certification-scheme/

[23] Protocol buffers. Accessed on 06-10-2020. [Online]. Available: https://developers.google.com/protocol-buffers/

Enabling Defensive Deception by Leveraging Software Defined Networks

Ilias Belalis*, Georgios Kavallieratos†, Vasileios Gkioulos†, Georgios Spathoulas †
*Department of Computer Science and Biomedical Informatics
University of Thessaly
Lamia, Greece
ibelalis@uth.gr
†Department of Information Security and Communications Technology
Norwegian University of Science and Technology
Gjøvik, Norway
{georgios.kavallieratos, vasileios.gkioulos, georgios.spathoulas}@ntnu.no

***Abstract*—Computer networks are critical for modern society and protecting their security is of high importance. Due to their increasing size and complexity providing the required cyber security counter measures has become a very difficult task. One of the most recent approaches is to employ defensive deception techniques, in order to provide to the attacker a false perception about the protected network and thus increase the effort that is needed to carry on a successful intrusion. In this paper we present a comprehensive literature review and a comparison of existing SDN based defensive deception methods. Additionally, we propose a novel deception mechanism that combines moving target and honeypots approaches and carry out extensive tests of its functionality.**

***Index Terms*—network security, SDN, deception, defense, moving target, honeypots**

I. Introduction

Nowadays, the complexity of computer networks and our dependence on them are continuously increasing, also projected as increasing system interconnections and interdependencies [1]. Networking becomes imperative, even across previously isolated domains such as critical infrastructures, due to fundamental data flows that are essential for accomplishing novel functionalities and business models. Nevertheless, this practice enables additional attack vectors, not only from novel attacks but also from those that are considered common within ICT. A plethora of cyber-attacks, such as Distributed Denial of Service (DDoS) is reported daily. These attacks target computer networks to compromise devices and execute malicious actions [2]. Although various works in the literature aim to mitigate such attacks [3], [4] the complexity and heterogeneity of the networks impede the implementation of traditional techniques.

Software-Defined Networks (SDN) are a novel technology aiming to facilitate the management and the programming of large-scale networks. Notably, the control and data planes are grouped in traditional networks. In a more flexible approach, the SDN technology separates the control plane from the data plane and enables the programmability of the network. Thus, the routers and the switches can be programmed via the control plane and therefore, the network management and evolution are better facilitated. Furthermore, computer network challenges such as resilience, scalability, performance, security and dependability can also be addressed by SDN technology.

In this article, we argue that the combination of existing defensive deception techniques and the dynamicity provided by the SDN technology can be utilised for enhancing the security, the robustness and the scalability of contemporary computer networks. Furthermore, the dynamic reprogramming of the network and the monitoring of the data flows are impractical by leveraging existing defensive deception techniques such as honeypots and Moving Target Defense (MTD). On the other hand, SDN allows overcoming such limitations and enables the implementation of defensive deception techniques.

The contribution of this work is twofold:

- A comprehensive survey of existing defensive deception techniques on SDN technology is provided. The analysis is focused on the most prominent techniques considering five distinct properties.
- A Defensive Deception mechanism based on SDN technology is presented. This mechanism aims at misleading malicious activities in a computer network by presenting a virtual network topology and hiding the real network along with possible vulnerabilities that attackers can exploit. Furthermore, by using this Defensive Deception mechanism defenders are able to track malicious activities in time and respond before adversaries are able to succeed in their attacks.

The rest of the paper is structured as follows : Section II presents related work while Section III discusses SDN technology and defensive deception techniques in general. The two main sections of the paper are Section IV which thoroughly analyses and compares current state of the art methods for SDN based defensive deception and Section V which presents the proposed novel defensive deception mechanism. Finally, Section VI presents the results obtained through experiments and Section VII discusses our conclusions.

II. Related work

Various approaches exist in the literature analyzing the application of defensive deception techniques in contemporary systems and networks. Hoffman et al. in [5] proposed a framework to identify potential attacks and defence mechanisms in repudiation systems. Furthermore, Jajodia et al. in [6] analyzed the implementation of the moving target defence technique in order to protect modern computer networks. Nevertheless, the implementation of MTD on SDN by leveraging its capabilities is not considered. Furthermore, Lei et al. in [7] conducted a survey on different moving target defence techniques. Through their work, they analyzed the design principles and system architecture of MTD. Ward et al. in [8] provide an overview of different cyber moving target techniques, their threat models and their technical details. However, none of the previous works has focused on the MTD implementation on SDN. Additionally, the SDN implementations and capabilities have been studied in the literature. Specifically, Rowshanrad et al. in [9] analyzed the different SDN application and different southbound interfaces, also discussing potential SDN applications on Cloud, wireless, and mobile networks. In addition, a comprehensive survey for the SDN has been conducted by Kreutz et al. in [1]. Although various surveys examined the SDN technology, none of them has considered it in combination with the implementation of defensive deception techniques in their architectures and how such techniques affect the security in contemporary networks. Further, the application of defensive deception techniques has been studied extensively [10]–[21]. These are analyzed in detail in Section IV towards the identification of the most appropriate defensive deception mechanism explained and applied in Sections V and VI respectively.

III. Background

In this section, the basic notions on SDN technology and defensive deception techniques are presented.

A. SDN Technology

Traditional networks consist of a three-layer architecture; (i) Data plane, (ii) control plane and (iii) management plane where the last two layers are to some extent considered as one [1]. In particular, the data plane consists of the necessary network devices that are responsible for data forwarding. Further, the control plane contains network protocols that are used by network devices while the management plane consists of the software services which enable the remote monitoring and configuration of the network. Various management and configuration challenges arise from this architectural paradigm since deploying elaborate policies and adjusting the network in case of faults and changes can become cumbersome.

SDN proposes a different network architecture where different abstraction layers facilitate network management and configuration. The motivation behind SDN technology is to differentiate the control from the data plane. Particularly, SDN technology was proposed a couple of years ago, where both academia and industry were trying to build programmable networks. Two distinct approaches have been proposed in [22], [23] for active networks: (1) programmable switches and (2) capsules. Further, different approaches have arisen regarding programmable networks [24]–[27]. Recent initiatives such as ForCES [28], OpenFlow [29] and POF [30] have been described in [1]. These approaches propose the separation of the control plane from the data plane without significant adjustments to the network's infrastructure. Furthermore, one of the major approaches in the field of network virtualization was presented in [31] in the Tempest project. In particular, this project proposed the concept of switches in ATM networks in order to facilitate network management, allowing the ATM networks to communicate under the same physical resources. Further, different projects such as Planet lab [32], MBone [33], GENI [34], and VINI [35] proposed architectures for virtual network topologies. SDN technology arose by the OpenFlow work at Stanford University, CA, USA [36].

According to Kreutz et al. in [1], the forwarding state of the data plane is managed by a remotely controlled plane in SDN architecture. Further, eight different layers have been developed in the SDN architecture. These are listed below:

- Network Infrastructure: Different physical systems are installed which are responsible for forwarding packets.
- Southbound Interface: The connections between control and forwarding elements, which is one of the major SDN's advantages, are represented.
- Network Hypervisor: Using contemporary virtualization tools, SDN can virtualize machines and typologies to share the same hardware components.
- Network Operating Systems – NOS: Programmed APIs which provide services to the programmers in order to facilitate the network management. Through NOS, programmers are able to control APIs to generate the network configuration according to specific policies.
- Northbound Interface: A software system which promotes the application's portability and interoperability among the different control platforms.
- Language-based Virtualization: Different programming languages such as Pyretic and Splendid can be used in order to virtualize network topologies to enable the SDN's interoperability.
- Programming Languages: High-level programming languages are used by programmers in order to configure an SDN topology.
- Network Applications: The application in this layer implements the control logic for the SDN. Namely, such systems compile the commands which must be implemented in the data plane.

B. Defensive deception techniques

The development and application of the SDN has been studied extensively in the literature [37]–[39]. However, different security techniques have been developed that could be applied in such infrastructures in order to ensure their operations. Defensive deception techniques are able to increase security and dependability of Software Defined Networks.

In the following section, we will present and describe such techniques.

Fraunholz et al. in [40] conducted a comprehensive survey of deception technologies. Notably, different security mechanisms have been categorized considering the application layer of each technique; (i) Network, (ii) System, and (iii) Data layer. Furthermore, Han et al. in [41] examined deception techniques in computer security and categorized existing works according to the unit of deception, the layer where deception is applied, the goal of the deception solution, and the deployment mode.

This work focuses on network-based deception technologies in order to examine their application to the SDN. According to [41], network-based deception technologies aim to mitigate three threat categories: network fingerprinting, eavesdropping, and infiltration and attack propagation. To this end, ten different techniques have been identified. These are listed below:

- Network Tarpit: This technique focuses on sticky connections aiming to slow or stall automated network scanning in order to confuse attackers.
- Traffic forging: This technique increases the traffic flow in the network to slow down adversary's actions.
- Deceptive topology: This technique aims to distort network topology through traffic forging to slow the attacker.
- OS obfuscation: Through this technique, a mimic of the network behaviour of fake operating systems is created in order to deceive potential attackers.
- Honeytokens: Honeytokens consist of honey passwords, honey URL parameters, database honeytokens and honey permissions.
- Deceptive attack graphs: This technique uses attack graph representations to lead adversaries to follow a rouge attack path in order to distract them from their real targets.
- Deceptive simulation: The simulation enables the monitoring of the network topology and the creation of false attack targets in order to deceive adversaries.
- Decoy services: The defender share fake protocol messages, respond delays and crafted error messages in order to delay the attacker.
- Moving Target Defense: MTD is an asymmetric situation which keeps moving the attack surface of protected systems through dynamic shifting, which can be controlled and managed by the administrator [42].
- Honeypots: Honeypots are built to intentionally expose vulnerable resources to attackers by emulating or simulating systems such as databases, servers and file systems and services such as authentication [13].

Existing works considering defensive deception techniques for computer networks are depicted in Table I, while the classification has been adopted from [41]. As can be seen, various approaches for defensive deception have been applied in traditional computer networks.

TABLE I
DEFENSIVE DECEPTION TECHNIQUES.

Reference	Technique
[43]–[45]	Network Tarpit
[46]	Traffic forging
[47]	Deceptive Technology
[48]	OS obfuscation
[49], [50]	Honeytokens
[51], [52]	Deceptive attack graph
[53]	Decoy services
[54]	Deceptive simulation
[20]	Moving Target Defense
[13]	Honeypots

IV. DEFENSIVE DECEPTION TECHNIQUES ON SDN IMPLEMENTATIONS

The application of defensive deception techniques by leveraging the SDN technology has been extensively studied in the literature. The research papers analyzed in this work are identified by searching in the ACM Digital Library, Science Direct, Scopus, IEEE Xplore and Semantic Scholar databases with appropriate keywords. For the selection of the articles we consider the criterion that the proposed approach should be exclusively related to defensive deception techniques on SDN implementations. These approaches are analyzed below considering their core elements such as the *used systems*, *defensive deception technique*, and the *outcome/results*.

Achleitner et al. in [10] simulate network topologies based on SDN in order to deceive potential attackers targeting the network. The core element in this deception technique is the Reconnaissance Deception System – RDS. The RDS is a reconnaissance deception system which aims to defend the network from potential adversaries. By leveraging a software-defined network virtual network topologies, including its physical components, are simulated. In particular, SDN is responsible to dynamically generate flow rules, analyze flow statistics of the switch rules in order to identify malicious activity and steer and control network traffic by generating rules upon the arrival of the packet.

Zhao et al. in [11] propose a decoy chain deployment (DCD) method based on SDN and NFV as a defensive technique against penetration attacks. The decoy chain consists of a sequence of virtual machines which could operate as decoy switches, middleboxes or terminal hosts. As long as an attacker runs into a decoy chain will continue to penetrate decoy nods without any intrusion to the network. Therefore, the adversary's malicious actions are slowed down, and sensitive targets are protected, while at all times, the SDN controller monitors the security status of the whole network.

Kyung et al. in [12] designed an SDN-based honeynet to globally monitor all internal traffic with the help of the SDN controller. An advance honeynet named HoneyProxy has been proposed to improve data capture capabilities by leveraging the SDN controller. Hence, honeynet provides more flexibility in terms of network access management. Particularly, a honeyproxy using SDN controller monitors the data flows over the network and performs the necessary intervention to the proxy servers when a honeypot is compromised. Although honeypots constitute one of the most prominent defensive deception techniques, their implementation based on SDN technology is limited.

Han et al. in [13] proposed an SDN-based intelligent honeynet in order to attract attackers and learn about their scope, tactic and behaviour. By leveraging SDN technologies, honeynets can avoid fingerprinting attacks. Namely, HoneyMix leverages the SDN technology in different layers of its architecture toward a more efficient and effective data control. The programmability of the SDN offers a dynamic reconfiguration of the network rules depending on each situation. Furthermore, the SDN switch allows the direct connection among honeypots and hence, increases the protection from honeypot fingerprinting attacks.

Chowdhary et al. in [14] propose a MTD technique based on shuffle strategy using an SDN controller in order to dynamically reconfigure the network and hence, make harder for an attacker to understand the network topology. SDN is prefered due to its ability to reconfigure a cloud-based network topology continuously. In this work, a shuffle based MTD technique has been deployed where the port number for each service or the IP address of a VM are continuously changing.

Kampanakis et al. in [15] studied the application of the SDN technology in network-based MTD techniques. The use of SDN in MTD techniques aims to obfuscate the attacker's actions. SDN implementations improve the defence against port scanning either TCP port scan or UDP and ICMP scans. The proposed implementation clarifies that the SDN could open fault ports which are related to actual services in the network and hence confuse the attacker consistently.

Steinberger et al. in [16] discuss the combination of MTD and SDN in order to reduce the effects of a large-scale cyber-attack. The static configuration of traditional computer networks jeopardizes the infrastructure since attackers can reconnaissance the network and choose the most effective attack in order to cause damage to the network. SDN and MTD aim to address the issues above due to the scalability of SDN. The MTD technique is implemented by leveraging the carrier-grade SDN network operating systems, named ONOS. Two MTD techniques are used in this defensive solution: (i) the network-level MTD, and (ii) the host-level MTD. The former is based on BGP routes and multiple routers while the latter performs IP hopping in order to set up a honeypot.

Makanju et al. propose an Evolutionary Computation (EC) technique for MTD in combination with the SDN technology in [17]. Particularly, EC algorithms have been designed in order to search large spaces for optimal solutions efficiently. The MTD technique facilitates the deployment of a new configuration for the network, considering the network status indicators and the intrusion alerts.

Debroy et al. in [18] proposed an implementation of MTD technique in an SDN in cloud infrastructure. An adequate VM location is proposed by using the SDN controller which directs OpenFlow switches over the cloud infrastructure. The MTD technique's goal is to allow the proactive migration of target nodes in a VM. Additionally, the control module initiates the migration process through the migration initiator module, and thus, the clients are rerouted to a VM using OpenFlow switches. The intrusion detection module ensures the migration process by detecting DoS attacks.

TABLE II
SDN IMPLEMENTATIONS USING DEFENSIVE DECEPTION TECHNIQUES.

SDN	Defensive Deception Techniques
[10]	Deceptive Technologies
[11]	Decoy Services
[12], [13]	Honeypots, Honeytokens
[14]–[17], [17]–[21]	Moving Target Defense

Jafarian et al. in [19] developed a MTD architecture using an SDN controller in order to change the IP addresses of each host dynamically. The OpenFlow Random Host Mutation (OF-RHM) technique assigns a random virtual IP which is translated to/from the real IP of the host in order to overcome the static configuration of the traditional computer networks. The aim of the technique is to protect the network's topology for stealthy scanning, worm propagation and other scanning based attacks.

Macfarland et al. in [20] proposed a MTD application using SDN technology In particular, their technique aims to service unmodified clients while avoiding scalability limitations. An SDN controller provides to defenders the ability to distinguish trustworthy and untrustworthy clients by using pre-shared keys, cryptographic MACs, or embedding passwords into hostnames. The anonymity and unlinkability are ensured by utilizing the SDN controller since it prevents the revocation of the flows across movements over the network.

Aydeger et al. in [21] proposed a defensive mechanism for Crossfire DDoS attacks. By leveraging the SDN technology and MTD technique, the dynamic reconfiguration of the network environment is achieved. The SDN controller enables the management of the traffic flow over the network and is capable of protecting the network from both proactive and reactive attacks. However, this work focuses particularly on crossfire attacks. The defensive deception mechanism consists of four inter-related SDN modules; (i) ICMP monitoring, (ii) Traceroute profiling, (iii) Route mutation, and (iv) Congestion-link monitoring.

Table II depicts current SDN applications considering defensive deception techniques. It can be noticed that defense deception techniques in SDN is immature state since only four out of ten techniques have been applied.

Table IV depicts twelve of the existing techniques considering the five properties of defensive deception techniques. These properties have been adopted from [55] and are depicted in Table III.

Particularly, five out of twelve implementations fulfilled four properties while seven met three out of five properties. We can conclude that MTD techniques aim to increase the attacker's workload and uncertainty. On the other hand, techniques such as honeypots or honeyproxies facilitate the identification of the attack before adversaries succeed. Moreover, five out

TABLE III
DEFENSIVE DECEPTION TECHNIQUES PROPERTIES.

Property	Description
P1	Increase the attacker's workload
P2	Allow defenders to better track attacks and respond before adversaries succeed
P3	Exhaust adversary's resources
P4	Increase the sophistication required for an attack
P5	Increase the attacker's uncertainty

TABLE IV
COMPARISON OF ANALYZED IMPLEMENTATIONS.

Reference	P1	P2	P3	P4	P5
[10]	✓	✓			✓
[11]	✓	✓	✓		
[12]		✓		✓	
[13]	✓	✓		✓	✓
[14]	✓		✓	✓	✓
[15]			✓	✓	✓
[16]	✓	✓	✓		
[17]	✓		✓	✓	✓
[18]	✓	✓		✓	✓
[19]	✓			✓	✓
[20]	✓			✓	✓
[21]	✓	✓		✓	✓
12	10	7	5	9	9

of twelve analyzed studies aim to exhaust the adversary's resources. Although SDN technology can meet the aforementioned defensive deception properties, the fulfilment of all five properties is challenging. To the best of our knowledge, there are not implementations that consider all these properties.

V. DEFENSIVE DECEPTION MECHANISM

Due to the static nature of computer networks, intruders are able to detect their structure and identify vulnerabilities which they can then exploit through advanced attacks. The attackers initially examine a target networks, in order to identify hosts, open ports and map the network topology and to find known or unknown (zero-day) vulnerabilities that will enable them to continue their attack.

The approach proposed herein, aims at misleading such malicious activities by presenting a virtual network topology while it also hides the real network along with possible vulnerabilities that attackers can exploit. Presenting a virtual network falsifies all the information an intruder collects from examining a network and delays the rate of identification of actual vulnerable servers. Delaying the intruder is critical as the extra time given before the actual attack is executed, can facilitate the detection of the intruder and the timely reaction for protecting the network.

In the threat model of this work, it is assumed that the intruder is trying to locate the computers on the network and collect as much information as possible about each computer in order to continue the attack. The main purpose of our deception mechanism is to face those malicious network activities regardless of whether they come from a compromised or a non-compromised host.

Important part of the deception mechanism is the virtual network composition in order to delay and mislead intruders from locating real and possibly vulnerable computers. Furthermore, each host has a different view of the virtual network, so the Deception mechanism is independent of the compromised computer.

The deception mechanism consists of four essential elements:

- an **SDN Controller** responsible for dynamically creating and managing the flow rules in order to direct and control network traffic
- a **Packet Handler** responsible for handling network packets and for simulating specific virtual network resources
- a **Virtual Network Generator** that contains a description of the virtual network components and their connectivity
- as well as **a Honeypot Server** responsible for the services that honeypots will provide to the attacker after a port scanning

When a packet arrives at a switch, the SDN Controller applies a flow rule according to the virtual network topology. Thus, the controller forwards ARP, ICMP, UDP packets to the Packet Handler while it forwards TCP packets to the destination host. When the Packet Handler receives a packet, it creates a response packet according to the virtual topology and sends it back to the source. The source of the packet may be classified as an intruder according to at least one of the following criteria:

- A packet is destined for a honeypot;
- Multiple SYN messages are sent from one source to multiple destination ports of another network host.

The proposed defence deception mechanism has been implemented in the Mininet, which is a SDN Simulator and the POX SDN controller has been used. As mentioned above, the proposed defensive deception mechanism consists of four basic components the functionality of which is analyzed as follows:

SDN Controller is responsible for dynamically creating and managing the flow rules of switches. It is also responsible for creating and periodically updating the virtual network topology. The SDN Controller is able to create flow rules for routing ARP, ICMP, UDP and TCP packets.

As regards the ARP packets, when the switch receives an ARP request it forwards it to the Packet Handler. Then, the Packet Handler creates an ARP reply based on the virtual topology and sends it to the switch. The switch in turn forwards the ARP reply to the switch port from which it received the ARP request.

For ICMP packets, when the switch receives an ECHO request it forwards it to the Packet Handler. Then, the Packet Handler creates an ECHO reply based on the virtual topology and sends it to the switch. The switch in turn forwards the ECHO reply to the switch port from which it received the ECHO request.

For UDP packets, the packet destination port is first checked. If the destination port is 53 then the switch should forward the DNS query to the Packet Handler. Then, the Packet Handler will create a reply based on the virtual topology and send it back to the switch. The switch in turn must forward the reply to the switch port from which it received the DNS query. If the destination port is between 33434 and 33523, that is, the traceroute command has been used; the switch should forward the request to the Packet Handler. Then, the Packet Handler will create a reply based on the virtual topology and send it to the switch. The reply could be ICMP time exceeded or ICMP destination/port unreachable. The switch in turn must forward the reply to the switch port from which it received the request.

In the case of TCP packets, when a switch receives a TCP packet it will forward it to its destination given that the source of the packet has not been identified as an intruder from the SDN controller. A host can be identified as an intruder by the SDN Controller in two cases. The first case is if a host interacts with a honeypot through ping or traceroute commands. The second case is if a host makes a port scanning attempt against another host on the network. In order to detect port scanning attempts, the number of SYN messages sent from a host along with the corresponding destination ports are examined. In the case that a host is classified as an intruder, its network activity is forwarded to the Honeypot Server. Actually, when the switch receives a TCP packet from such a host it replaces its destination IP and MAC addresses with those of the Honeypot Server. Then, in the Honeypot Server response the switch replaces the source IP and MAC addresses with the original addresses and forward it to the switch port where the intruder is connected. The main reason that TCP packets are forwarded to the Honeypot Server instead of the Packet Handler is because in that case we can increase the level of deception for the intruder by using a honeypot. The Honeypot server allows for more interaction with the intruder, which in the case of complex TCP connections can end up to with the intruder having a largely false perception of the network.

Packet Handler is responsible for generating and sending packets, according to the virtual topology created by the virtual topology generator, when this is required. Packet Handler has been implemented in Python while the Scapy Framework has also been used. The role of the packet handler is taken up by one of the hosts created in Mininet. Thus, the packets will be forwarded by the switch to the Packet Handler, which in turn will generate a response and send it back to the switch.

Honeypot Server is responsible for generating the virtual set of services for each host, that will be provided to the attacker after a port scanning attempt. As mentioned above, it is not allowed to an intruder to perform a port scanning on the actual network and the network traffic will be routed to a honeypot. Thus, the need arises to present a different set of services for each scanned computer. One of the hosts created in the Mininet has the role of Honeypot Server. Honeypot Server has also been implemented in Python and starts services on the computer on which is running. Also, it should be mentioned that these services are periodically updated.

Virtual topology generator is responsible for creating the virtual topology as well as periodically updating the virtual IP and MAC addresses of the Mininet hosts and honeypots. This generator creates a text file that is accessible from the SDN controller and Packet Handler. Each line of this file corresponds to a component of the deception mechanism. Specifically, there are four types of entities, the Packet Handler, the hosts, the fake-routers and the routes.

The Packet Handler is unique to the network and is connected at port 1 of the switch. In addition, the text file contains information about the real IP and MAC addresses and about the virtual IP and MAC addresses.

As regards hosts, they can either be Mininet hosts or honeypots. In addition, the text file contains information about real IP and MAC addresses, virtual IP and MAC addresses as well as the switch port in which is connected the Packet Handler. If the entity is a Mininet host, then there is information about the port that is connected to the switch. If the entity is a honeypot, there is information about the port that the Honeypot Server is connected to the switch. From the information contained in host-type rows, the Packet Handler can respond to ARP, ICMP and UDP requests. The SDN controller knows the IP addresses of honeypots in order to designate a host as an intruder. Also, there is information on routing TCP packets.

The fake-router rows contain information about virtual routers that the deception mechanism will use to deceive the traceroute command. This information is about the router interface, the virtual IP and MAC addresses as well as the switch port that the Packet Handler is connected to.

Route rows contain information about virtual routes from one host to another. As well as, fake routers are used to mislead the traceroute command. This information is about a source host, a destination host, and the intermediate hops which are the fake router's interfaces mentioned above.

As mentioned above, one of the functions of the virtual topology generator is to periodically update the IP and MAC addresses in order to increase the attacker's uncertainty about the target host. However, there is a limitation regarding the termination of the TCP connections by changing the IP and MAC addresses. The number of subnets created by this mechanism is static and the optimal way to create a virtual topology given a real topology is a future track of research.

In order to present the functionality of the Defensive Deception Mechanism components as a whole, two different scenarios are described, one for an attacker scanning hosts in a network and a second one for an attacker scanning services on a host.

In the first scenario, we assume that an attacker will interact with a host on the network via the ping command. Thus, the switch will receive an ARP request which will be forwarded to the SDN Controller. The SDN Controller will send two flow rules to the switch. According to the first flow rule the switch will forward the ARP request to the Packet Handler. In turn, Packet Handler will generate an ARP reply and send it to the switch. According to the second flow rule the switch will forward the ARP reply to the switch port from which it received the ARP request. After that, an ECHO request will

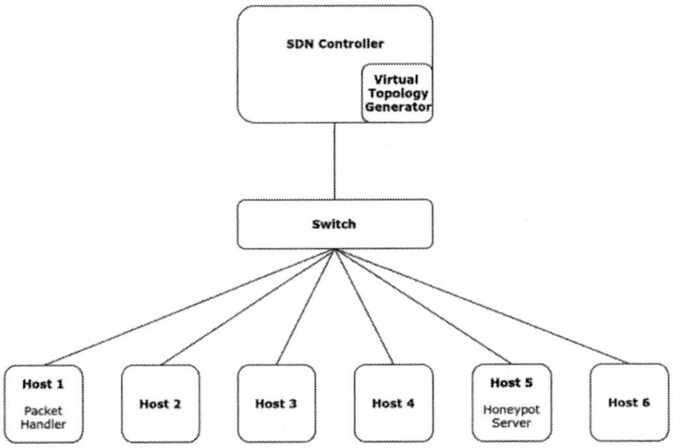

Fig. 1. Topology of implementation

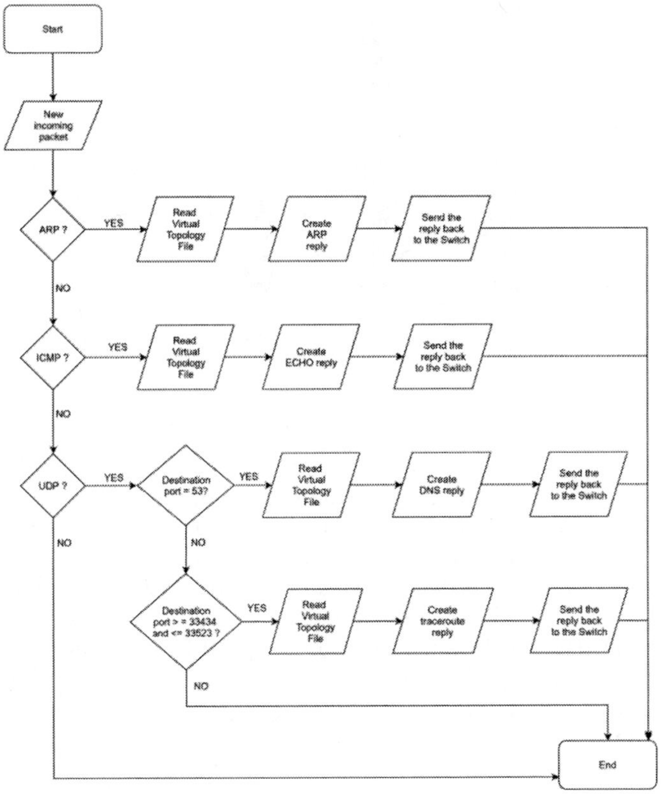

Fig. 2. Packet handler flowchart

be sent from the attacker's computer. The switch will forward it to the SDN Controller and the SDN Controller will create two flow rules. According to the first flow rule, the switch will forward the ECHO request to the Packet Handler. In turn, Packet Handler will generate an ECHO reply and send it back to the switch. According to the second flow rule the switch will forward the ECHO reply to the switch port from which it received the ECHO request. Figure 4 depicts the sequence diagram for the aforementioned scenario.

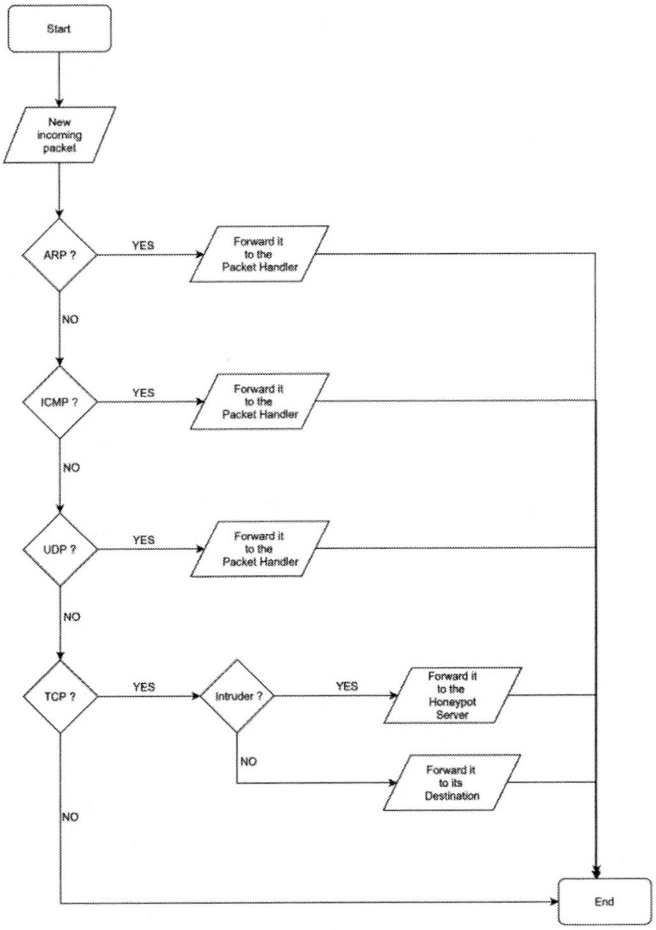

Fig. 3. SDN controller flowchart

In the second scenario, we assume that the attacker will interact with a host on the network through the nmap program. Based on the function of the nmap program, several SYN-type messages will be sent from the attacker's computer to many host's ports. All of these messages will be forwarded from the switch to the SDN Controller, and once the number of those SYN messages surpasses a specified limit for a multitude of different ports then the SDN Controller will create two flow rules. According to the first flow rule, when the switch receives a TCP packet, from the attacker's computer, it replaces its destination IP and MAC addresses with those of the Honeypot Server. According to the second flow rule, in the Honeypot Server response the switch replaces the source IP and MAC addresses with the original addresses and forward it to the switch port where the attacker is connected. Figure 5 depicts the sequence diagram for the second scenario.

VI. Results

In this section, the effectiveness of the deception defense mechanism discussed above is examined. For this purpose the nmap port scan tool was used, in order to scan a network protected by the proposed defensive deception mechanism.

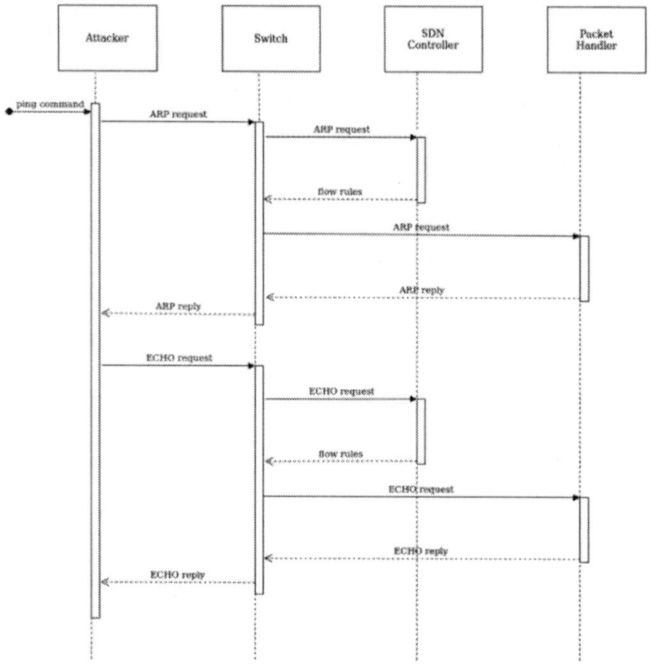

Fig. 4. Ping command sequence diagram

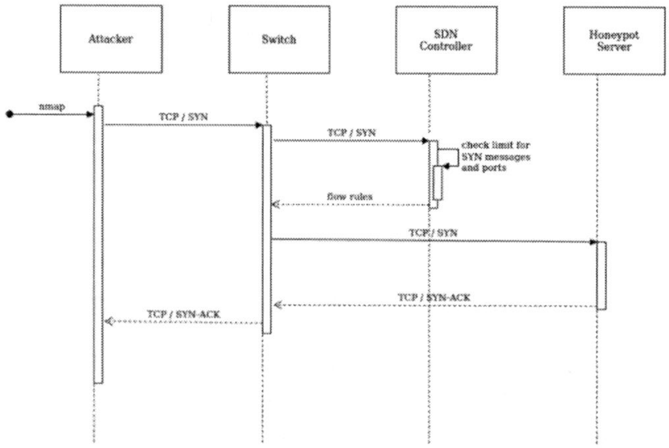

Fig. 5. Nmap sequence diagram

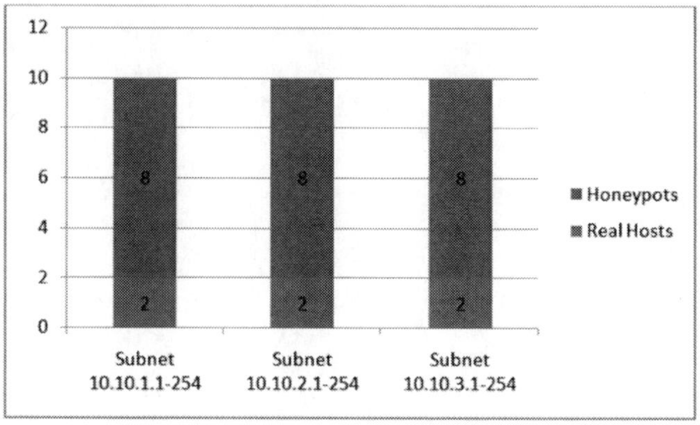

Fig. 6. Nmap ping sweep results (computers per subnet)

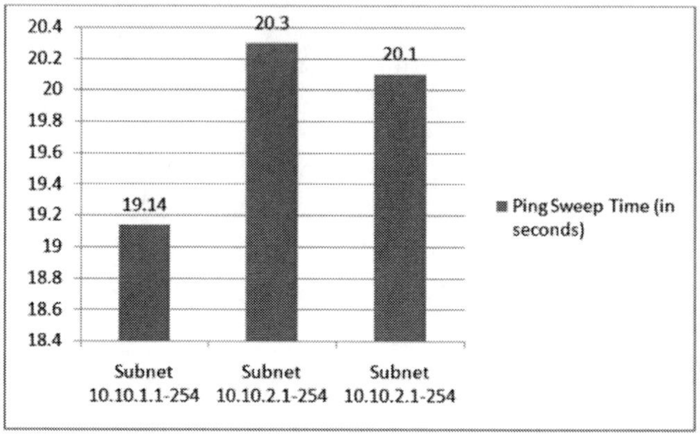

Fig. 7. Nmap ping sweep time (in seconds)

The results will be based on the defensive deception techniques properties presented in Table III.

Initially, an SDN network consisting of a switch and six computers was created in Mininet. The defensive deception mechanism created three sub-networks, each consisting of eight honeypots and two real computers. In total there are twenty four honeypots and six real computers. The ping sweep function of the nmap tool will be used to locate the computers running on the network. The results of the scans on the three subnets as well as the time taken for each scan are presented in Figure 6 and Figure 7.

In these scans it was observed that we can increase the number of computers in a network by increasing the number of honeypots. Thus, we increase the workload (P1) and uncertainty (P5) of the attacker. Also, we are able to track attacks and respond before attackers succeed (P2).

Each of the network computers that responded to the ping sweep will then be examined separately. For this reason, the nmap tool will be used again to identify the services that each computer hosts. The following graphs, Figure 8 and Figure 9, show the number of services that each computer runs and the time required for each scan.

In these scans it has been observed that we can vary the number of services running on a computer. Thus, we increase the workload (P1) and uncertainty (P5) of the attacker. Also, We are able to detect attacks and respond before attackers succeed (P2).

VII. Conclusions

As computer networks become more complex and attacks against those become more sophisticated, the mitigation efficiency of passive static countermeasures is going to decline. In order to be able to cope up with protecting modern computer networks from attackers we are required to come up with more sophisticated solutions such as SDN based deceptive defense techniques, that can delay and reveal the attacker.

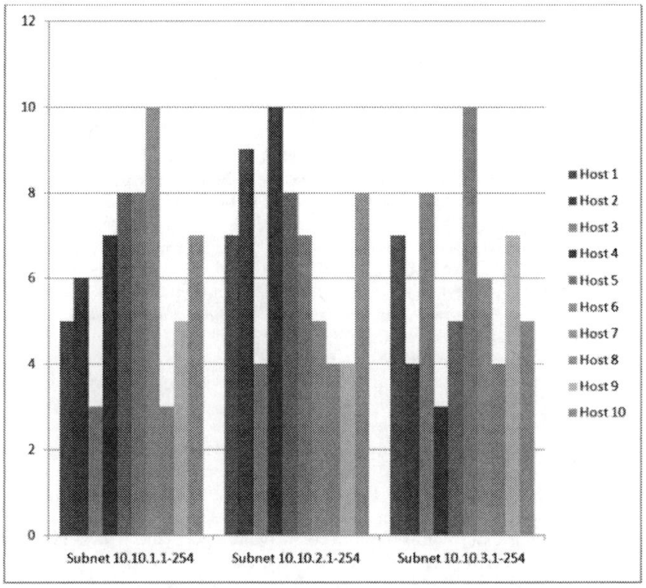

Fig. 8. Nmap scan results (open ports per computer)

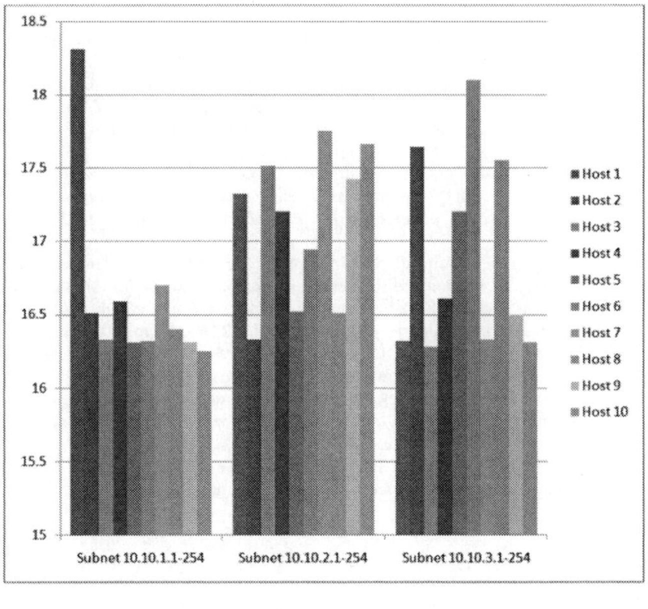

Fig. 9. Nmap scan time (in seconds)

Our comprehensive literature review showed that there are multiple efforts to set up such deceptive defense mechanisms based on SDN and the results are promising. The different methods have been analysed with respect to their main properties according to Table III.

Furthermore, we introduce a novel defensive deception mechanism that leverages the capabilities provided by SDN technologies. The proposed mechanism combines components from multiple defensive deception techniques as identified in the examined prior studies (see Table II), namely Deceptive Technologies, Honeypots, and Moving Target Defense. Finally, we have implemented the proposed mechanism and evaluated its capacity to satisfy the defensive deception mechanisms properties (see Table III), and more specifically to increase the attacker's workload, to allow defenders to better track attacks and respond before adversaries succeed, and to increase the attacker's uncertainty.

As future work, the proposed system is going to be enhanced both in terms of detection capabilities and prevention mechanisms. Detection is going to be expanded through the use of machine learning techniques. Prevention is going to be revised, to enable deception techniques to adapt to each protected network in terms of size and type of connected hosts or devices.

REFERENCES

[1] D. Kreutz, F. M. Ramos, P. E. Verissimo, C. E. Rothenberg, S. Azodolmolky, and S. Uhlig, "Software-defined networking: A comprehensive survey," *Proceedings of the IEEE*, vol. 103, no. 1, pp. 14–76, 2014.

[2] C. Layne, "Cyber attacks against critical infrastructure," Ph.D. dissertation, Utica College, 2017.

[3] D. Wenda and D. Ning, "A honeypot detection method based on characteristic analysis and environment detection," in *2011 International Conference in Electrics, Communication and Automatic Control Proceedings*. Springer, 2012, pp. 201–206.

[4] O. Schneider and N. Giller, "Method for mitigation of cyber attacks on industrial control systems," Jul. 3 2018, uS Patent 10,015,188.

[5] K. Hoffman, D. Zage, and C. Nita-Rotaru, "A survey of attack and defense techniques for reputation systems," *ACM Computing Surveys (CSUR)*, vol. 42, no. 1, pp. 1–31, 2009.

[6] S. Jajodia, A. K. Ghosh, V. Swarup, C. Wang, and X. S. Wang, *Moving target defense: creating asymmetric uncertainty for cyber threats*. Springer Science & Business Media, 2011, vol. 54.

[7] C. Lei, H.-Q. Zhang, J.-L. Tan, Y.-C. Zhang, and X.-H. Liu, "Moving target defense techniques: A survey," *Security and Communication Networks*, vol. 2018, 2018.

[8] B. C. Ward, S. R. Gomez, R. Skowyra, D. Bigelow, J. Martin, J. Landry, and H. Okhravi, "Survey of cyber moving targets second edition," MIT Lincoln Laboratory Lexington United States, Tech. Rep., 2018.

[9] S. Rowshanrad, S. Namvarasl, V. Abdi, M. Hajizadeh, and M. Keshtgary, "A survey on sdn, the future of networking," *Journal of Advanced Computer Science & Technology*, vol. 3, no. 2, pp. 232–248, 2014.

[10] S. Achleitner, T. F. La Porta, P. McDaniel, S. Sugrim, S. V. Krishnamurthy, and R. Chadha, "Deceiving network reconnaissance using sdn-based virtual topologies," *IEEE Transactions on Network and Service Management*, vol. 14, no. 4, pp. 1098–1112, 2017.

[11] Q. Zhao, C. Zhang, and Z. Zhao, "A decoy chain deployment method based on sdn and nfv against penetration attack," *PloS one*, vol. 12, no. 12, 2017.

[12] S. Kyung, W. Han, N. Tiwari, V. H. Dixit, L. Srinivas, Z. Zhao, A. Doupé, and G.-J. Ahn, "Honeyproxy: Design and implementation of next-generation honeynet via sdn," in *2017 IEEE Conference on Communications and Network Security (CNS)*. IEEE, 2017, pp. 1–9.

[13] W. Han, Z. Zhao, A. Doupé, and G.-J. Ahn, "Honeymix: Toward sdn-based intelligent honeynet," in *Proceedings of the 2016 ACM International Workshop on Security in Software Defined Networks & Network Function Virtualization*, 2016, pp. 1–6.

[14] A. Chowdhary, A. Alshamrani, D. Huang, and H. Liang, "Mtd analysis and evaluation framework in software defined network (mason)," in *Proceedings of the 2018 ACM International Workshop on Security in Software Defined Networks & Network Function Virtualization*, 2018, pp. 43–48.

[15] P. Kampanakis, H. Perros, and T. Beyene, "Sdn-based solutions for moving target defense network protection," in *Proceeding of IEEE International Symposium on a World of Wireless, Mobile and Multimedia Networks 2014*. IEEE, 2014, pp. 1–6.

[16] J. Steinberger, B. Kuhnert, C. Dietz, L. Ball, A. Sperotto, H. Baier, A. Pras, and G. Dreo, "Ddos defense using mtd and sdn," in *NOMS 2018-2018 IEEE/IFIP Network Operations and Management Symposium.* IEEE, 2018, pp. 1–9.

[17] A. Makanju, A. N. Zincir-Heywood, and S. Kiyomoto, "On evolutionary computation for moving target defense in software defined networks," in *Proceedings of the Genetic and Evolutionary Computation Conference Companion*, 2017, pp. 287–288.

[18] S. Debroy, P. Calyam, M. Nguyen, A. Stage, and V. Georgiev, "Frequency-minimal moving target defense using software-defined networking," in *2016 international conference on computing, networking and communications (ICNC).* IEEE, 2016, pp. 1–6.

[19] J. H. Jafarian, E. Al-Shaer, and Q. Duan, "Openflow random host mutation: transparent moving target defense using software defined networking," in *Proceedings of the first workshop on Hot topics in software defined networks*, 2012, pp. 127–132.

[20] D. C. MacFarland and C. A. Shue, "The sdn shuffle: creating a moving-target defense using host-based software-defined networking," in *Proceedings of the Second ACM Workshop on Moving Target Defense*, 2015, pp. 37–41.

[21] A. Aydeger, N. Saputro, K. Akkaya, and M. Rahman, "Mitigating crossfire attacks using sdn-based moving target defense," in *2016 IEEE 41st Conference on Local Computer Networks (LCN).* IEEE, 2016, pp. 627–630.

[22] D. L. Tennenhouse, J. M. Smith, W. D. Sincoskie, D. J. Wetherall, and G. J. Minden, "A survey of active network research," *IEEE communications Magazine*, vol. 35, no. 1, pp. 80–86, 1997.

[23] N. Feamster, J. Rexford, and E. Zegura, "The road to sdn," *Queue*, vol. 11, no. 12, pp. 20–40, 2013.

[24] A. T. Campbell, I. Katzela, K. Miki, and J. Vicente, "Open signaling for atm, internet and mobile networks (opensig'98)," *ACM SIGCOMM Computer Communication Review*, vol. 29, no. 1, pp. 97–108, 1999.

[25] A. Doria, F. Hellstrand, K. Sundell, and T. Worster, "General switch management protocol (gsmp) v3," 2002.

[26] J. Biswas, A. A. Lazar, J.-F. Huard, K. Lim, S. Mahjoub, L.-F. Pau, M. Suzuki, S. Torstensson, W. Wang, and S. Weinstein, "The ieee p1520 standards initiative for programmable network interfaces," *IEEE Communications Magazine*, vol. 36, no. 10, pp. 64–70, 1998.

[27] M. Casado, T. Garfinkel, A. Akella, M. J. Freedman, D. Boneh, N. McKeown, and S. Shenker, "Sane: A protection architecture for enterprise networks." in *USENIX Security Symposium*, vol. 49, 2006, p. 50.

[28] A. Doria, J. H. Salim, R. Haas, H. M. Khosravi, W. Wang, L. Dong, R. Gopal, and J. M. Halpern, "Forwarding and control element separation (forces) protocol specification." *RFC*, vol. 5810, pp. 1–124, 2010.

[29] N. McKeown, T. Anderson, H. Balakrishnan, G. Parulkar, L. Peterson, J. Rexford, S. Shenker, and J. Turner, "Openflow: enabling innovation in campus networks," *ACM SIGCOMM Computer Communication Review*, vol. 38, no. 2, pp. 69–74, 2008.

[30] H. Song, "Protocol-oblivious forwarding: Unleash the power of sdn through a future-proof forwarding plane," in *Proceedings of the second ACM SIGCOMM workshop on Hot topics in software defined networking*, 2013, pp. 127–132.

[31] J. E. Van der Merwe, S. Rooney, L. Leslie, and S. Crosby, "The tempest-a practical framework for network programmability," *IEEE network*, vol. 12, no. 3, pp. 20–28, 1998.

[32] B. Chun, D. Culler, T. Roscoe, A. Bavier, L. Peterson, M. Wawrzoniak, and M. Bowman, "Planetlab: an overlay testbed for broad-coverage services," *ACM SIGCOMM Computer Communication Review*, vol. 33, no. 3, pp. 3–12, 2003.

[33] M. R. Macedonia and D. P. Brutzman, "Mbone provides audio and video across the internet," *Computer*, vol. 27, no. 4, pp. 30–36, 1994.

[34] L. L. Peterson, T. Anderson, D. Blumenthal, D. Casey, D. Clark, D. Estrin, J. Evans, D. Raychaudhuri, M. Reiter, J. Rexford *et al.*, "Geni design principles," *Computer*, vol. 39, no. 9, pp. 102–105, 2006.

[35] A. Bavier, N. Feamster, M. Huang, L. Peterson, and J. Rexford, "In vini veritas: realistic and controlled network experimentation," in *Proceedings of the 2006 conference on Applications, technologies, architectures, and protocols for computer communications*, 2006, pp. 3–14.

[36] S. Ortiz, "Software-defined networking: On the verge of a breakthrough?" *Computer*, no. 7, pp. 10–12, 2013.

[37] S. Shin, Y. Song, T. Lee, S. Lee, J. Chung, P. Porras, V. Yegneswaran, J. Noh, and B. B. Kang, "Rosemary: A robust, secure, and high-performance network operating system," in *Proceedings of the 2014 ACM SIGSAC conference on computer and communications security*, 2014, pp. 78–89.

[38] P. Porras, S. Shin, V. Yegneswaran, M. Fong, M. Tyson, and G. Gu, "A security enforcement kernel for openflow networks," in *Proceedings of the first workshop on Hot topics in software defined networks*, 2012, pp. 121–126.

[39] K. Benton, L. J. Camp, and C. Small, "Openflow vulnerability assessment," in *Proceedings of the second ACM SIGCOMM workshop on Hot topics in software defined networking*, 2013, pp. 151–152.

[40] D. Fraunholz, S. D. Anton, C. Lipps, D. Reti, D. Krohmer, F. Pohl, M. Tammen, and H. D. Schotten, "Demystifying deception technology: A survey," *arXiv preprint arXiv:1804.06196*, 2018.

[41] X. Han, N. Kheir, and D. Balzarotti, "Deception techniques in computer security: A research perspective," *ACM Computing Surveys (CSUR)*, vol. 51, no. 4, pp. 1–36, 2018.

[42] G.-l. Cai, B.-s. Wang, W. Hu, and T.-z. Wang, "Moving target defense: state of the art and characteristics," *Frontiers of Information Technology & Electronic Engineering*, vol. 17, no. 11, pp. 1122–1153, 2016.

[43] T. Liston, "Labrea:"sticky" honeypot and ids," 2001.

[44] K. Borders, L. Falk, and A. Prakash, "Openfire: Using deception to reduce network attacks," in *2007 Third International Conference on Security and Privacy in Communications Networks and the Workshops-SecureComm 2007.* IEEE, 2007, pp. 224–233.

[45] L. Shing, "An improved tarpit for network deception," Naval Postgraduate School Monterey United States, Tech. Rep., 2016.

[46] E. Le Malécot, "Mitibox: camouflage and deception for network scan mitigation," in *Proceedings of the 4th USENIX conference on Hot topics in security.* USENIX Association, 2009, pp. 4–4.

[47] S. T. Trassare, "A technique for presenting a deceptive dynamic network topology." Naval Postgraduate School Monterey United States, Tech. Rep., 2013.

[48] M. Smart, G. R. Malan, and F. Jahanian, "Defeating tcp/ip stack fingerprinting." in *Usenix Security Symposium*, 2000.

[49] B. M. Bowen, V. P. Kemerlis, P. Prabhu, A. D. Keromytis, and S. J. Stolfo, "Automating the injection of believable decoys to detect snooping," in *Proceedings of the third ACM conference on Wireless network security*, 2010, pp. 81–86.

[50] S. Chakravarty, G. Portokalidis, M. Polychronakis, and A. D. Keromytis, "Detecting traffic snooping in tor using decoys," in *International Workshop on Recent Advances in Intrusion Detection.* Springer, 2011, pp. 222–241.

[51] F. Cohen, I. Marin, J. Sappington, C. Stewart, and E. Thomas, "Red teaming experiments with deception technologies," *IA Newsletter*, 2001.

[52] F. Cohen and D. Koike, "Leading attackers through attack graphs with deceptions," *Computers & Security*, vol. 22, no. 5, pp. 402–411, 2003.

[53] N. Provos *et al.*, "A virtual honeypot framework." in *USENIX Security Symposium*, vol. 173, no. 2004, 2004, pp. 1–14.

[54] J. L. Rrushi, "An exploration of defensive deception in industrial communication networks," *International Journal of Critical Infrastructure Protection*, vol. 4, no. 2, pp. 66–75, 2011.

[55] F. Cohen, "The use of deception techniques: Honeypots and decoys," *Handbook of Information Security*, vol. 3, no. 1, pp. 646–655, 2006.

Handoff Characterization of Multipath Video Streaming

Kazuya Fujiwara, Shinichi Nagayama, Dirceu Cavendish, Daiki Nobayashi, Takeshi Ikenaga
Department of Computer Science and Electronics
Kyushu Institute of Technology
Fukuoka, Japan
e-mail: {q108107k@mail, o108076s@mail}.kyutech.jp {cavendish@ndrc, nova@ecs, ike@ecs}.kyutech.ac.jp

***Abstract*—Video streaming has become the major source of Internet traffic nowadays. Considering that content delivery network providers utilize Video over Hypertext Transfer Protocol/Transmission Control Protocol (HTTP/TCP) as the preferred protocol stack for video streaming, understanding TCP performance in transporting video streams has become paramount. Recently, multipath transport protocols have allowed streaming of video over multiple paths. In this paper, we analyze the impact of handoffs on multipath video streaming and network performance on WiFi and cellular paths. We utilize network performance measures, as well as video quality metrics, to characterize the performance and interaction between network and application layers of video data for various network scenarios.**

Keywords*—*Video streaming; high speed networks; TCP congestion control; TCP socket state; Multipath TCP; Packet retransmissions; Packet loss.

I. INTRODUCTION

Transmission Control Protocol (TCP) has become the most widely deployed transport protocol of the Internet, providing reliable data transmission for the overwhelming majority of applications. For data applications, the perceived quality of service can be summarized as the total transport time of a given file. For streaming applications, the perceived quality of experience involves the amount of data discarded at the client due to excessive transport delays, as well as rendering stalls due to lack of timely playout data. These performance measures, namely transport delays and data starvation, depend on how TCP handles flow control and packet retransmissions.

Motivated by the evolution of multiple device interfaces, multipath transport has been developed, allowing video streaming over multiple IP interfaces and network paths. Multipath streaming not only increases aggregated bandwidth capacity, but also increases reliability at the transport level session when a specific radio link coverage gets compromised. Moreover, an important issue in multipath transport is the path (sub-flow) selection; a path scheduler is needed to split traffic to be injected on a packet by packet basis onto available paths. Head of line blocking across different paths may cause incomplete or late frames to be discarded at the receiver, as well as stream stalling, compromising video rendering performance. In this work, we analyze the effect of path handoffs from a primary path to a secondary path on the quality of video stream delivery. As streaming session lasts long enough to experience path disconnection in many use cases, such as WiFi to Cellular handoffs, it is important to study such events from an application performance viewpoint.

The material is organized as follows. Related work is discussed on Section II. Section III details how video streaming is supported over TCP transport protocol. Section IV introduces widely deployed TCP variants utilized as transport for each path. Section V characterizes handoff effects on multiple path video delivery via WiFi and cellular paths via network emulation, addressing performance evaluation using a default path scheduler and a recently proposed sticky scheduler, for each TCP variant. Our empirical results show that Video streaming using coupled TCP variants may be impacted by handoffs, particularly on WiFi-Cellular scenarios. Section VI addresses directions we are pursuing as follow up to this work.

II. RELATED WORK

Although there have been several multipath transport studies in the literature, few have focused on video performance over multiple paths. In what follows, we classify these efforts according to their scope, and comment on representative ones.

A. Multipath Video streaming on ad-hoc networks

These works are motivated by vehicular communication use cases emerging for assisted driving systems. A representative research effort within this scope is [2], which proposes an interference aware multipath video streaming in Vehicular Adhoc Networks (VANETs). They consider vehicle interference within neighbors, as well as shadowing effects onto Signal to Noise ratio, data delay and throughput of video streams over multiple paths. They also provide a good survey of recent work on multipath video streaming over VANETs. From a scope's perspective, even though the ultimate objective is reliable transport of high quality video streams, minimizing video freezes and dropped frames, these efforts are link layer approaches, such as channel interference, coupled with efficient routing strategies on ad-hoc vehicular networks. In contrast, our scope is video streaming over regular Internet, where channel and route optimization opportunities are limited.

B. Application driven path selection on heterogeneous paths

The scope here is in coupling application layer with transport protocol to increase video streaming quality. For instance, [1] proposes a path-and-content-aware path selection approach to couple MPEG Media Transport (MMT) protocol with multipath transport protocol. They estimate path quality condition of each subflow, and selectively avoid sending I-frames on paths of low quality. They evaluate video layer quality via Peak Signal to Noise (PSNR) tracing, as well as network layer goodput. A similar approach, at which different sub-flows are used for segregating prioritized packets of Augmented Reality/Virtual Reality streams has been proposed by Silva et al.

[21]. In contrast, our previous and current work do not couple application with multipath transport, as the coupling would require different transport protocols for different applications.

C. Multipath path selection of data transport within MPTCP

Here, the scope is smart path selection via sub-flow transport chanracterization. Arzani et al. [4] present a modelling of multipath transport in which they explain empirical evaluations of the impact of selecting a first sub-flow in throughput performance. Hwang et al. [10] propose a blocking scheme, where a slow path is not used when delay difference between paths is large, to improve data transport completion time on short lived flows. Ferlin et al. [7] introduce a path selection scheme based on a head-of-line blocking predictor of paths. They carry out emulation experiments of their scheduler against minimum Round Trip Time (RTT) default scheduler, in transporting bulk data, Web transactions and Constant Bit Rate (CBR) traffic. Performance evaluation metrics are goodput, completion time and packet delays, respectively.

More recently, Kimura et al. [12] have shown throughput performance improvements on schedulers driven by path sending rate and window space, focusing on bulk data transfer applications. Xue et al. [23] has proposed a path scheduler based on prediction of the amount of data a path is able to transmit and evaluated it on simulated network scenarios with respect to throughput performance. Also, Frommgen et al. [9] have shown that stale round trip time (rtt) information interferes with path selection of small streams such as HTTP traffic. The authors propose an rtt probing and one way delay based path selection to improve latency and throughput performance of thin streams. Finally, [22] has addressed the WiFi/Cellular(LTE) handoff scenario when transferring data over MPTCP. They propose a radio/transport cross-layer approach, where TCP layer receives indication of a threshold SNR event crossing, indicating likely handoff. Via simulations, they show transport layer (throughput, RTT, retransmissions) improvements when WiFi/LTE handoffs occur, for Reno, Lia and Olia TCP variants on data transfers. In contrast, our handoff characterization focuses on impact of handoffs on video streaming quality.

D. Multipath path selection of Video Streams within MPTCP

Dong et al. [6] have proposed a path loss estimation approach to select paths subject to high and bulk loss rates. Although they have presented some video streaming experiments, they do not measure streaming performance from an application perspective.

By contrast, in our previous work, we have proposed multipath path scheduling principles that can be applied to different path schedulers to specifically improve the quality of video streams. In [13], we have proposed Multipath TCP path schedulers based on dynamic path characteristics, such as congestion window space and estimated path throughput, and evaluated multipath video streaming using these proposed schedulers. Recently [14], we have also proposed to enhance path schedulers with TCP state information, such as whether a path is in fast retransmit and fast recovery, to improve

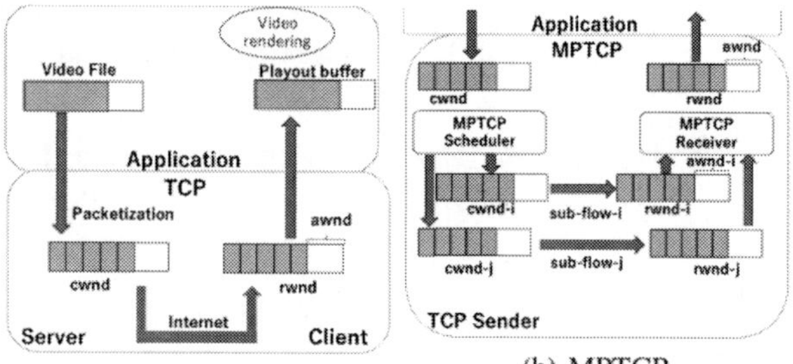

(a) TCP (b) MPTCP

Figure 1: Video Streaming over TCP/MPTCP

video quality in lossy network scenarios. In [15], we have introduced the concept of a sticky scheduling, where once a path switch occurs, we stay with the new path until its bandwidth resources become exhausted. In this work, we have included sticky scheduler as part of our handoff performance evaluation using widely deployed TCP variants on open source network experiments over WiFi and cellular paths. We focus on most commonplace scenario of handoffs between WiFi and cellular networks on video streaming sessions originated at home and lasting way after the user leaves its WiFi network.

III. Video Streaming Over TCP

At application layer, a video streaming over HTTP/TCP typically uses an HTTP server, where video files are made available for streaming upon HTTP requests, and a video client, which places HTTP requests to the server over the Internet, for video streaming. At transport layer, a TCP variant is used to store and reliably transport video data over IP packets between the two end points. Figure 1 (a) illustrates video streaming components. The HTTP server stores encoded video files, making them available upon HTTP requests. Upon HTTP video request, a TCP sender is instantiated to transmit packetized data to the client machine, making a TCP socket available to the application at both end points. At TCP transport layer, a congestion window is used at the sender for flow controlling the amount of data injected into the network. The size of the congestion window, $cwnd$, is adjusted dynamically, according to the level of congestion in the network, as well as the space available for data storage, $awnd$, at the TCP client receiver buffer. Congestion window space is freed only when data packets are acknowledged by the receiver, so that lost packets are retransmitted by the TCP layer. At the client side, in addition to acknowledging arriving packets, the TCP receiver informs the sender its current available space $awnd$, so that at the sender side, $cwnd \leq awnd$ condition is enforced at all times. At client application layer, a video player extracts data from a playout buffer, filled with packets delivered by the TCP receiver from its socket buffer. The playout buffer serves to smooth out variable data arrival rate.

A. Interaction between Video streaming and TCP

At the server side, HTTP server injects data into the TCP sender buffer according to $cwnd$ space availability. Hence, the injection rate of video data into the TCP socket is dictated by the congestion network condition, and thus different than the video variable encoding rate. Moreover, TCP throughput performance is affected by the round trip time of the TCP session. This is a direct consequence of the congestion window mechanism of TCP, where only up to a $cwnd$ worth of data can be delivered without acknowledgements. Hence, for a fixed $cwnd$ size, from the sending of a first packet until the first acknowledgement arrives, a TCP session throughput is capped at $cwnd/RTT$. For each TCP congestion avoidance scheme, according to the TCP variant, the size of the congestion window is computed by a specific algorithm at time of packet acknowledgement reception by the TCP source. However, for all variants, the size of the congestion window is capped by the available TCP receiver space $awnd$ sent back from the TCP client. At the client side, the video data is retrieved from TCP client socket by the video player into a playout buffer, before delivering to the video renderer. However, client playout buffer may underflow, if TCP receiver window empties out. On the other hand, playout buffer overflow does not occur, since the player will not pull more data into the playout buffer than it can handle.

IV. Transport Protocols

We now describe single/multipath transport protocols.

A. Multipath TCP

MPTCP is an IETF supported transport layer protocol which allows data transport over multiple TCP sessions [8]. The multipath nature of the transport session is hidden to upper layers via a single TCP socket use per application session. At the transport layer, however, MPTCP works with TCP variant sub-flows, each of which unaware of the multipath nature of the overall transport session. Connecting the application facing socket with transport sub-flow is a path scheduler, which extracts packets from the MPTCP socket exposed to applications, selects a sub-flow, and injects them into TCP sockets belonging to the selected sub-flow. MPTCP transport architecture is represented in Figure 1 (b).

The most widespread path scheduler (Linux implementation) selects the path with shortest round trip time (rtt) among paths with congestion window space for new packets. We refer to this path scheduler as default scheduler. In addition to this path scheduler, we include evaluation of a sticky scheduler [15], as follows. At the start of a new video streaming session, the path with smallest rtt is chosen, as per default scheduler. However, once a new path is selected (due to congestion of a previously selected path), the scheduler remains selecting the same path until it can no longer inject new packets. We call this path strategy as Greedy Sticky scheduler - GR-STY.

In addition, a MPTCP packet scheduler is supported, which adjusts the congestion window of each subflow according to some strategy. The packet scheduler may work in one of two different configuration modes: uncoupled and coupled. In uncoupled mode, each sub-flow congestion window $cwnd$ is adjusted independently. In coupled mode, MPTCP couples the congestion control of the sub-flows, by adjusting the congestion window $cwnd_k$ of a sub-flow k according with parameters of all sub-flows. Although several coupled mechanisms exist, we focus on Linked Increase Algorithm (LIA) [18] and Opportunistic Linked Increase Algorithm (OLIA) [11].

MPTCP supports the advertisement of IP interfaces available between two endpoints via specific TCP option signalling. As IP option signalling may be blocked by intermediate IP boxes such as firewalls, paths that cross service providers may require VPN protection. Morever, both endpoints require MPTCP to be running for the establishment of multiple transport paths. In addition, IP interfaces may be of diverse nature: WiFi, cellular, etc.

B. TCP variants

TCP protocol variants can be classified into delay and loss based. Loss based TCP variants use packet loss as primary congestion indication signal, performing window regulation as $cwnd_k = f(cwnd_{k-1})$, hence being ack reception paced. Most f functions follow an Additive Increase Multiplicative Decrease (AIMD) strategy, with various increase and decrease parameters. TCP NewReno [3] and Cubic [19] are examples of AIMD strategies. Delay based TCP variants, on the other hand, use queue delay information as the congestion indication signal, increasing/decreasing the window if the delay is small/large, respectively. Compound [20] and Capacity and Congestion Probing (CCP) [5] are examples of delay based protocols. Most TCP variants follow a slow start, congestion avoidance, fast retransmit and fast recovery phase framework. For TCP variants widely used, congestion avoidance is sharply different.

Cubic TCP Congestion Avoidance: TCP Cubic is a loss based TCP that has achieved widespread usage as the default TCP of the Linux operating system. During congestion avoidance, its congestion window is adjusted as follows (1):

$$\begin{aligned} AckRec:\quad cwnd_{k+1} &= C(t-K)^3 + Wmax \\ K &= (Wmax\frac{\beta}{C})^{1/3} \\ PktLoss:\quad cwnd_{k+1} &= \beta cwnd_k \\ Wmax &= cwnd_k \end{aligned} \quad (1)$$

where C is a scaling factor, Wmax is the cwnd value at time of packet loss detection, and t is the elapsed time since the last packet loss detection. K parameter drives the cubic increase away from Wmax, whereas β tunes how quickly cwnd is reduced on packet loss. This adjustment strategy ensures that its $cwnd$ quickly recovers after a loss event.

Compound TCP Congestion Avoidance: Compound TCP is the TCP variant used in most deployed Wintel machines. This variant implements a hybrid loss/delay based congestion avoidance scheme, by adding a delay congestion window $dwnd$ to the congestion window of NewReno [20]. Compound TCP $cwnd$ adjustment is as follows (2):

$$\begin{aligned} AckRec:\quad cwnd_{k+1} &= cwnd_k + \frac{1}{cwnd_k + dwnd_k} \\ PktLoss:\quad cwnd_{k+1} &= \frac{cwnd_k}{2} \end{aligned} \quad (2)$$

where the delay component is computed as:

$$\begin{aligned} AckRec: dwnd_{k+1} &= dwnd_k + \alpha dwnd_k^K - 1, \text{if } diff < \gamma \\ & dwnd_k - \eta diff, \quad \text{if } diff \geq \gamma \\ PktLoss: dwnd_{k+1} &= dwnd_k(1-\beta) - \frac{cwnd_k}{2} \end{aligned} \quad (3)$$

TABLE I: EXPERIMENTAL NETWORK SETTINGS

Element	Value
Video size	409 MBytes
Video rate	5.24 Mbps
Playout time	10 mins 24 secs
Video Codec	H.264 MPEG-4 AVC
MPTCP variants	Cubic, Compound, LIA, OLIA
MPTCP schedulers	DFT, GR-STY

where parameter $diff$ is the estimated number of backlogged packets, γ is a threshold parameter which drives congestion detection sensitivity and α, β, η and K are parameters chosen as a tradeoff between responsiveness, smoothness and scalability. Compound TCP behavior is dominated by its loss based component, featuring a slow responsiveness to path bandwidth variations, which may cause playout buffer underflows.

Linked Increase Congestion Control: LIA [18] window adjustment couples the congestion control algorithms of different sub-flows by linking their congestion window increasing functions, while halving $cwnd$ window upon packet loss detection. LIA $cwnd$ adjustment scheme is as follows (4):

$$AckRec: cwnd^i_{k+1} = cwnd^i_k + min\left(\frac{\alpha B_{ack} Mss^i}{\sum_0^n cwnd^p}, \frac{B_{ack} Mss^i}{cwnd^i}\right)$$

$$PktLoss: cwnd^i_{k+1} = \frac{cwnd^i_k}{2} \quad (4)$$

where parameter α regulates the aggressiveness of the protocol, B_{ack} represents the number of acknowledged bytes, Mss^i is the maximum segment size of sub-flow i and n is the number of sub-flows. Equation (4) adopts $cwnd$ in bytes, rather than in packets (Maximum Segment Size - MSS), in contrast with other TCP variants equations, because here we have the possibility of diverse MSSs on different sub-flows. However, the general idea is to increase $cwnd$ in increments that depend on $cwnd$ size of all sub-flows, for fairness, but with total increase no more than a single TCP Reno flow. The min operator in the increase adjustment equation guarantees that the increase is at most the same as if MPTCP was running on a single TCP Reno sub-flow. In practical terms, each LIA sub-flow increases $cwnd$ at a slower pace than TCP Reno, still cutting $cwnd$ in half at each packet loss.

Opportunistic Linked Increase Congestion Control: OLIA [11] congestion window adjustment also couples the congestion control algorithms of different sub-flows, but with the increase based on the quality of the available paths. OLIA cwnd adjustment scheme is as follows (5):

$$AckRec: cwnd^i_{k+1} = cwnd^i_k + \frac{\frac{cwnd^i}{(RTT^i)^2}}{(\sum_0^n \frac{cwnd^p}{RTT^p})^2} + \frac{\alpha^i}{cwnd^i},$$

$$PktLoss: cwnd^i_{k+1} = \frac{cwnd^i_k}{2} \quad (5)$$

where α is a positive parameter for all paths. The idea is to tune $cwnd$ to an optimal congestion balancing point (Pareto optimal sense). In practical terms, each OLIA sub-flow increases $cwnd$ at a pace related to the ratio of each sub-flow RTT and the RTT of other subflows, still cutting $cwnd$ in half at each packet loss.

V. STREAMING PERFORMANCE UNDER PATH HANDOFF

Figure 2 describes two network testbeds used for emulating network paths with WiFi and Cellular (LTE) wireless access links. In WiFi only testbed (a), an HTTP Apache video server

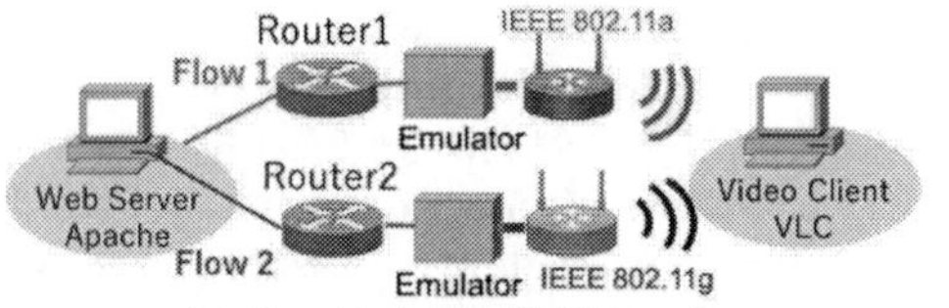

(a) Two Path Wi-Fi Network

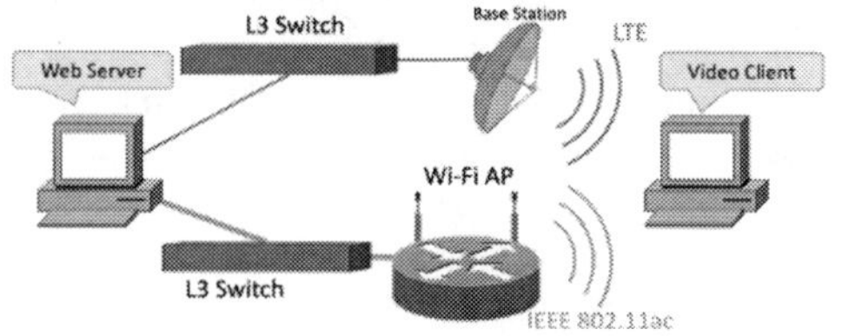

(b) Cellular and Wi-Fi Network

Figure 2: Video Streaming Emulation Network

TABLE II: EXPERIMENTAL NETWORK SCENARIOS

Scenario	Path properties (RTT, Bandwidth)
Limited BW Scenario Each path BW is close to video rate	Flow1) RTT 50 ms, BW 6 Mb/s Flow2) RTT 100 ms, BW 6 Mb/s
Large BW Scenario Each path BW is 3 times video rate	Flow1) RTT 50 ms, BW 18 Mb/s Flow2) RTT 100 ms, BW 18 Mb/s
Cellular Scenario (Interface BW speed)	Cellular) RTT 3.3ms, BW 24 Mb/s Wi-Fi) RTT 2.9ms, BW 433 Mb/s

is connected to two access routers, which are connected to link emulators, used to adjust path delays. A VLC client machine is connected to two Access Points, a 802.11a and 802.11g, on different bands (5GHz and 2.4GHz, respectively). In WiFi-Cellular testbed (b), an HTTP Apache video server is connected to two L3 switches, one of which directly connected to an 802.11ac router, and the other connected to an LTE base station via a cellular network card. The simple topologies and isolated traffic allow us to better understand the impact of differential delays, TCP variants, and path schedulers on streaming performance. Handoff is forced by cutting off WiFi primary path, simulating a break down of router to client communication.

Network settings and scenarios under study are described in Tables I and II, respectively. Video settings are typical of a video stream, with size short enough to run multiple streaming trials within a short amount of time. For WiFi only scenario, path bandwidth capacity is tuned to support a limited bandwidth and large bandwidth scenarios to stream a video playout rate of 5.24Mbps. TCP variants used are: Cubic, Compound, LIA and OLIA. Performance measures are:

- **Picture discards:** number of frames discarded by the video decoder.
- **Buffer underflow:** number of buffer underflow events at video client buffer.
- **Sub-flow throughput:** the value of TCP throughput on each sub-flow.
- **Packet retransmissions:** number of packets retransmitted by TCP.

We organize our video streaming experimental results in three network scenarios (Table II): i) A WiFi-WiFi limited bandwidth scenario, with 6Mbps capacity on each path and differential delay; ii) A WiFi-WiFi large bandwidth scenario,

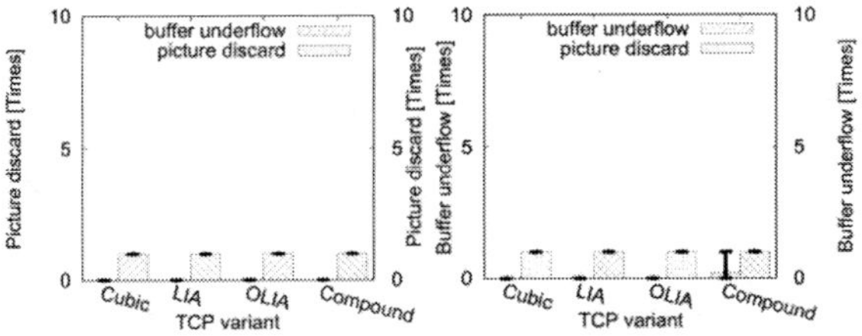

(a) Limited BW Scenario (b) Large BW Scenario

Figure 3: WiFi: no Handoff with DFT

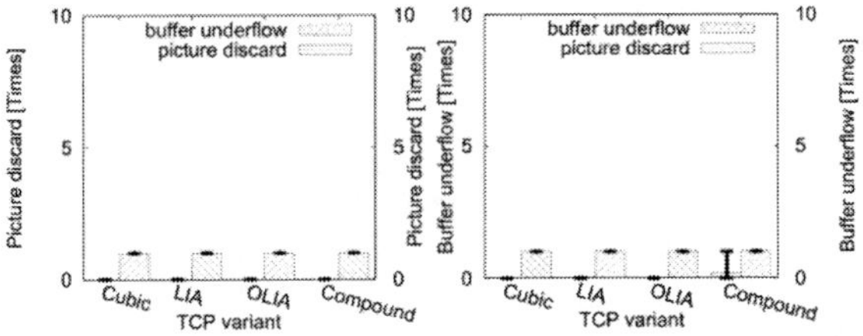

(a) Limited BW Scenario (b) Large BW Scenario

Figure 4: WiFi Handoff: video performance with DFT

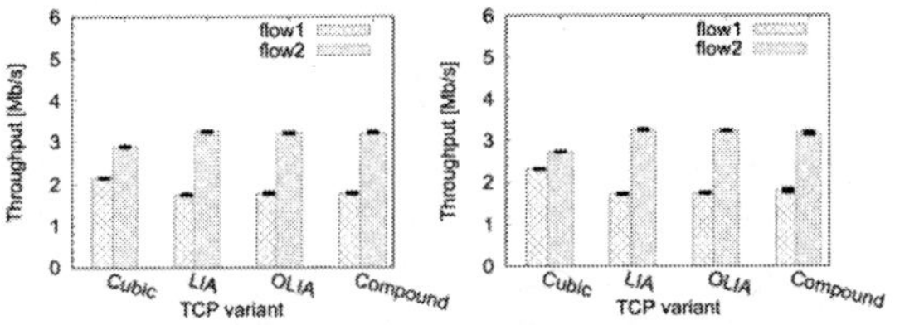

(a) Limited BW Scenario (b) Large BW Scenario

Figure 5: WiFi Handoff: transport throughput with DFT

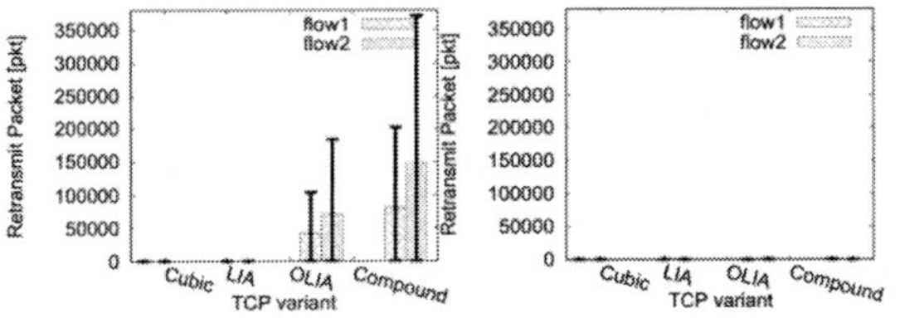

(a) Limited BW Scenario (b) Large BW Scenario

Figure 6: WiFi Handoff: transport retransmissions with DFT

with 18Mbps capacity on each path; iii) A WiFi-Cellular(LTE) scenario, with practically unlimited capacity on each path (path bandwidth is limited only by interfaces speed). Results are reported as average and min/max deviation bars.

A. WiFi Scenarios

Figures 3 a and b report on video streaming and TCP performance of baseline scenario with no handoff, where flow 1 and 2 have 50, 100msec round trip times, respectively, and default packet scheduler. We see that picture discards and buffer underflows are as small as they can be, even when per flow bandwidth is limited (a). Figures 4 present same network scenario, but with WiFi-WiFi handoff. We see that for both limited and large bandwidth scenarios, video performance is not disturbed by handoffs. Figures 5 (a) and (b) report throughput of each flow, verifying that a larger throughput results on flow 2, with is the sole flow carrying traffic after handoff. Finally, for this handoff scenario, Figures 6 report

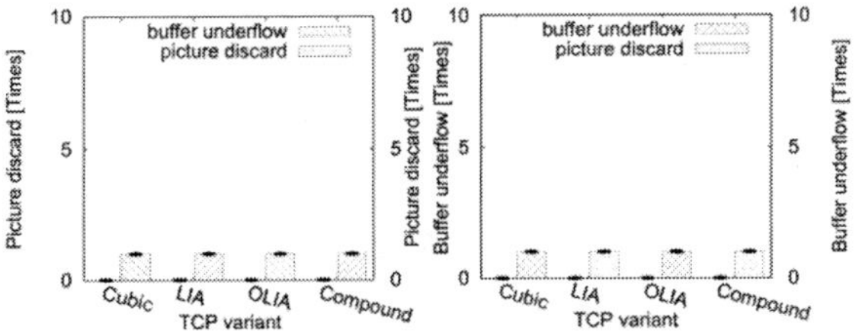

(a) Limited BW Scenario (b) Large BW Scenario

Figure 7: WiFi: No Handoff with GR-STY

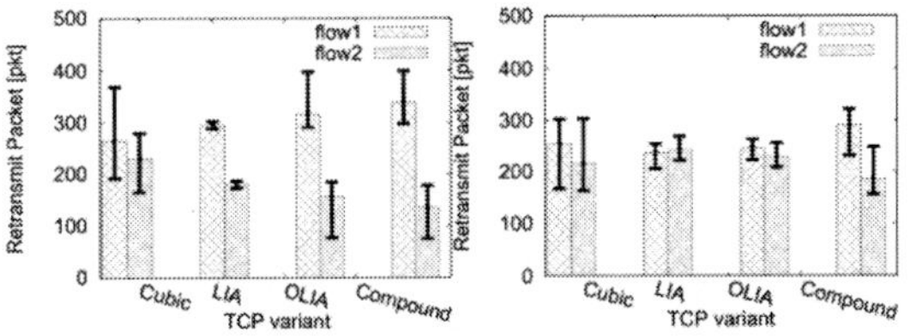

(a) Limited BW Scenario (b) Large BW Scenario

Figure 8: WiFi Handoff: transport retransmissions with GR-STY

on TCP layer packet retransmissions. Interestingly, in limited (tight) bandwidth scenario, significant retransmissions occur on both flow 1 and flow 2 for OLIA and Compound TCP variants. We notice that these two are the slowest variants to have their congestion window *cwnd* recover from packet loss, as per respective equations of Section IV.

We have repeated handoff experiments using sticky scheduler instead of default scheduler, for comparison. Video performance results are similar to Figures 4, and hence are omitted for space's sake, as well as throughput results. However, transport retransmissions (Figures 8) show very little retransmissions on both flow 1 and flow 2 triggered by handoffs for all TCP variants (notice scale change of y-axis), including slow OLIA and Compound. From these and previous default scheduler retransmission results, we verified that large number of retransmissions occur prior to handoff, when both flow 1 and flow 2 are used, since the level of retransmissions is affected by the path scheduler used, with sticky scheduler alleviating retransmissions. Once handoff to flow 2 occurs, which occurs quickly due to both paths being available simultaneously, some extra retransmissions, no longer caused by the scheduler, also occur for OLIA and Compound TCP variants.

B. Cellular Scenario

Figures 9 a and b report on video streaming performance of WiFi - cellular network scenario with no handoff, under default and sticky path schedulers. We can verify perfect video streaming. In contrast, when handoffs from WiFi to cellular occur (Figures 10), buffer underflow and picture discards are significant for OLIA using default scheduler (a) , and LIA using sticky scheduler (b). Cubic and Compound TCP variants do not suffer video level performance degradation on under either path schedulers. In addition, Figures 11 confirm handoff from cellular link to WiFi link. Finally, Figures 12 show that most of retransmissions occur in the LTE path, for Compound and OLIA variants, again the least responsive variants to congestion window recovery.

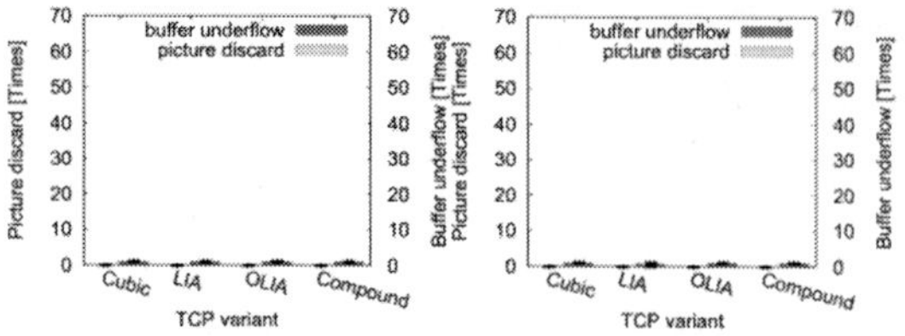

(a) DFT (b) GR-STY

Figure 9: WiFi-Cellular: No Handoff

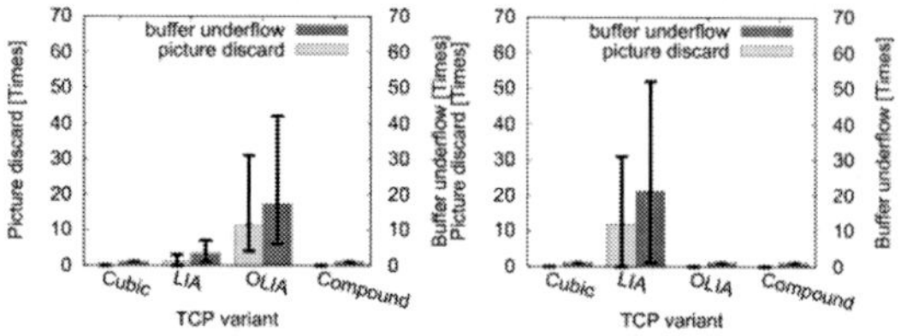

(a) DFT (b) GR-STY

Figure 10: WiFi-Cellular Handoff: video performance

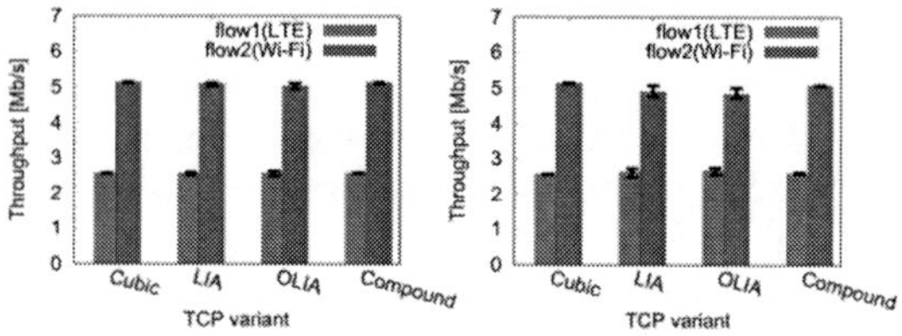

(a) DFT (b) GR-STY

Figure 11: WiFi-Cellular Handoff: transport throughput

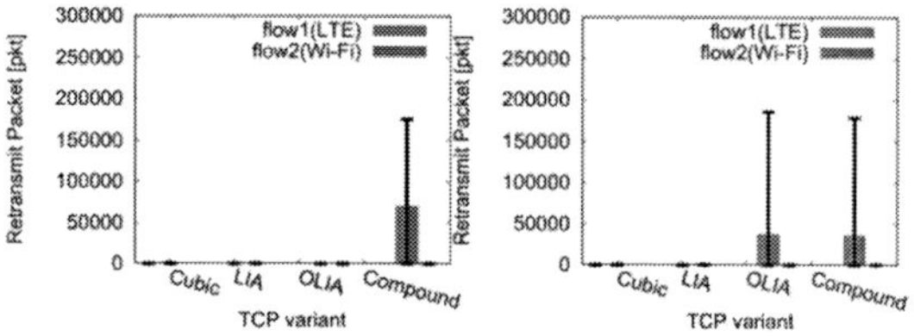

(a) DFT (b) GR-STY

Figure 12: WiFi-Cellular Handoff: transport retransmissions

Overall, the results show that video streaming over multiple paths may sustain handoffs between WiFi and cellular paths without significant performance degradation. In addition, sticky scheduler helps reduce retransmissions on slow to recover TCP variants such as OLIA and Compound.

VI. Conclusion and Future work

We have analyzed the impact of handoffs on video streaming performance over multiple paths. On a WiFi only scenario, we have shown that video streaming does not get affected by handoffs even on tight path bandwidth conditions. For WiFi-LTE cellular handoff, by using a VPN approach to overcome the issue of MPTCP signalling being dropped at intermediate nodes, we have shown video performance degradation for LIA and OLIA TCP variants. The path coupling of these TCP variants, where congestion window size depends on all active paths, slows down their recovery from packet losses during handoffs. We are currently investigating how coupled TCP variants may be made more robust to handoffs. We are also planning a handoff study on 5G cellular links.

Acknowledgments

Work supported by JSPS KAKENHI Grant # 16K00131.

References

[1] S. Afzal et al., "A Novel Scheduling Strategy for MMT-based Multipath Video Streaming," In Proceedings of IEEE Global Communications Conference - GLOBECOM, pp. 206-212, 2018.

[2] A. Aliyu et al., "Interference-Aware Multipath Video Streaming in Vehicular Environments," In IEEE Access Special Section on Towards Service-Centric Internet of Things (IoT): From Modeling to Practice, Volume 6, pp. 47610-47626, 2018.

[3] M. Allman, V. Paxson, and W. Stevens, "TCP Congestion Control," IETF RFC 2581, April 1999.

[4] Arzani et al., "Deconstructing MPTCP Performance," In Proceedings of IEEE 22nd ICNP, pp. 269-274, 2014.

[5] D. Cavendish, K. Kumazoe, M. Tsuru, Y. Oie, and M. Gerla, "Capacity and Congestion Probing: TCP Congestion Avoidance via Path Capacity and Storage Estimation," IEEE Second International Conference on Evolving Internet, pp. 42-48, September 2010.

[6] E. Dong et. al., "LAMPS: A Loss Aware Scheduler for Multipath TCP over Highly Lossy Networks," *Proceedings of the 42th IEEE Conference on Local Computer Networks*, pp. 1-9, October 2017.

[7] S. Ferlin et. al., "BLEST: Blocking Estimation-based MPTCP Scheduler for Heterogeneous Networks," In Proceedings of IFIP Networking Conference, pp. 431-439, 2016.

[8] A. Ford et. al., "Architectural Guidelines for Multipath TCP Development," IETF RFC 6182, 2011.

[9] A. Frommgen, J. Heuschkel and B. Koldehofe, "Multipath TCP Scheduling for Thin Streams: Active Probing and One-way Delay-awareness," IEEE Int. Conference on Communications (ICC), pp.1-7, May 2018.

[10] J. Hwang and J. Yoo, "Packet Scheduling for Multipath TCP," IEEE 7th Int. Conference on Ubiquitous and Future Networks, pp.177-179, July 2015.

[11] R. Khalili, N. Gast, and J-Y Le Boudec, "MPTCP Is Not Pareto-Optimal: Performance Issues and a Possible Solution," IEEE/ACM Trans. on Networking, Vol. 21, No. 5, pp. 1651-1665, Aug. 2013.

[12] Kimura et al., "Alternative Scheduling Decisions for Multipath TCP," IEEE Communications Letters, Vol. 21, No. 11, pp. 2412-2415, Nov. 2017.

[13] Matsufuji et al., "Multipath TCP Packet Schedulers for Streaming Video," IEEE Pacific Rim Conference on Communications, Computers and Signal Processing (PACRIM) , August 2017, pp. 1-6.

[14] Nagayama et al., "TCP State Driven MPTCP Packet Scheduling for Streaming Video," IARIA 10th International Conference on Evolving Internet, pp. 9-14, June 2018.

[15] Nagayama et al., "Path Switching Schedulers for MPTCP Streaming Video," IEEE Pacific Rim Conference on Communications, Computers and Signal Processing (PACRIM) , August 2019, pp. 1-6.

[16] R. K. P. Mok, E. W. W. Chan, and R. K. C. Chang, "Measuring the Quality of Experience of HTTP Video Streaming," Proceedings of IEEE International Symposium on Integrated Network Management, Dublin, Ireland, pp. 485-492, May 2011.

[17] Z. Lu, V. S. Somayazulu, and H. Moustafa, "Context Adaptive Cross-Layer TCP Optimization for Internet Video Streaming," In Proceedings of IEEE ICC 14, pp. 1723-1728, 2014.

[18] C. Raiciu, M. Handly, and D. Wischik, "Coupled Congestion Control for Multipath Transport Protocols," IETF RFC 6356, 2011.

[19] I. Rhee, L. Xu, and S. Ha, "CUBIC for Fast Long-Distance Networks," Internet Draft, draft-rhee-tcpm-ctcp-02, August 2008.

[20] M. Sridharan, K. Tan, D. Bansal, and D. Thaler, "Compound TCP: A New Congestion Control for High-Speed and Long Distance Networks," Internet Draft, draft-sridharan-tcpm-ctcp-02, November 2008.

[21] F. Silva, D. Bogusevschi, and G-M. Muntean, "A MPTCP-based RTT-aware Packet Delivery Prioritization Algorithm in AR/VR Scenarios," In Proceedings of IEEE Intern. Wireless Communications & Mobile Computing Conference - IWCMCC 18, pp. 95-100, June 2018.

[22] H. Sinky, B. Hamdaoui, M. Guizani, "Proactive Multipath TCP for Seamless Handoff in Heterogeneous Wireless Access Networks," In Proceedings of IEEE Transactions on Wireless Communications, Volume 15, Issue 7, pp. 4754-4764, 2016.

[23] Xue et al., "DPSAF: Forward Prediction Based Dynamic Packet Scheduling and Adjusting With Feedback for Multipath TCP in Lossy Heterogeneous Networks," IEEE/ACM Trans. on Vehicular Technology, Vol. 67, No. 2, pp. 1521-1534, Feb. 2018.

Loop Users in: The Key to Cross-Platform Data Interoperability

Han Su, Jialing Wu, Lifeng Liu,
Yingxuan Zhu, Jian Li

Futurewei Technologies
Boston, Massachusetts
Email: (hsu, jwu3,
lifeng.liu, yingxuan.zhu,
jian.li)@futurewei.com

Liyang Zhu, Boyan Xu

New York University
New York, USA
Email: (bx376, tomzhu)@nyu.edu

Abstract—**The lack of data interoperability on today's Internet platforms has led to data ownership problems, which further lead to the deprivation of netizen participation and representation in the data economy. In this paper, we conclude that user-oriented data interoperability is the key to change the siloed app ecosystem toward a more decentralized direction. This paper examines the various attempts made by the industry to increase interoperability at different levels: software level, platform level, and infrastructure level. Web 1.0 granted netizens the right to view online content and Web 2.0 (Apps) has given netizens the right to publish in a participatory manner. In this paper, we envision that the next-generation Internet platforms will enable netizens to access personal storage and computation, which can recuperate netizens' right for data ownership and representation in the data economy.**

Keywords–Data Interoperability; Web 3.0; Data Ownership; App Ecosystem; Data Economy; Privacy.

I. INTRODUCTION

With the rise of Internet companies, Internet platforms have become more centralized in terms of data storage, which has led to myriad problems including data ownership [1]-[3] and privacy issues [4]-[6]. The rise of apps and the decline of the World Wide Web exacerbate the problem [7], [8]. A major drawback of the app ecosystem where Internet companies control most resources is the lack of data interoperability between platforms [9], making the current app ecosystem de facto app silos. Data interoperability [10], [11] not only means different platforms sharing data between each other, but also addresses the ability of users, platforms and other agencies who create, exchange and consume data to have clear, shared expectations for the usage, context, and meaning of the data [12].

App silos (see Figure 1) depict the ill status quo of different apps practicing their own data standards while leaving users out of the loop. The lack of data interoperability has led to two major issues. First, Internet companies have made the data generated on their platforms as private properties and make profits through which, e.g., by enhancing ads with data-driven micro-targeting means, or directly selling user data. Second, netizen online data are shattered on different platforms with different accounts. The popular narrative of big data is that platforms may learn your preferences to provide better-personalized services. However, the app silo status quo thwarts the ideal, since an app can only learn about a limited part of the user. None of them can see the whole picture, nor could the user themselves, which makes it less possible to maximize the potential value from user data.

Moreover, the lack of data interoperability also exacerbates the unvirtuous deeds and competitions in the internet industry, for big companies will always be in an advantageous, if not hegemonic position in data collections and data trades. Since users are left out of the loop of the sales and future usages of their data, these kinds of data sales and analysis deeds in the capitalism market will ultimately commodify personal information and let corporations prey back on users.

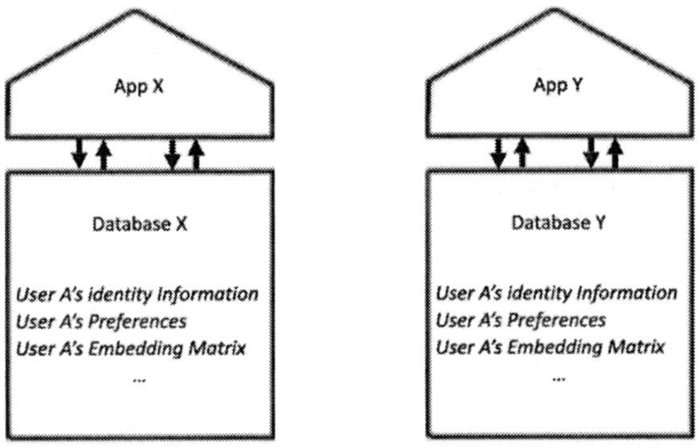

Figure 1. App Silo.

Dissatisfied with the status quo, innovators in the Internet field have been developing new forms of protocols or technologies to increase interoperability between different agents, e.g., the decentralized web movement and linked-data platforms in the Web field [13], [14], and the burgeoning use of Application Program Interface (API) [15] in the Internet industry.

The purpose of this paper is to introduce an ongoing project. Our aim is to protect user privacy, facilitate data management online and enhance data interoperability among web apps. This paper will cover the theories, methods and products of our project.

The paper is structured as follows: Section II describes the three levels of data interoperability with real-world examples. Section III illustrates the architecture and characteristics of our end-user customizable platform design proposed in the Alora project and incorporated in its web based portal app called Alora.

TABLE I. THREE MAJOR ISSUES ON TODAY'S INTERNET

Issue	Description
Online Privacy	Without resorting to third party services, netizens cannot tell if a website is collecting certain cookies or using trackers, nor could netizens disable them.
Data Storage	Online activities only enrich the databases of Internet companies, rather than the power of netizens to control what they want to see. Moreover, the databases of different apps are not interoperable.
Micro-targeting Advertising	Although most of the Internet is free to browse for netizens, yet we are paying with our attention to the free services, which may eventually cost more due to the asymmetric information in the market.

II. Three Levels of Data Interoperability and Existing Examples

The prevailing data ownership issues stem from when Internet companies make it a norm to collect and privatize user data, which has led to the rise of advertising-supported business models. As scrutinized by Wu [16], Internet platforms provide user free diversion in exchange for user attention, which is monetized through advertising, and the efficiency of which is enhanced by micro-targeting and recommendation systems based on the data collected by internet companies. Internet companies play the role of "attention merchants", a term coined by Wu to describe the role played by Internet companies in the advertising model [16]. We have listed three major problems faced by today's Internet users due to the lack of data interoperability in today's Internet platforms, as shown in Table 1.

A. Software Level Interoperability

Software level interoperability refers to the scenario that the owner of the software designs data interoperability protocol and defines how their data will be accessed by outside parties.

The app ecosystem has been constantly making progress towards software level data interoperability. We are seeing an ever-growing API ecosystem. With API, outside developers can access data in the API providers' servers with the provided calls and requests. For example, team collaboration app Slack [17] has integrated more than 2000 frequently used services into their platform, including Office 365®, GitHub, and Google Drive.

Emerging products like Zapier and IFTTT, whose slogan is "get all your apps and devices talking to each other", are de facto a combination of APIs. There are plenty of explorations to improve the interoperability between apps, and API is the best representative of which, yet software level interoperability also has the app itself as the limit–making things beyond the app out of reach.

B. Platform Level Interoperability

Platform level interoperability denotes a parent platform that defines the data interoperability protocol adopted by agencies residing on the platform.

In platform level interoperability, the parent platform promotes platform level interoperability in a top-down manner by enforcing standardized developing languages, data formats, and user interaction components. One recent popular instance is the Mini Program inside a platform. The Chinese social media platform WeChat [18], [19] first published its Mini Program platform in 2017, followed by Baidu and Alipay. The parent platform provides a slew of developing standards and functioning modules, so that all functions are accessible to developers and there is no need to reproduce existing solutions: authentication and authorization, QR code scanning, augmented reality modules, online payment, map and location service, etc. Moreover, data storage is also partially interoperable between Mini Programs and the parent platform. With the help of various interoperable functions, Mini Programs can stay light in size and focus on functions the main platform does not provide. According to the 2019 year-end report, WeChat has more than 3 million Mini Programs on its platform with 330 million daily active users. Moreover, users on average have used 60 different Mini Programs in 2019.

C. Infrastructure Level Interoperability

Infrastructure level interoperability refers to a thorough set of protocols from the front-end interface to back-end computing and storage, which all agents need to have a consensus on the use of the data.

One and probably the only prevailing Internet platform that meets infrastructure level interoperability is the World Wide Web. Backed by W3C standards, the web is an immense platform where netizens read data and write data. However, the interoperability of the web has been declining with the prevalence of platforms with private databases when most of the data collecting actions are underwater.

In this section, we analyze three projects aiming at providing infrastructure level interoperability to internet services: SoLiD, Brave, and Blockstack.

Social Linked Data (SoLiD) [20], [21] is the new project proposed by Sir Tim Berners-Lee, the inventor of the World Wide Web. SoLiD targets at improving data interoperability in the infrastructure level by granting users access to their data storage with the Personal Data Pod, which gives read/write permissions to different apps. Social linked data also guarantees social connections to be a secured property linked with users' WebID [22], [23], which makes authentication and social connection infrastructures on the web. SoLiD aims to rejuvenate the web through solving problems, which we have concluded below: privacy, storage, and advertising.

Brave is an open-sourced browser known for its novel solutions to privacy and advertising issues. Brave aims to build the infrastructure for online content production and consumption business model. As Brave points out on its website, the foremost problem on today's Internet for Brave to solve is: "[a]s a user, access to your web activity and data is sold to the highest bidder. Internet giants grow rich, while publishers go out of business. And the entire system is rife with ad fraud [24]." Brave helps its users to block data-grabbing ads and trackers [25]. Moreover, Brave introduces the Brave Attention Token, a cryptocurrency issued by Brave that allows users to earn frequent flier-like tokens for browsing and support web creators with the tokens. In this way, contents on the Internet will get matched with economic values without resorting to the advertisement. Brave envisions Brave Attention Token as a new infrastructure for linking valuable content with user attention and money.

Blockstack is a platform with the overarching mission of giving users direct ownership of their internet assets and protecting user privacy [26]. Blockstack is trying to achieve the goal of infrastructure level interoperability for dApps by providing a suite of developer tools and protocols intended to lower the start-up barriers of dApp development [27]. The most important feature is its enforcement of universal login with Blockstack ID. Blockstack keeps a record of user identity on a blockchain database and then asks its user to set up accounts with apps built on Blockstack [28].

III. Architecture and Characteristics of our End-user Customizable Platform–Alora

As discussed, Alora is a web-based platform being developed by our team [29]. Alora addresses the three problems aforementioned, i.e., data privacy, personal storage, and advertising, in a user-friendly way with existing web technologies. Figure 2 is a screenshot of the current version of Alora extension. The code is open-sourced [30].

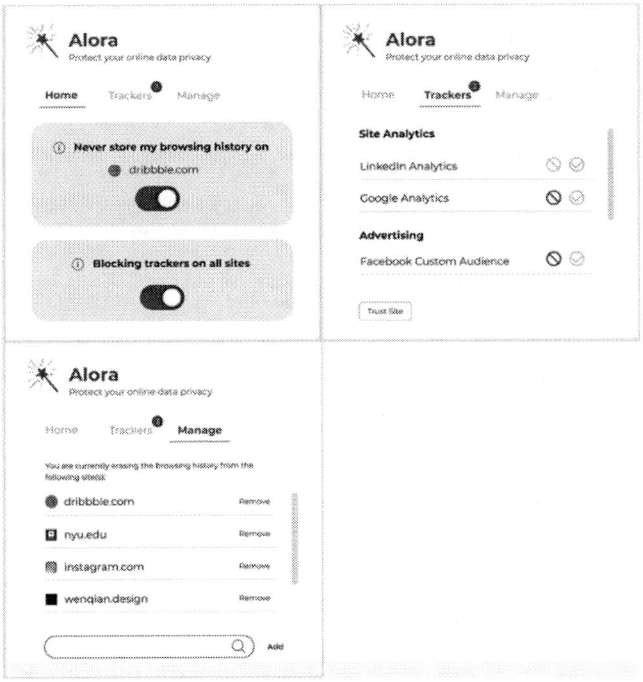

Figure 2. Alora Privacy Extension.

A. Data Privacy

Alora provides a digital footprint management system in the form of a browser extension, as shown in Fig. 3. Based on EFF's privacy badger project [31], the extension can detect third party trackers and automatically block it for the users. Moreover, Alora also automates users' preference on managing privacy-related data on chosen sites including cache, cookies, history, etc. For example, if a user does not want to save history nor cookies on www.amazon.com, the user can switch on the button on Alora, and the extension will delete cookies and history data related to the selected URL automatically. Alora also provides an email for every user to do account management.

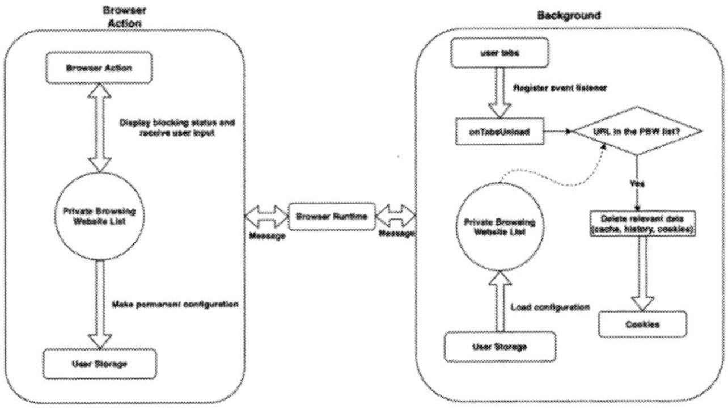

Figure 3. Alora's Customizable Personal Portal User Interface.

B. Personal Data Management.

Alora provides a personal portal page that serves as the homepage of our users, where frequently visited websites will be prioritized into a cluster of lists, as shown in the left column in Figure 4. Furthermore, with the help of APIs of the frequently used services of the user, users are able to maintain a customizable portal–e.g, email notifications, Twitter feeds, messages, etc. In this way, the features of different services are interoperable with the user's Alora homepage. Moreover, Alora affords users the function to add User Generated Paratext upon resources (see Fig. 4), which means users can save, like, comment, annotate the resources they have browsed online. In this way, user data and metadata are guarded inside the user's personal data zone at the local storage or user's Alora personal cloud, which is analogous to the Personal Data Pod in SoLiD, rather than Internet companies' servers. In future work, Alora also plans to generate user embedding with locally stored user data, or lets users allow third-party services to run federated learning models on certain local user data [32]. The strength of Alora is that the data structure is a thorough one that contains all aspects of the user's online activities, rather than a biased one restricted to a single service. What's more, users have full knowledge and control of the data collecting and management process.

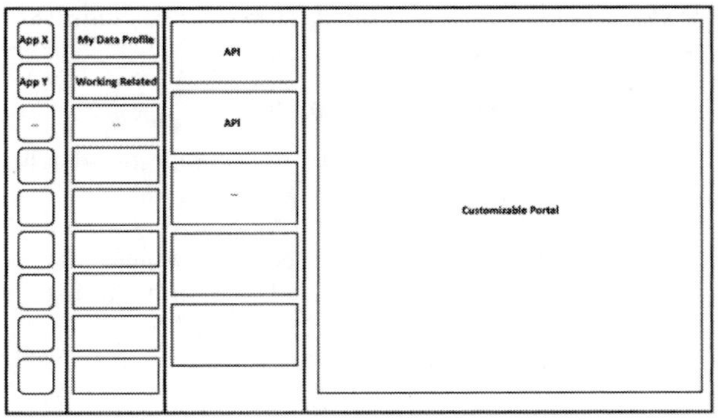

Figure 4. Alora's Automation for User Private Data Management.

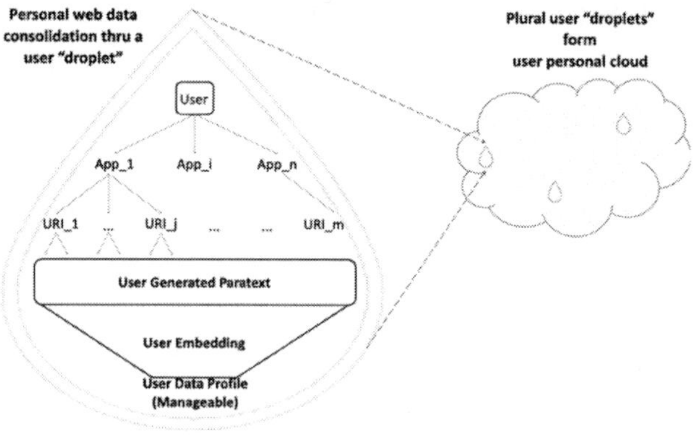

Figure 5. Alora's Customizable Personal Portal User Interface.

As shown in Figure 5, Internet resources generated through Alora include the User Generated Paratext and the User Embedding with a user manageable data profile, which are controlled by the user and accessible by third parties through Alora APIs–which users have the right to decide the read/write accessibility of their resources. Therefore, with the help of Alora, user online data is at the fingertips of users in their personal data storage rather than in custody by cloud service vendors. Such an in-app approach elevates the visibility of privacy control and grants the user convenient control of their personal data management.

C. Data Profile Management (Work in progress)

Based on the user metadata including browsing history, user action data, and the user-generated paratext including likes, comments, and annotations, Alora will be able to train a user embedding, and generate a user-readable and -manageable data profile. The profile will include different tags as in Figure 6. User embedding is a popular method used in today's recommendation systems, yet most labels are latent [33]. The goal of Alora's user data profile design above is to make the latent labels transparent to the users, and users will also have the right to manage their data profile and assign accessibilities to their profile and metadata. Furthermore, third party services will no longer need to resort to trackers to collect user data, which is hard to be comprehensive especially for small and medium businesses. We believe the impacts of Alora on the next-generation Internet are huge by looping users back in the game. Data economy and the advertising business model of Internet companies will be fundamentally changed by looping users in the data mining process. The data monopoly by giant Internet companies will get destroyed by granting users the right to maintain a more comprehensive user data profile. Last but not least, the realization of data ownership and willingness to pay for content online will go hand in hand–if users are willing to pay for better data ownership, they will also appreciate the value of information and will be willing to get information as a service.

TABLE II. USER DATA PROFILE EXAMPLE

Key	Value
Age	18-24 years old
Gender	Male
Interests	Fitness, Adventure Games
Work	Internet Industry

IV. Conclusion

This paper scrutinized the compelling problems faced by Internet users today: the privatization of user data has led to the ill status quo of today's Internet–lack of data interoperability between platforms and users, myriad data breaches, and various data ownership issues. The quintessential problem is not technical bottlenecks, but a lack of user-oriented infrastructure that protects the data ownership of Internet users, the sources of data that are ironically left out of today's data economy. Alore aims to provide open-sourced, transparent, secure, user-oriented personal cloud computing solutions. By looping users in the data collection and mining process, the latent data collection and data mining process will become transparent to users, resulting in better data interoperability between users and services.

Acknowledgment

This research was partially supported by Futurewei Technologies. We thank our team members from MIT, NYU, CMU who contribute to the Alora project with their expertise, and the global contributors of Alora.

References

[1] H. Kopka and P. W. Daly, *A Guide to LaTeX*, 3rd ed. Harlow, England: Addison-Wesley, 1999.

[2] S. Bertram and C.-P. Georg, "A privacy-preserving system for data ownership using blockchain and distributed databases," arXiv preprint-arXiv:1810.11655, 2018

[3] S. M. Khan and K. W. Hamlen, "Anonymous cloud: A data ownership privacy provider framework in cloud computing," in 2012 IEEE 11thInternational Conference on Trust, Security and Privacy in Computing and Communications. IEEE, 2012, pp. 170–176.

[4] S. Zuboff, "Big other: surveillance capitalism and the prospects of an information civilization," Journal of Information Technology, vol. 30,no. 1, 2015, pp. 75–89.

[5] D. Kifer and A. Machanavajjhala, "No free lunch in data privacy," inProceedings of the 2011 ACM SIGMOD International Conference onManagement of data, 2011, pp. 193–204.

[6] M. S. Ali, K. Dolui, and F. Antonelli, "Iot data privacy via block chains and ipfs," in Proceedings of the seventh international conference on the internet of things, 2017, pp. 1–7.

[7] Pentina, L. Zhang, H. Bata, and Y. Chen, "Exploring privacy paradox in information-sensitive mobile app adoption: A cross-cultural comparison," Computers in Human Behavior, vol. 65, 2016, pp. 409–419.

[8] V. M. Wottrich, E. A. van Reijmersdal, and E. G. Smit, "The privacy trade-off for mobile app downloads: The roles of app value, intrusive-ness, and privacy concerns," Decision Support Systems, vol. 106, 2018,pp. 44–52.

[9] A. Kadadi, R. Agrawal, C. Nyamful, and R. Atiq, "Challenges of data integration and interoperability in big data," in 2014 IEEE international conference on big data (big data). IEEE, 2014, pp. 38–40.

[10] J. Buck, S. J. Bainbridge, E. F. Burger, A. C. Kraberg, M. Casari,K. S. Casey, L. Darroch, J. D. Rio, K. Metfies, E. Delory et al.,"Ocean data product integration through innovation-the next level of data interoperability," Frontiers in Marine Science, vol. 6, 2019, p. 32.

[11] R. Nawaratne, D. Alahakoon, D. De Silva, P. Chhetri, and N. Chilamkurti, "Self-evolving intelligent algorithms for facilitating data interoperability in iot environments," Future Generation Computer Systems,vol. 86, 2018, pp. 421–432.

[12] "What Is 'Data Interoperability?'." [cited 12 July 2020] The Data Interoperability Standards Consortium , datainteroperability.org/.

[13] N. Vogel, "The great decentralization: How web 3.0 will weaken copyrights," J. Marshall Rev. Intell. Prop. L., vol. 15, 2015, p. 136.

[14] Zuboff, Shoshana. "Google as a Fortune Teller: The Secrets of Surveillance Capitalism." FAZ.NET. [cited 12 July 2020] https://www.faz.net/aktuell/feuilleton/debatten/the-digitaldebate/ shoshana-zuboff-secrets-of-surveillance-capitalism - 14103616.html?printPagedArticle=true.

[15] A. W. Smith, A. J. Moore, D. S. Ebbo, E. B. Christensen, E. B. Olson,F. A. Yeon, J. V. Rajan, K. W. Ballinger, M. Vasandani, M. T. Anderset al., "Application program interface that enables communication for a network software platform," Oct. 3 2006, US Patent 7,117,504.

[16] T. Wu, The attention merchants: The epic scramble to get inside our heads. Vintage, 2017.

[17] J. Hill, R. LaFollette, R. Grosso, D. Axelson, K. Hart, and E. McDonough, "Using slack to facilitate virtual small groups for individualized interactive instruction," AEM education and training, vol. 3, no. 1,2019, pp. 92–95.

[18] Lin, J. Qiu, and P. Chen, "Exploration and practice on intelligent teaching patterns based on wechat mini program," in Proceedings of the 2020 9th International Conference on Educational and InformationTechnology, 2020, pp. 153–157.

[19] L. Hao, F. Wan, N. Ma, and Y. Wang, "Analysis of the development of wechat mini program," in J. Phys.: Conf. Ser, vol. 1087, 2018, p.062040..

[20] A. V. Sambra, E. Mansour, S. Hawke, M. Zereba, N. Greco, A. Ghanem,D. Zagidulin, A. Aboulnaga, and T. Berners-Lee, "Solid: a platform for decentralized social applications based on linked data," TechnicalReport, MIT CSAIL Qatar Computing Research Institute, Tech. Rep.,2016.

[21] J. Werbrouck, P. Pauwels, J. Beetz, and L. van Berlo, "Towards a decentralised common data environment using linked building data andthe solid ecosystem," in 36th CIB W78 2019 Conference, 2019, pp.113–123..

[22] G. Huang and K. Mak, "Webid: A web-based framework to support early supplier involvement in new product development," Robotics andComputer-Integrated Manufacturing, vol. 16, no. 2-3, 2000, pp. 169–179.

[23] P. Mainini and A. Laube-Rosenpflanzer, "Access control in linked data using webid," arXiv preprint arXiv:1611.03019, 2016.

[24] Secure, Fast Private Web Browser with Adblocker — Brave Browser [Internet]. Brave Browser. 2020 [cited 12 July 2020]. Available from: https://brave.com/?ref=soc369.

[25] Tung, Liam. "Brave defies Google's moves to cripple ad-blocking with new 69x faster Rust engine". ZDNet. Retrieved 1 July 2020.

[26] About [Internet]. Blockstack.org. 2020 [cited 12 July 2020]. Available from: https://blockstack.org/about.

[27] Popper N. Tech Thinks It Has a Fix for the Problems It Created: Blockchain [Internet]. Nytimes.com. 2020 [cited 12 July 2020]. Available from: https://www.nytimes.com/2018/04/01/technology/blockch ain-uses.html

[28] Buchko S. What Is Blockstack (STX)? — The First SEC-Qualified Token Offering [Internet]. CoinCentral. 2020 [cited 12 July 2020]. Available from: https://coincentral.com/blockstack-stx/

[29] The Privoce Project [Internet]. Privoce.com. 2020 [cited 12 July 2020]. Available from: http://privoce.com.

[30] The Privoce Project [Internet]. . 2020 [cited 7 Oct 2020]. Available from: https://github.com/privoce

[31] Privacy Badger [Internet]. Electronic Frontier Foundation. 2020 [cited 12 July 2020]. Available from: https://privacybadger.org

[32] D. Zhang, J. Yin, X. Zhu, and C. Zhang, "User profile preserving social network embedding," in IJCAI International Joint Conference on Artificial Intelligence, 2017.

[33] X. He, L. Liao, H. Zhang, L. Nie, X. Hu, and T.-S. Chua, "Neural collaborative filtering," in Proceedings of the 26th international conference on world wide web, 2017, pp. 173–182.

Efficient Intrusion Detection Using Evidence Theory

Islam Debicha

Royal Military Academy
and Université Libre de Bruxelles
Brussels, Belgium
Email: debichasislam@gmail.com

Thibault Debatty

Royal Military Academy
Brussels, Belgium
Email: thibault.debatty@rma.ac.be

Wim Mees

Royal Military Academy
Brussels, Belgium
Email: wim.mees@rma.ac.be

Jean-Michel Dricot

Université Libre de Bruxelles
Brussels, Belgium
Email: jdricot@ulb.ac.be

***Abstract*—Intrusion Detection Systems (IDS) are now an essential element when it comes to securing computers and networks. Despite the huge research efforts done in the field, handling sources' reliability remains an open issue. To address this problem, this paper proposes a novel contextual discounting method based on sources' reliability and their distinguishing ability between normal and abnormal behavior. Dempster-Shafer theory, a general framework for reasoning under uncertainty, is used to construct an evidential classifier. The NSL-KDD dataset, a significantly revised and improved version of the existing KDD-CUP'99 dataset, provides the basis for assessing the performance of our new detection approach. While giving comparable results on the KDDTest+ dataset, our approach outperformed some other state-of-the-art methods on the KDDTest-21 dataset which is more challenging.**

Keywords–Intrusion detection; machine learning; evidence theory; contextual discounting.

I. INTRODUCTION

As computer network usage grows rapidly along with the significant increase in the number of applications running on it, the importance of network security is increasing. As dedicated tools designed to identify anomalies and attacks on the network, Intrusion Detection Systems (IDS) are becoming more valuable. Detection techniques based on anomalies and misuse have long been the principal subject of research in the field of intrusion detection [1].

Misuse-based IDSs operate quite similarly to most antivirus systems. Maintaining a signature database that could identify specific types of attacks and checking all incoming traffic against these signatures. Overall, this approach performs well, although it does not work properly when dealing with new attacks, or those that were specifically crafted to mismatch existing signatures.

On the other hand, anomaly-based IDSs operate generally on a baseline of normal activities and network traffic. This allows them to assess the current state of network traffic against this baseline so that abnormal patterns can be identified. While such an approach could be quite effective in detecting new attacks or those that have been intentionally crafted to evade IDSs, it can also result in a higher number of false positives compared to misuse-based IDSs.

Dempster-Shafer Theory (DST), also known as evidence theory [2] is one of the most versatile mathematical frameworks, extending Bayesian theory by (i) providing each source with the ability to integrate information at various scales of detail, thus addressing uncertainty; and (ii) offering a robust decision-making tool to make a consensus-based decision. This theory was later widely applied in several domains [3][4][5]. Regardless of this popularity, mass function generation and source reliability estimation remain an ongoing challenge.

Probabilistic frameworks for mass generation take advantage of the extensive research literature of the traditional probabilistic classifiers. These approaches usually represent the information associated with each attribute through Probability Density Functions (PDF), typically Gaussian [6][7]. Such densities are then transformed into beliefs that can subsequently be merged to form a joint decision. One can attribute masses to the compound hypotheses by subtracting the mass values related to the simple hypotheses involved [6] or by mixing the distributions associated with these hypotheses [7]. It should be noted that for most applications, Gaussian densities have been widely assumed due to their simplicity. Nevertheless, in the case where this assumption fails, the decision-making performance may be influenced considerably. More sophisticated approaches can be used to surmount this limitation by transforming data attributes into an equivalent normal space [8].

This paper offers a more effective way to overcome this disadvantage by constructing PDFs that are better suited to the original data histograms instead of projecting them into a new Gaussian-like space. On a more explicit level, a kernel smoothing estimation [9] is used on the training data to derive an approximate PDF for each data attribute and each simple hypothesis. These PDFs may be of any shape. Notably, they might be non-Gaussian. During the classification phase, a given datum is associated with a set of masses that are generated in an elaborated way from the aforementioned densities. Using the proposed contextual discounting method, mass functions are then weakened differently depending on the ability of each source to discriminate between classes. Mass functions of the different sources are then merged to have a consensual mass function using a suitable fusion rule. A final decision is then deduced using the so-called "pignistic transform" [10].

The rest of this paper is organized as follows: Section II recalls the theoretical tools used in the proposed approach. Section III describes the NSL-KDD dataset. A description of Boosted PR-DS architecture is introduced in Section IV. Section V discusses the experimental results by comparing them with those of some previous studies using the NSL-KDD dataset. Final remarks and further suggestions for improvement are given in Section VI.

II. RELATED BACKGROUND

We succinctly outline some fundamentals of Dempster-Shafer theory, Parzen-Rosenblatt density estimation and contextual discounting.

A. Dempster-Shafer theory

Suppose that $\Omega = \{\omega_1, ..., \omega_K\}$, and $\mathcal{P}(\Omega) = \{A_1, ..., A_Q\}$ is its power set, where $Q = 2^K$. A defined mass function M ranging from $\mathcal{P}(\Omega)$ to $[0, 1]$ is named a "basic belief assignment" (*bba*) if $M(\emptyset) = 0$ and $\sum_{A \in \mathcal{P}(\Omega)} M(A) = 1$. A *bba* M therefore defines a "plausibility" function Pl ranging from $\mathcal{P}(\Omega)$ to $[0, 1]$ by $Pl(A) = \sum_{A \cap B \neq \emptyset} M(B)$, and a "credibility" function Cr ranging from $\mathcal{P}(\Omega)$ to $[0, 1]$ by $Cr(A) = \sum_{B \subset A} M(B)$. In addition, the two functions mentioned above are bound by $Pl(A) + Cr(A^c) = 1$. Moreover, a probability function p could be regarded as a particular case wherein $Pl = Cr = p$.

In case where two *bbas* M_1 and M_2 denote two elements of evidence, we can combine them together using the "Dempster-Shafer fusion" (DS fusion), which results in $M = M_1 \oplus M_2$ that is defined by:

$$M(A) = (M_1 \oplus M_2)(A) \propto \sum_{B_1 \cap B_2 = A} M_1(B_1) M_2(B_2) \quad (1)$$

Lastly, through Smets' technique[10], an evidential *bba* M can be converted into a probabilistic one, whereby every belief mass $M(A)$ is evenly distributed over all elements of A, resulting in the so-called "pignistic probability", Bet , given by:

$$Bet(\omega_i) = \sum_{\omega_i \in A \subseteq \Omega} \frac{M(A)}{|A|} \quad (2)$$

where $|A|$ is the number of elements of Ω in A.

It is worth mentioning that there are various evidential fusion rules in the literature that deal differently with the issue of conflicting sources [11][12][13].

B. Parzen-Rosenblatt density estimation

As a statistical tool, the Parzen-Rosenblatt window technique [14][15], otherwise known as kernel density estimation, is a way to smooth data by making population inferences based on a finite sample. This technique can be perceived as a non-parametric method to construct the PDF f, of an unknown form, linked to a random variable X. Suppose $(x_1, x_2, ..., x_N)$ an example of the realizations of such a random variable. The challenge is to estimate the f values at multiple points of interest. The smoothing of the kernel can then be seen as a generalization of the histogram smoothing where a window, of a predetermined shape, centered at every point is utilized to approximate the value of density at the given point. This is done by using the following estimator:

$$\hat{f}_h(x) = \frac{1}{Nh} \sum_{i=1}^{N} K\left(\frac{x - x_i}{h}\right) \quad (3)$$

where $K(\cdot)$ is the kernel - a zero-mean non-negative function that integrates to one - and $h > 0$ is a smoothing parameter known as "kernel width". Furthermore, it is possible to use a variety of kernel functions like Uniform (Box), Gaussian (Normal), Triangle, Epanechnikov [16], Quartic (Biweight), Tricube [17], Triweight, Logistic, Quadratic [18], and others.

C. Discounting methods

Such methods can be used to estimate the weakening coefficients assigned to a source in order to correct its decision. These adjustments differ depending on whether it is a classic or contextual weakening.

1) Classical discounting: The weakening of mass functions makes it possible to model sources' reliability by introducing a coefficient α^s where for each source s we have:

$$\begin{cases} m'^s(A) = \alpha^s.m^s(A) & \forall A \in 2^\Omega, A \neq \Omega \\ m'^s(\Omega) = (1 - \alpha^s) + \alpha^s.m(\Omega) \end{cases} \quad (4)$$

α^s is the weakening coefficient of the sth source. Among the classical weakening methods, we find [19] and [5].

2) Contextual discounting: The idea behind the contextual weakening is that the reliability of a source can vary depending on the truth of the object to be recognized (the context). For example, a sensor responsible for recognizing flying targets may be more or less able to discern certain types of aircraft. The method we propose belongs to this category and is described below.

Weakening using F-score: In this method, we evaluate the ability of each attribute (source) to classify elements belonging to different hypotheses -simple or composite-. This is done by considering each attribute separately to classify a new element. Using a cross-validation process, a confusion matrix is obtained. From this matrix, the "F-score" performance is calculated for all the hypotheses. These measures will be used as weakening coefficients and the equation 5 is applied to weaken the mass function of each source s.

$$\begin{cases} m'^s(A) = \alpha^s_A m^s(A) & A \in \{2^\Omega / \Omega\} \\ m'^s(\Omega) = m^s(\Omega) + \sum_{A \in \{2^\Omega / \Omega\}} (1 - \alpha^s_A) m^s(A) \end{cases} \quad (5)$$

α^s_A is the weakening coefficient of hypothesis A for the sth source.

III. NSL-KDD DATASET DESCRIPTION

In addition to the fact that attack patterns are constantly evolving and changing, the challenge in building a robust Network Intrusion Detection System (NIDS) is that a real-time pattern of network data consisting of both intrusions and normal traffic is out of reach. This is why many recent works are still using the NSL-KDD dataset to evaluate the performance of their approaches [20][21].

One of the most frequently used datasets for intrusion detection tests is the NSL-KDD dataset which was released in 2009 [22]. In addition to addressing efficiently redundant records' issue in the KDDCUP'99 dataset, NSL-KDD is designed by reducing the number of records in the training and test sets in a sophisticated manner to prevent the classifier from biasing towards frequent records.

There are three datasets within NSL-KDD. One for training which is KDDTrain+ and two for testing with an increasing difficulty respectively KDDTest+ and KDDTest-21, all of which having normal records as well as four distinct types of attack records, as shown in Table I. KDDTest-21 which is a subset of the KDDTest+ is designed to be a more challenging dataset by removing the often correctly classified records. For more details about how KDDTest-21 was conceived, the reader may refer to [22].

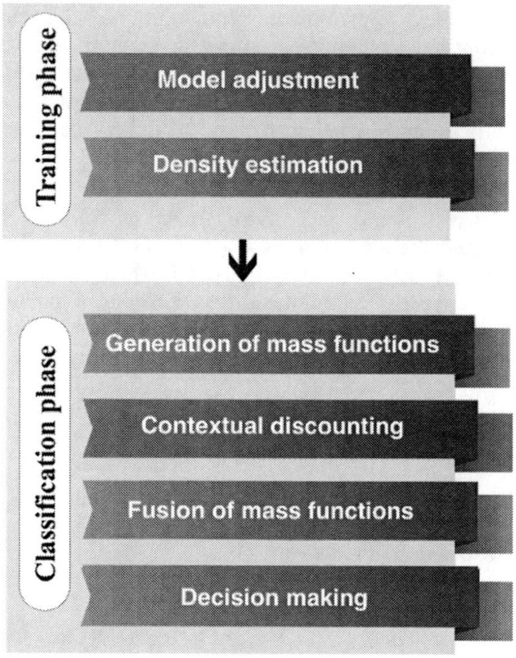

Figure 1. Proposed Boosted PR-DS framework

TABLE I. DIFFERENT CLASSES OF THE NSL-KDD DATASET.

	Normal	Dos	Probe	R2L	U2R
KDDTrain+	67343	45927	11656	995	52
KDDTest+	9711	7458	2421	2754	200
KDDTest-21	2152	4342	2402	2754	200

Each record has 41 attributes and a class label as well. These attributes are divided into basic features, content features, and traffic features. Attacks in the dataset are grouped into four categories based on their characteristics: DoS (denial of service attacks), Probe (Probing attacks), R2L (root-to-local attacks) and U2R (user-to-root attacks). Some specific types of attacks are included in the test set but are not included in the training set. This makes it possible to provide a more realistic testing ground.

IV. BOOSTED PR-DS

This section describes the theoretical basis of the proposed intrusion detection scheme called Boosted Parzen-Rosenblatt Dempster-Shafer (Boosted PR-DS). To do this, suppose we have a sample of N pre-tagged multiattribute data $(Z_1, ..., Z_N)$ where each datum $Z_n = (X_n, Y_n)$ with $X_n \in \Omega = \{\omega_1, ..., \omega_K\}$ being the tag, and $Y_n = (Y_n^1, ..., Y_n^P) \in \mathbb{R}^P$ being the P-attribute observation. The challenge is then to determine the tag of any new observation $Y_{n'}$.

As shown in Figure 1, we begin by briefly outlining the training process carried out on the pre-tagged data sample $(Z_1, ..., Z_N)$. Next, we illustrate the way our approach assigns a new observation $Y_{n'}$ to one of the K classes (tags).

A. Training phase

Consider the pre-tagged multi-attribute data above $(Z_1, ..., Z_N)$. Under our Boosted PR-DS scheme, the training phase involves two steps. The first is model adjustment which consists of determining the optimal kernel and fusion rule for the data along with the computing of weakening coefficients for each hypothesis. The second step is density estimation where the previously chosen kernel is used to estimate the Probability Density Functions (PDF) of each class for all attributes.

1) Model adjustment: In the first step, while changing kernels and fusion rules, basic PR-DS is used in a cross-validation process on the training data. The kernel and fusion rule giving the highest accuracy are then selected. To compute the weakening coefficients, we propose to use the F-score measures obtained from classifying each attribute (taken alone) as explained in paragraph Section II-C2.

2) Density estimation: In this step, we use the kernel chosen during the previous step to estimate densities using the Parzen-Rossenblatt method as described in Section II-B instead of considering that they follow a normal distribution as in the classical case. We thus obtain, for each class $\omega_k \in \Omega$ and for each attribute p $(1 < p < P)$, a Parzen-Rosenblatt density $\hat{f}_k^p$.

Eventually, in addition to the estimated densities, the trained model includes the weakening coefficients and the best-fit fusion rule.

B. Classification phase

Given a new observation $Y_{n'}$, a mass function M^p for each attribute is constructed based on the estimated densities. The proposed contextual discounting mechanism is then applied using the previously calculated weakening coefficients. Subsequently, the weakened mass functions are combined to obtain a consensual report M. The final decision is made using the so-called Pignistic Transform. In what follows, we describe these different steps.

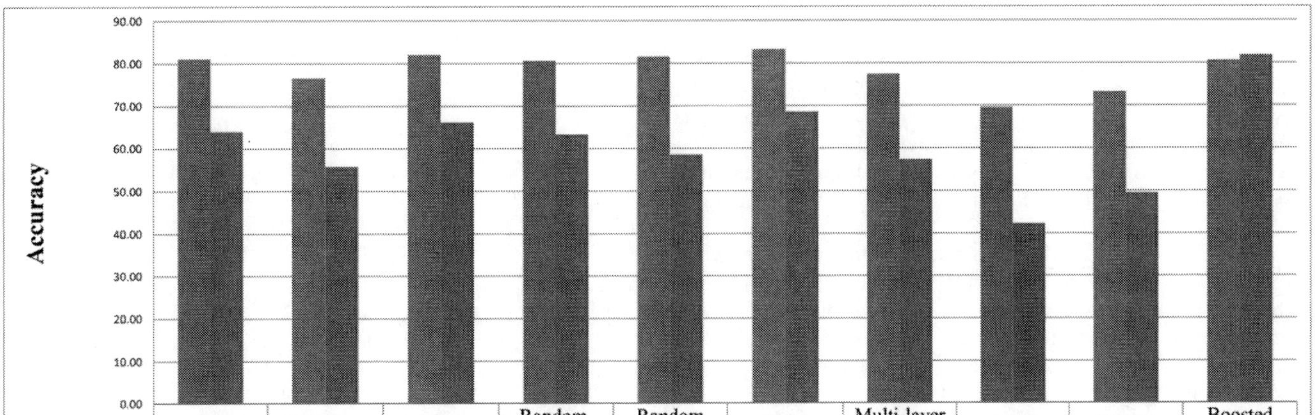

	J48	Naive Bayes	NB Tree	Random Forest	Random Tree	RNN	Multi-layer Perceptron	SVM	PR-DS	Boosted PR-DS
KDDTest+	81.05	76.56	82.02	80.67	81.59	83.28	77.41	69.52	73.28	80.62
KDDTest-21	63.97	55.77	66.16	63.26	58.51	68.55	57.34	42.29	49.48	81.84

Figure 2. Performance of Boosted PR-DS and the other models on KDDTest+ and KDDTest-21.

1) Generation of mass function: In order to determine the mass $\mathcal{M}^p$ assigned to the attribute p, we will consider the rank function δ_p which is defined from $\{1, .., K\}$ to Ω so that $\delta_p(k)$ is the $k-$ranked element of Ω in terms of $\hat{f}^p$, i.e. $\hat{f}^p_{\delta_p(1)}(Y^p_{n'}) \leq \hat{f}^p_{\delta_p(2)}(Y^p_{n'}) \leq ... \leq \hat{f}^p_{\delta_p(K)}(Y^p_{n'})$. Then, $\mathcal{M}^p$ is determined as follows:

$$\begin{cases} \mathcal{M}^p(\Omega) \propto \hat{f}^p_{\delta_p(1)}(Y^p_{n'}) \\ \mathcal{M}^p(\{\omega_{\delta_p(k)}, ..., \omega_{\delta_p(K)}\}) \propto \hat{f}^p_{\delta_p(k)}(Y^p_{n'}) - \hat{f}^p_{\delta_p(k-1)}(Y^p_{n'}) \end{cases} \quad (6)$$

2) Contextual discounting: To fine-tune the ultimate mass assigned to the p attribute, a weakening process based on the proposed contextual discounting mechanism mentioned in paragraph II-C2 is applied.

3) Fusion of mass functions: Mass Functions assigned to different attributes are then merged into a single consensus mass $M = \bigoplus_{p=1}^{P} M^p$ using the fusion rule selected on the training phase.

4) Decision making: The final decision is made based on the Pignistic transformation of M:

$$\hat{X}_{n'} = \arg\max_{\omega_k} \sum_{A \ni \omega_k} \frac{M(A)}{|A|} \quad (7)$$

It is worth noting that the novelty of Boosted PR-DS with respect to those using similar architectures is based on the steps of model adjustment, generation of mass function, and contextual discounting.

V. Experimental results

To assess the performance of the proposed boosted PR-DS method, experimental tests are conducted on the NSL-KDD dataset containing two test sets of increasing difficulty, KDDTest+ and KDDTest-21 respectively, as described in Section III.

A comparative analysis is made with regard to nine methods: J48 decision tree learning [23], Naive Bayes [24], NBTree[25], Random Forest [26], Random Tree [27], Multi-layer Perceptron [28], Support Vector Machine (SVM) [29], and Recurrent Neural Networks (RNN) [21], Parzen-Rosenblatt Dempster-Shafer (PR-DS) [30].

While giving a comparable accuracy on the KDDTest+ dataset, Boosted PR-DS outperforms the other state-of-the-art methods on the KDDTest-21 testing set as shown in Figure 2. This is mainly due to taking the estimated reliability into account by using the contextual discounting mechanism along with adjusting the model by selecting the most suitable kernel and fusion rule for a given training dataset.

To demonstrate the effect of kernel selection, we assess our approach on the KDDTest-21 dataset by changing the kernel each time, while maintaining the other parameters. Figure 3 shows that three kernels at least are getting better results than the Normal kernel which confirms the relevance of choosing an adapted kernel to suitably constructing our densities instead of using the normality assumption.

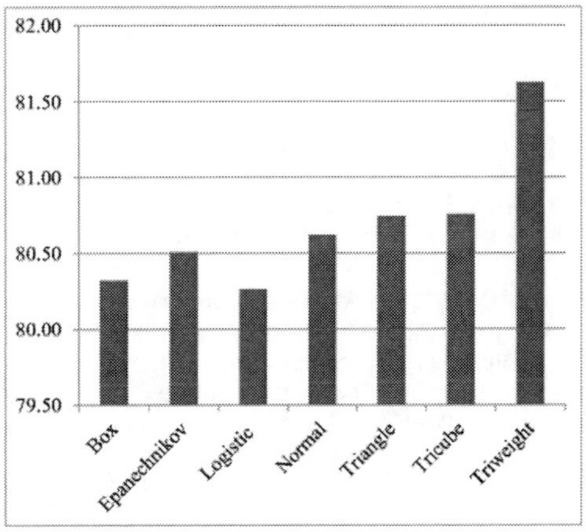

Figure 3. Boosted PR-DS on the KDDTest-21 dataset using different kernels

VI. Conclusion and Future Work

As a conclusion, we can consider Boosted PR-DS as a combination of multiple classifiers where each attribute (source) is a classifier. By using contextual discounting, one may prioritize the decision of an individual classifier regarding those classes in which its accuracy was high in the training phase and be doubtful regarding those classes it did not classify well. Furthermore, Boosted PR-DS choose a suitable fusion rule to take advantage of each individual classifier's knowledge to achieve a consensus decision. Experimental results validate the interest of this approach with respect to other state-of-the-art intrusion detection models. As a possible future direction, it would be interesting to consider handling conflicting sources with a more sophisticated fusion rule.

References

[1] J. Andress, The basics of information security: understanding the fundamentals of InfoSec in theory and practice. Syngress, 2014.

[2] G. Shafer, A Mathematical Theory of Evidence. Princeton: Princeton University Press, 1976.

[3] R. W. Jones, A. Lowe, and M. J. Harrison, "A framework for intelligent medical diagnosis using the theory of evidence," Knowledge-Based Systems, vol. 15, no. 1, 2002, pp. 77–84.

[4] M. E. Y. Boudaren, L. An, and W. Pieczynski, "Dempster–Shafer fusion of evidential pairwise Markov fields," International Journal of Approximate Reasoning, vol. 74, 2016, pp. 13–29.

[5] H. Guo, W. Shi, and Y. Deng, "Evaluating sensor reliability in classification problems based on evidence theory," IEEE Transactions on Systems, Man, and Cybernetics, Part B (Cybernetics), vol. 36, no. 5, 2006, pp. 970–981.

[6] F. Salzenstein and A.-O. Boudraa, "Unsupervised multisensor data fusion approach," in Signal Processing and its Applications, Sixth International, Symposium on. 2001, vol. 1. IEEE, 2001, pp. 152–155.

[7] A. Bendjebbour, Y. Delignon, L. Fouque, V. Samson, and W. Pieczynski, "Multisensor image segmentation using Dempster—Shafer fusion in Markov fields context," Geoscience and Remote Sensing, IEEE Transactions on, vol. 39, no. 8, 2001, pp. 1789–1798.

[8] P. Xu, Y. Deng, X. Su, and S. Mahadevan, "A new method to determine basic probability assignment from training data," Knowledge-Based Systems, vol. 46, 2013, pp. 69–80.

[9] M. P. Wand and M. C. Jones, Kernel smoothing. Crc Press, 1994.

[10] P. Smets and R. Kennes, "The transferable belief model," Artificial intelligence, vol. 66, no. 2, 1994, pp. 191–234.

[11] D. Dubois and H. Prade, "Representation and combination of uncertainty with belief functions and possibility measures," Computational intelligence, vol. 4, no. 3, 1988, pp. 244–264.

[12] P. Smets, "The combination of evidence in the transferable belief model," IEEE Transactions on Pattern Analysis and Machine Intelligence, vol. 12, no. 5, May 1990, pp. 447–458.

[13] F. Sebbak, F. Benhammadi, S. Bouznad, A. Chibani, and Y. Amirat, "An evidential fusion rule for ambient intelligence for activity recognition," in International Conference on Belief Functions. Springer, 2014, pp. 356–364.

[14] E. Parzen, "On estimation of a probability density function and mode," The annals of mathematical statistics, vol. 33, no. 3, 1962, pp. 1065–1076.

[15] M. Rosenblatt, "Remarks on some nonparametric estimates of a density function," The Annals of Mathematical Statistics, 1956, pp. 832–837.

[16] V. A. Epanechnikov, "Non-parametric estimation of a multivariate probability density," Theory of Probability & Its Applications, vol. 14, no. 1, 1969, pp. 153–158.

[17] N. S. Altman, "An introduction to kernel and nearest-neighbor nonparametric regression," The American Statistician, vol. 46, no. 3, 1992, pp. 175–185.

[18] W. S. Cleveland and S. J. Devlin, "Locally weighted regression: an approach to regression analysis by local fitting," Journal of the American statistical association, vol. 83, no. 403, 1988, pp. 596–610.

[19] Z. Elouedi, K. Mellouli, and P. Smets, "Assessing sensor reliability for multisensor data fusion within the transferable belief model," IEEE Transactions on Systems, Man, and Cybernetics, Part B (Cybernetics), vol. 34, no. 1, 2004, pp. 782–787.

[20] S. Gurung, M. K. Ghose, and A. Subedi, "Deep learning approach on network intrusion detection system using nsl-kdd dataset," International Journal of Computer Network and Information Security (IJCNIS), vol. 11, no. 3, 2019, pp. 8–14.

[21] C. Yin, Y. Zhu, J. Fei, and X. He, "A deep learning approach for intrusion detection using recurrent neural networks," Ieee Access, vol. 5, 2017, pp. 21 954–21 961.

[22] M. Tavallaee, E. Bagheri, W. Lu, and A. A. Ghorbani, "A detailed analysis of the kdd cup 99 data set," 2009 IEEE Symposium on Computational Intelligence for Security and Defense Applications, 2009, pp. 1–6.

[23] J. R. Quinlan, C4. 5: programs for machine learning. Elsevier, 2014.

[24] G. H. John and P. Langley, "Estimating continuous distributions in bayesian classifiers," in Proceedings of the Eleventh conference on Uncertainty in artificial intelligence. Morgan Kaufmann Publishers Inc., 1995, pp. 338–345.

[25] R. Kohavi, "Scaling up the accuracy of naive-bayes classifiers: A decision-tree hybrid." in Kdd, vol. 96. Citeseer, 1996, pp. 202–207.

[26] L. Breiman, "Random forests," Machine learning, vol. 45, no. 1, 2001, pp. 5–32.

[27] D. Aldous, "The continuum random tree. i," The Annals of Probability, 1991, pp. 1–28.

[28] D. W. Ruck, S. K. Rogers, M. Kabrisky, M. E. Oxley, and B. W. Suter, "The multilayer perceptron as an approximation to a bayes optimal discriminant function," IEEE Transactions on Neural Networks, vol. 1, no. 4, 1990, pp. 296–298.

[29] C.-C. Chang and C.-J. Lin, "Libsvm: a library for support vector machines," ACM Transactions on Intelligent Systems and Technology (TIST), vol. 2, no. 3, 2011, p. 27.

[30] A. Hamache, M. E. Y. Boudaren, H. Boukersoul, I. Debicha, H. Sadouk, R. Zibani, A. Habbouchi, and O. Merouani, "Uncertainty-aware parzen-rosenblatt classifier for multiattribute data," in International Conference on Belief Functions. Springer, 2018, pp. 103–111.

Identification of Fake Profiles in Twitter Social Network

Mário Antunes
CIIC, School of Technology and Management, Polytechnic of Leiria
Leiria, Portugal
e-mail: mario.antunes@ipleiria.pt

Hugo Baptista
School of Technology and Management, Polytechnic of Leiria
Leiria, Portugal
e-mail: hfontainhas@hotmail.com

Baltazar Rodrigues
School of Technology and Management, Polytechnic of Leiria
Leiria, Portugal
e-mail: baltazar.rodrigues@ipleiria.pt

Abstract— **Online social networks are being intensively used by millions of users, Twitter being one of the most popular, as a powerful source of information with impact on opinion and decision making. However, in Twitter as in other online social networks, not all the users are legitimate, and it is not easy to detect those accounts that correspond to fake profiles. In this work in progress paper, we propose a method to help practitioners to identify fake Twitter accounts, by calculating the "fake probability" based on a weighted parameter set collected from public Twitter accounts. The preliminary results obtained with a subset of an existing annotated dataset of Twitter accounts are promising and give confidence on using this method as a decision support system, to help practitioners to identify fake profiles.**

Keywords – online social networks; Twitter; fake profiles.

I. Introduction

The exponential growth of social networks and the role they play in today's society, both socially and in business, means that it is important to study in depth how they work. The popularity of these applications has led to the possibility of exposing confidential information, the spread of phishing and other cybercrime related activities.

One of the ways to enhance these cybercrime episodes is to use fake profiles, as the information conveyed through fake online social networks profiles may cause disastrous damage to individual and business entities. The cybercrime on online social networks is rising and the "real" authors are not usually punished [3]. These profiles are created for the purpose of anonymizing the account owner or to promote alienation, which challenges law enforcement to identify and trace the attacker.

Online social networks providers have implemented security mechanisms to mitigate these problems, by applying captchas or email validation, and also by requesting the mobile number to send a verification code. Research community is also aware of this issue and machine learning techniques have also been applied to mitigate the problem [10]-[12]. Despite the promising results obtained with some techniques, there are still limitations regarding the access to the public data and the lack of tools available to analyze the "fakeness probability" of an account.

A major challenge is to understand how fake profiles are created and how they work, in order to come up with a solution that may help and warn the users about a possible identified fake profile. The method proposed in this paper aims to contribute to identify a presumable Twitter fake profile, by calculating its fake probability. The developed method collects the values of a predefined set of parameters associated with a public profile, and further applies a weighted parameter set derived from the method published in [1], to calculate the likelihood of an account to be fake. The tests were based on published datasets with Twitter accounts classified as legitimate or associated to a fake profile. Other parameters, not previously mentioned, were added to the weighted parameter set, in order to enhance the results. A comparison between both approaches revealed the usefulness of these new parameters. This methodology and the algorithm may also be extended to other social networks, since the limitations on accessing and using the available Application Programming Interface (API) may be overcome.

The results obtained are promising both in performance and in the level of assertiveness. The datasets used for the tests have provided good indications regarding the level of accuracy to identify accounts related with fake profiles.

The paper is organized as follows: Section II describes the state of art related with the subject; Section III depicts the architecture and the methodology defined to process the Twitter profiles. Section IV describes the tests setup and the datasets used; Section V presents the results; and finally, in Section VI we delineate the conclusions and present actions for future work.

II. Background

This work is based on the method proposed by El Azab et al. [1]. The methodology presented was designed for Twitter, but it can be extended to other social networks. According to [1], the Twitter account analysis is based on a set of parameters and a corresponding assigned weight.

The authors' approach proposes the use of as few parameters as possible. Firstly, the factors that categorize a profile as fake were found. Secondly, a classification algorithm that uses the factors previously found to classify an account as corresponding to a fake profile was applied.

Other works have proposed different parameters set, as depicted in Table 1 [1][2][3]. It was found that unnecessarily high number of parameters were used, many of them were not used by social network users or had default values. However, more important than the number of parameters is their relevance in a fake profile detection scenario. In [1], the initial set was of 22 parameters (Table 2).

TABLE I. PARAMETER SET PROPOSED BY DIFFERENT RESEARCHERS (ADAPTED FROM [1]).

Benevenuto et al. [2]	Gurajala et al. [8]	Stringhini et al. [9]
• Number of followers • Number of followees • Followers / followees ration • Number of wweets • Age of the user account • Number of times the user was mentioned • Number of times the user was replied to • Number of times the user replied someone • Number of followees of the user's followers • Number of tweets received from followees • Existence of spam words on screen name • Minimum time between tweets • Maximum time between tweets • Average time between tweets • Median time between tweets • Number of tweets posted per day • Number of tweets posted per week	• Numer of followers • Identification • Friends count • Account verified • Date of creation • General description • Location • Account is updated • URL of profile image • Screen name	• Following / Followers ratio • URL ratio • Similarity among the messages sent by a user. • Friend Choice between screen names • Number of messages sent by a profile • Spammers that send less than 20 messages • Number of friends of a profile

After running the following five learning algorithms with k-fold cross-validation, against a dataset based on "the Fake project" [5], namely: Random Forest, Decision Tree, Naïve Bayes, Neural Network and Support Vector Machine, 19 parameters were chosen. By applying a gain measure algorithm, a weight for each parameter was calculated.

TABLE II. THE INITIAL PARAMETERS SET [1].

Attributes	Weight
The account has at least 30 followers	0.53
The account has been geo-localized	0.85
It has been included in another user's favourites	0.85
It has used a hashtag in at least one tweet	0.96
It has logged into Twitter using an iPhone	0.917
It was mentioned by a twitter user	1
It has written at least 50 tweets	0.01
It has been included in another user's list	0.45
Number of followers and friends' ratio	0.5
User have at least one favourite list	0.17
the profile contains a name	0.0
the profile contains an image	0.0
the profile contains a biography	0.0
the profile contains a URL	0.0
it writes tweets that have punctuation	0.0
it has logged into Twitter using an iPhone	0.0
it has logged into Twitter using an Android device	0.0
the profile contains a physical address	0.0
it has logged into twitter.com website	0.0
it is connected with Foursquare	N/A
it is connected with Instagram	N/A
it has logged into Twitter through different clients	N/A

By applying a comprehensive task list to choose the best parameters set [4][6], a list of the ten most relevant was obtained, which should be used to identify an account as fake [1]. From this list, the parameters whose weight is above 50% and which contribute heavily to the calculation, were identified. The seven parameters obtained, and their corresponding weight are the following [1]:

- The account has at least 30 followers. 0.53
- The account has been geo-located: 0.85
- It has been included in user's favorites: 0.85
- It has used a hashtag in at least one tweet: 0.85
- It has logged into Twitter using an iPhone: 0.96
- It was mentioned by a Twitter user: 1
- Numbers of followers and friends' ratio: 0.5

This set of seven parameters, and its corresponding values were tested in the proposed method described in Section III and benchmarked with other sets, with eight, ten, and eleven parameters.

III. PROPOSED METHOD

The algorithm receives a profile name ("screen name") or a set of profiles and processes them through Twitter API, available at [13]. The first step is to identify if an account with the "screen name" provided exists. Then, for each parameter, the method queries the available profile parameters through the Twitter API. After processing all the parameters, the probability of fakeness of the account is calculated, according to the weight value of each parameter, as described in Section II.

Tests have also been done for Facebook and Instagram, but due to the successive restrictions of the corresponding API, it has become inviable. Some restrictions were related with General Data Protection Regulation (GDPR) and other with successive privacy breaches that were exploited and addressed by various companies. Another limitation found on Twitter has to do with the privacy settings that the user can select. If the user limits access to the data by defining it as private, it becomes impossible to calculate the level of fakeness of a profile.

IV. DATASET

To perform the tests, two datasets, each one with 100 accounts, both in .CSV format, with the screen names of users to search, were prepared. One dataset has only genuine accounts (not fake) and another has accounts previously classified as fake. The datasets were collected from the My Information Bubble (MIB) Project [7] and a summary is shown in Table 3.

TABLE III. DATASETS INFORMATION FROM MIB PROJECT.

group name	Description	acc	tweets
genuine acc (2011)	Verified human operated accounts	3,474	8,377,522
social spambots #1 (2012)	retweets of an Italian political candidate	991	1,610,176
social spambots #2 (2014)	spammers of paid apps for mobile devices	3,457	428,542
social spambots #3 (2011)	spammers of products on sale at Amazon.com	464	1,418,626
traditional spambots #1 (2009)	training set of spammers used by Yang, et al. [14]	1,000	145,094
traditional spambots #2 (2014)	spammers of scam URLs	100	74,957
traditional spambots #3 (2013)	automated accounts spamming job offers	433	5,794,931
traditional spambots #4 (2009)	automated accounts of spamming job offer.	1,128	133,311
fake followers (2012)	accounts that inflate the number of followers of another account	3,351	196,027

The dataset used, which includes 100 examples of each class (fake and genuine) is a subset of the vast datasets of Twitter accounts, available at MIB. The examples used in our experiments were identified as being related with active Twitter accounts.

V. RESULTS

Table 4 illustrates the average of fake percentage for both genuine and fake accounts presented in the dataset, by calculating the parameters values with 7, 8, 10 and 11 parameters. That is, for genuine accounts the percentage of fake is expected to be low. However, for the fake accounts, the probability of fakeness should be high.

The average results obtained for each dataset were as follows. For the genuine accounts dataset, we have obtained 52.92% of fake probability with 11 parameters, 55.88% with 10 parameters, 41.38% with 8 parameters and, the best result, 33,59% with 7 parameters. For the fake accounts dataset, the best result was obtained with an average of 87.73%, by using the set with 11 parameters, 86.5% with 10 parameters, 83.13% with the 8 parameters and 80.71% with 7. This means that in the dataset with only genuine accounts, the lower the fake probability (33.59%) is, the better chance the account has to be genuine. Otherwise, in the dataset of fake accounts, the higher the fake probability (87.73%) is, the better chance the account has to be fake.

TABLE IV. AVERAGE OF FAKE PERCENTAGE.

	11 par.	10 par.	8 par.	7 par.
Genuine accounts	52,92	55,88	41,38	33,59
Fake accounts	87,73	86,50	83,13	80,71

In order to better understand the values obtained, the "fake probability" was sliced into six stripes, between 40% and 90% in intervals of 10%. The underpinning idea is to have a closer precision regarding the level of assertiveness which is intended to be considered in the analysis. In a decision support system approach, this analysis could tune the level of confidence of the decision maker.

Table 5 represents the number of accounts on each percentual range, for the dataset of genuine accounts. Analysing the table, it is possible to observe that, with 11 parameters, 9 accounts have a high probability of being fake (90%). This means that, in a dataset with genuine accounts, almost all of them have a low probability of being fake. For the same parameters set, it is also possible to observe that 96 accounts have a fake probability below 50%, which may infer they are legitimate.

TABLE V. RESULTS IN PREDEFINED INTERVALS FOR GENUINE ACCOUNTS

%	>=40	>=50	>=60	>=70	>=80	>=90
11 par.	96	66	41	24	15	9
10 par.	70	45	29	22	15	9
8 par.	64	41	29	19	11	7
7 par.	45	29	20	19	10	7

However, with a threshold >= 80% the number of false positives increases to 15, and with a percentage >= 70%, increases to 24 accounts misclassified.

The range of values with the largest difference is between 60% and 70%. For the 10 parameters set with a threshold of 40%, we obtained 70 accounts, with a value >= 50% the value decrease to 45, and with a value of >60% we registered 29 accounts. Finally, we obtained 22 accounts that have a fake probability >=70%, with 80% the value decreases to 15, and with a value >=90% only 9 were classified as fake. In this case, the interval with the largest decrease is between 40% and 50%.

Table 6 represents the values obtained for the fake dataset, identifying the accounts in each fake interval. For a fake threshold of 70% all accounts are classified as fake except for the set of 7 parameters which has classified 97 accounts as fake. For 11 parameters set and for a threshold < 90%, 99 accounts were classified as fake, and only one account was misclassified. Even for the threshold of 90%, that is a high level of sensitivity, the method classifies 40% of the accounts correctly.

TABLE VII. RESULTS IN PREDEFINED INTERVALS FOR FAKE ACCOUNTS

%	>=40	>=50	>=60	>=70	>=80	>=90
11 par.	100	100	100	100	99	40
10 par.	100	100	100	100	97	40
8 par.	100	100	100	100	97	33
7 par.	100	100	100	97	96	33

Considering the data represented in Table 5, for values >=80%, and in Table 6 for values >=90%, comparing the values of the different parameter sets, we may infer that some parameters have no impact on the overall values obtained in the experiments.

VI. CONCLUSIONS

It is important to give people the knowledge needed to identify fake accounts on social networks. For the police investigators, in a digital forensics' perspective, this kind of solutions helps to better deal with cybercrime and malicious activity in online social networks.

This work in progress aims to contribute to identify fake profiles in online social networks. The work provides an additional resource that may help deciding about the veracity of a Twitter profile. The sensitivity of the decision was calculated by the probability intervals defined in the analysis. For instance, if an account shows a fake probability of 90%, it is possible to infer that it is strongly fake; being legitimate means that an account shows a fake probability of 40% or less. This method does not give a guarantee that an account is fake or genuine, but it gives an additional help on the overall final decision.

Besides the proposed methodology and the preliminary tests carried on, it was also evaluated the impact of the number of parameters extracted from the Twitter profiles. The development of a web application that incorporates the method and work described in this paper, is now being carried on. The web application should be available to those who aim to evaluate the legitimacy of a Twitter account.

The research is now focused on two major directions: i) to explore others API besides Twitter, such as Facebook, LinkedIn and Instagram. It is important to explore the various directions that may lead to obtain more information from the API, even using a paid version; ii) to work on the optimization of the parameters set and its continuous evaluation, by applying machine learning techniques for optimization. Finally, the parameters set can also be improved, not only in the weights but also in the selected parameters, as some of them are directed towards a specific scope (e.g., users that have a specific equipment, like iPhone) and some adjustments can be made in this subject.

REFERENCES

[1] A. El Azab, A. Idrees, M. Mahmoud and H. Hefny, "Fake Account Detection in Twitter Based on Minimum Weighted Feature set," International Journal of Computer, Electrical, Automation, Control and Information Engineering, World Academy of Science, Engineering and Technology. WASET, vol. 10, No. 1, pp.13-18, Nov. 2015.

[2] F. Benevenuto, G. Magno, T. Rodrigues and V. Almeida, "Detecting spammers on twitter. In Collaboration, electronic messaging", anti-abuse and spam conference (CEAS), vol. 6, No. 2010, pp. 12, 2010

[3] X. Zheng, Z. Zeng, Z. Chen, Y. Yu, and C. Rong, "Detecting spammers on social networks," Neurocomputing, Elsevier vol. 159, pp. 27–34, Jul. 2015.

[4] D. Kagan, Y. Elovichi, and M. Fire, "Generic anomalous vertices detection utilizing a link prediction algorithm," Social Networks Analysis and Mining, vol. 8, no. 1, pp. 27, Dec. 2018.

[5] "The Fake Project.", http://wafi.iit.cnr.it/fake/fake/app/. [Retrieved: September, 2020].

[6] T. Yoshida, "Term weighting method based on information gain ratio for summarizing documents retrieved by IR systems", Journal of Natural Language Processing, vol.9, No.4, pp.3-32, 2001

[7] M. P. Fazzolari, "My Information Bubble project.", Available: http://mib.projects.iit.cnr.it/index.html. [Retrieved: September, 2020].

[8] S. Gurajala, J. S. White, B. Hudson, and J. Matthews, "Fake Twitter accounts: Profile characteristics obtained using an activity-based pattern detection approach," in SMSociety , Toronto, ON, Canada, 2015

[9] G. Stringhini, C. Kruegel, and G. Vigna, "Detecting spammers on social networks," in Proceedings of the 26th Annual Computer Security Applications Conference, pp. 1–9, 2010

[10] A. Meligy, H. Ibrahim, and M. Torky, "Identity verification mechanism for detecting fake profiles in online social networks." *Int. J. Comput. Netw. Inf. Secur.(IJCNIS)*, vol.9, no. 1, pp.31-39, 2017

[11] A. K. Ojo, "Improved Model for Detecting Fake Profiles in Online Social Network: A Case Study of Twitter." Journal of Advances in Mathematics and Computer Science, vol. 33(4), pp.1-17, 2019

[12] S. R. Sahoo, and B. B. Gupta. "Hybrid approach for detection of malicious profiles in twitter." Computers & Electrical Engineering, vol. 76, pp. 65-81, 2019

[13] "Use cases, tutorials and documentation – Twitter developer"; https://developer.twitter.com/en. [Retrieved: September 2020]

[14] C. Yang, R. Harkreader and G. Gu, "Empirical Evaluation and New Design for Fighting Evolving Twitter Spammers,", IEEE Transactions on Information Forensics and Security, vol. 8, no. 8, pp. 1280-1293, 2013

An Intelligent Energy-driven System for Mobile Health Management

Jialing Wu, Yingxuan Zhu, Lifeng Liu, Han Su, Yizhuo Chen and Jian Li

Email: jialing.wu@live.com, {Yingxuan.zhu, hsu, ychen8, jian.li}@futurewei.com, lifeng.lifengliu@gmail.com,
Futurewei Technologies Inc.
Framingham, Massachusetts 01701

Abstract—**Pets have difficulties in communicating with their owners or veterinarians on healthcare problems. Mobile sensing can consistently detect their health problems and deliver the problems to their owners, so the owners can help them out. Data transferring and battery usage are two major challenges in mobile sensing, especially when continuous and long-term data transmission are needed if pets get lost. In this paper, we develop an intelligent energy-driven system for conditional data analysis and transferring, so sensing devices can work longer and more efficiently without recharging. Our system can be applied to the sensing devices used in other agents, such as babies, animals, and patients.**

Keywords–Mobile sensing; Healthcare monitoring; Energy aware system; Feature embedding.

I. INTRODUCTION

In mobile sensing field, data transferring and battery consumption are major issues to continuous data tracking and uploading [1] [2], especially when devices are in the wild without charge stations. That is why most of mobile sensing-based health data tracking are mainly operated under experimental environment where humans intensively control the sensing devices [3]. The sensing data transmitted to the cloud are usually raw data, which can consume large amount of transmission resources with low efficiency. However, unlike human beings who can manually adjust sensor devices and watch out for battery usage [4] [5] [6], pets (and monitored animals) are agents who have communication difficulty and cannot operate devices, especially when they get lost in the wild without power charge stations.

Most of people can communicate with families, friends and doctors when they are not feeling well. But pets cannot directly tell their owners when they are sick or in danger. In some situations, pet owners cannot stay with their pets all day long because they have to work or travel to other places. However, pet owners want to make sure the safety of their pets when they are not around.

As far as we known, there is limited work on developing an intelligent energy aware system to efficiently transfer sensing data based on real time battery level and help find the lost pets in the wild [7]. In this paper, we use pet as the agent example, but our methods can be applied to any agents that have communication difficulties, including but not limited to babies, wild animals, patients, etc.

After this introductory section, in Section II, we explain a framework to help find lost pets using energy aware mobile sensing. In Section III, we introduce an energy-driven mobile sensing system for pets.In Section IV, we further go through how the model is automatically trained and optimized through feature embedding on the cloud end and then be applied to the agent device.

II. FINDME: A MODEL TO FIND LOST PETS BY ENERGY AWARE MOBILE SENSING

With the prevalence of mobile devices using worldwide, mobile sensing are widely applied in different areas varying from GPS tracking [8], activity recognition [5], sleep quality measuring [9], daily social media usage [10] to personality traits [6], working performance evaluation [11], and mental health detection including depression [12] [13], anxiety [14] [15], and schizophrenia [4] [16]. Sensor equipped devices are also applied to monitor the health of pets, such as dogs and cats [17]. But all sensing based devices can not avoid one essential issue on saving battery and dealing with large raw data uploading and computing, which is a challenge to continuous data tracking and recording. This issue will be even more profound when the pets get lost without power charger. Once battery is out, there are limited ways to help owners find their pets. Based on real situations, we want to answer the question: How to prioritize battery consumption and data processing of mobile sensors in the wild?

1) Sensors applied in the system: Sensors in our system can be put into two groups: personal sensors embedded in a device and environmental sensors equipped at home. Personal sensors refer to thermometer, pulsimeter, sphygmomanometergravity sensor, GPS, Bluetooth, photoplethysmography, electrocardiogram, etc. Environmental sensors include beacon, camera, microphone ambient light detector, etc. With these two kinds of sensors, we can record and track agent behaviors both at home and in the wild, when the agent carries the device.

2) FindMe function applied in different situations: Figure 1 shows the functions of a FindMe model applied in different situations, at home and in the wild. A wearable device with integrated sensors will capture pets GPS locations and record their sound and environment features as well as their health conditions. When pets are at home, environmental sensors, such as beacon and camera are also included. When a beacon detects that a pet is getting into danger, such as standing beside an open window, it will send an alarm directly to the owner's phone. When a camera combined with health sensors detects that a pet's health is at risk, such as bleeding or in pains at home, it will also send warning to the owner. In the wild, if the sensors in a pet's device detect that the pet is getting lost

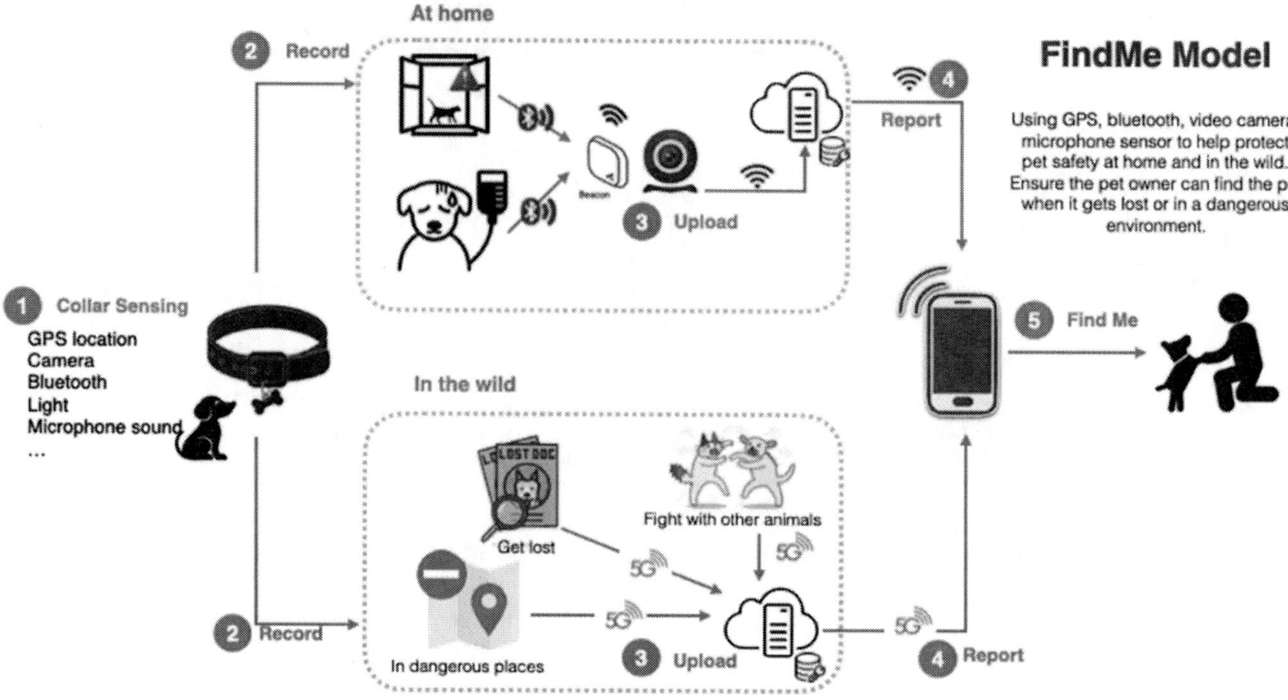

Figure 1. The FindMe model applied in the sensing system

or reported lost, the device will report to the owner about the pet's location and provide timely updates of the pet's safety.

III. An Energy-Driven Mobile Sensing System for Pets

Regarding the FindMe model discussed in Section II, energy consumption is a challenge especially when the agents are in places without power chargers nearby. Unlike human-beings who can speak with each other and ask for help, pets cannot speak human languages or ask for help as easily as us. Instead, they are very dependent and not able to control the devices manually. A system with energy-driven adaptive data analysis and upload that can improve battery life of mobile sensing devices is essential to help these agents get back home safely.

A. The battery level

Different batteries have different voltage decreasing rates. They have different discharge curves for real battery test [18]. To develop an energy aware system to save battery intelligently and automatically, we need to first understand their voltage rate during consumption by time. And what we can do here is that the battery level can be defined into a lookup table in the device ROM. We can use lookup table to know battery consumption and control sensors according to battery levels. Taking the battery consumption into consideration, the battery usage is not likely to be decreasing in a linear trend but a sharp drop after it reaches a certain level. However, with the lookup table written in the device ROM, a system will get timely updates about its battery usage rate and make adjustment to current working sensors.

B. An energy-driven system design and development

In order to prioritize tasks, when the battery level decreased, a system should reduce data processing to save power, i.e., the lower the battery, the less unimportant conditions should be processed. Let a_i be a parameter showing if data of sensor i can be processed, i.e., $a_i = 1$, depending on battery level. Assuming a device has m battery levels, the higher the level, the more power left. Let $b_i = 1, ..., m$ be the cutoff battery level of a sensor, which is predefined for each sensor. Note that the higher the cutoff level, the less chance a sensor will work when battery level is low, i.e., a sensor will only work when the battery level is higher than its cutoff level. Let b_t be the battery level at time t, H be the Heaviside function, and

$$a_i = H(m - b_i) = \begin{cases} 1, & if\, b_i < b_t \\ 0, & if\, b_i >= b_t \end{cases}$$

Note that a_i will be normalized based on the available sensors in the integration process, the green rectangle in the figure. The goal of using a_i is to only process the important conditions when battery level is low, Figure 2.

In Figure 3, another innovation of this system design is about using Long Short-term Memory (LSTM) to automatically learn the time-series data continuously from the multiple sensors. Facilitated by the deep learning model of LSTM, this system can intelligently react to the battery level by opening or shut down certain sensors to save energy and make the device working longer. Usually, some less important sensors with high data transferring demands will be shut down or decreased usage when the battery is running out in the wild. Not like the manually controlling and decision making of which sensor

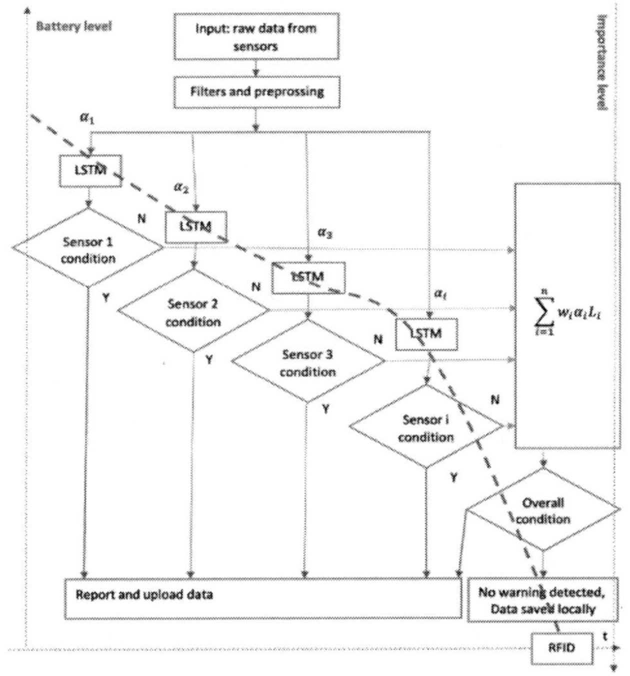

Figure 2. An energy-driven system for adaptive data profile and upload

should be first shut down or decrease usage frequency to what extent, our system aims to automatically learn from the data and making intelligent decision from the sensors, environment and battery level. This could be very helpful and essential for lost pets or agents to get more support and protection in the wild.

In our model, LSTM network is applied to track the changes in sensor data. Other machine learning methods can be applied to this modal too. Because each agent is different, so not only the values but the value changes are important features to tell how an agent's conditions change. Thus, a machine learning method that can track changes will help track the conditions of an agent.

IV. Feature Embedding On The Cloud-End

How could our system automatically learn when to lower the frequency or shut down certain sensors? On the agent's device, we utilized feature embedding trained on the cloud service and then applied to local end (agent's device) after a fine-tuned model is achieved. Feature embedding [19] is an emerging research area which intends to transform features from the original space into a new space to support effective learning. A generalized feature embedding algorithm (GEL) can learn feature embedding from any type of data or data with mixed feature types [20]. Specifically, multi-modal sensor data (i.e., time-series data from various sensors) are uploaded to the cloud where a feature embedding encoder can be trained based on the data from all devices. Note this step can be unsupervised that does not require any user input. Eventually, we obtain feature embedding algorithms for each sensor (or a combination of several related sensors), where a time series data can be represented as a special point in a multidimensional space. Similar time series (that most probably have similar semantics) will be mapped to close areas in the space. Such embedding algorithm are updated online and synced to the portable devices regularly.

Once the edge has downloaded the embedding algorithm from the cloud, it can generate features for its own sensor data using the model. In this way, it utilizes the patterns learned from the cloud. Locally on the edge, a customized decision tree model is trained using the embedded features and user labels. The owners or doctors can label some period as risky, so that the model can learn local thresholds for sensor data to classify risky behavior in the future.

V. Conclusion

Mobile sensing is important in health management. The FindMe model facilitates timely monitoring and health warning to owners when agents are in danger or get lost. To extend battery life and achieve intelligent sensing in the wild, we design an energy-driven system for conditional data analysis and transferring, so sensor device can work longer and more efficiently. This system can be utilized in devices for agents with communication difficulty. Agents, such as infants, toddlers, seniors or patients with dementia and Alzheimer's disease are vulnerable and dependent to caregivers and medical devices. Our model will make sure that these devices provide seamless cares to agents. In addition, our system and methods can extended to IoT scenarios, such as machine-to-machine(M2M) communications as well as edges and cloud nodes with communication challenges.

References

[1] Y. Kim, J. Sa, Y. Chung, D. Park, and S. Lee, "Resource-efficient pet dog sound events classification using lstm-fcn based on time-series data," Sensors, vol. 18, no. 11, 2018, p. 4019.

[2] G. M. Harari, W. Wang, S. R. Müller, R. Wang, and A. T. Campbell, "Participants' compliance and experiences with self-tracking using a smartphone sensing app," in Proceedings of the 2017 ACM International Joint Conference on Pervasive and Ubiquitous Computing and Proceedings of the 2017 ACM International Symposium on Wearable Computers, 2017, pp. 57–60.

[3] B. Belda, M. Enomoto, B. Case, and B. Lascelles, "Initial evaluation of petpace activity monitor," The Veterinary Journal, vol. 237, 2018, pp. 63–68.

[4] W. Wang, S. Mirjafari, G. Harari, D. Ben-Zeev, R. Brian, T. Choudhury, M. Hauser, J. Kane, K. Masaba, S. Nepal et al., "Social sensing: Assessing social functioning of patients living with schizophrenia using mobile phone sensing," in Proceedings of the 2020 CHI Conference on Human Factors in Computing Systems, 2020, pp. 1–15.

[5] R. Wang, W. Wang, A. DaSilva, J. F. Huckins, W. M. Kelley, T. F. Heatherton, and A. T. Campbell, "Tracking depression dynamics in college students using mobile phone and wearable sensing," Proceedings of the ACM on Interactive, Mobile, Wearable and Ubiquitous Technologies, vol. 2, no. 1, 2018, pp. 1–26.

[6] W. Wang, G. M. Harari, R. Wang, S. R. Müller, S. Mirjafari, K. Masaba, and A. T. Campbell, "Sensing behavioral change over time: Using within-person variability features from mobile sensing to predict personality traits," Proceedings of the ACM on Interactive, Mobile, Wearable and Ubiquitous Technologies, vol. 2, no. 3, 2018, pp. 1–21.

[7] D. Ben-Zeev, R. Brian, R. Wang, W. Wang, A. T. Campbell, M. S. Aung, M. Merrill, V. W. Tseng, T. Choudhury, M. Hauser et al., "Crosscheck: Integrating self-report, behavioral sensing, and smartphone use to identify digital indicators of psychotic relapse." Psychiatric rehabilitation journal, vol. 40, no. 3, 2017, p. 266.

[8] S. Van der Spek, J. Van Schaick, P. De Bois, and R. De Haan, "Sensing human activity: Gps tracking," Sensors, vol. 9, no. 4, 2009, pp. 3033–3055.

[9] N. D. Lane, M. Lin, M. Mohammod, X. Yang, H. Lu, G. Cardone, S. Ali, A. Doryab, E. Berke, A. T. Campbell et al., "Bewell: Sensing sleep, physical activities and social interactions to promote wellbeing," Mobile Networks and Applications, vol. 19, no. 3, 2014, pp. 345–359.

[10] J. F. Huckins, A. W. DaSilva, W. Wang, E. Hedlund, C. Rogers, S. K. Nepal, J. Wu, M. Obuchi, E. I. Murphy, M. L. Meyer et al., "Mental health and behavior of college students during the early phases of the covid-19 pandemic: Longitudinal smartphone and ecological momentary assessment study," Journal of Medical Internet Research, vol. 22, no. 6, 2020, p. e20185.

[11] S. Mirjafari, K. Masaba, T. Grover, W. Wang, P. Audia, A. T. Campbell, N. V. Chawla, V. D. Swain, M. D. Choudhury, A. K. Dey et al., "Differentiating higher and lower job performers in the workplace using mobile sensing," Proceedings of the ACM on Interactive, Mobile, Wearable and Ubiquitous Technologies, vol. 3, no. 2, 2019, pp. 1–24.

[12] R. Wang, W. Wang, M. S. Aung, D. Ben-Zeev, R. Brian, A. T. Campbell, T. Choudhury, M. Hauser, J. Kane, E. A. Scherer et al., "Predicting symptom trajectories of schizophrenia using mobile sensing," Proceedings of the ACM on Interactive, Mobile, Wearable and Ubiquitous Technologies, vol. 1, no. 3, 2017, pp. 1–24.

[13] J. F. Huckins, A. W. DaSilva, R. Wang, W. Wang, E. L. Hedlund, E. I. Murphy, R. B. Lopez, C. Rogers, P. E. Holtzheimer, W. M. Kelley et al., "Fusing mobile phone sensing and brain imaging to assess depression in college students," Frontiers in Neuroscience, vol. 13, 2019, p. 248.

[14] P. I. Chow, K. Fua, Y. Huang, W. Bonelli, H. Xiong, L. E. Barnes, and B. A. Teachman, "Using mobile sensing to test clinical models of depression, social anxiety, state affect, and social isolation among college students," Journal of medical Internet research, vol. 19, no. 3, 2017, p. e62.

[15] A. W. DaSilva, J. F. Huckins, R. Wang, W. Wang, D. D. Wagner, and A. T. Campbell, "Correlates of stress in the college environment uncovered by the application of penalized generalized estimating equations to mobile sensing data," JMIR mHealth and uHealth, vol. 7, no. 3, 2019, p. e12084.

[16] B. Buck, E. Scherer, R. Brian, R. Wang, W. Wang, A. Campbell, T. Choudhury, M. Hauser, J. M. Kane, and D. Ben-Zeev, "Relationships between smartphone social behavior and relapse in schizophrenia: a preliminary report," Schizophrenia research, vol. 208, 2019, pp. 167–172.

[17] M. Zakharov, A. Dagan, M. Bukchin, and A. Menkes, "Non-invasive automatic monitoring of pet animal's core temperature," Nov. 21 2017, uS Patent 9,823,138.

[18] P. Vyroubal, T. Kazda, J. Maxa, J. Vondrák, M. Sedlaříková, J. Tichý, and R. Cipín, "3d modelling and study of electrochemical characteristics and thermal stability of commercial accumulator by simulation methods," Int. J. Electrochem. Sci, vol. 11, 2016, pp. 1938–1950.

[19] Y. Jia, E. Shelhamer, J. Donahue, S. Karayev, J. Long, R. Girshick, S. Guadarrama, and T. Darrell, "Caffe: Convolutional architecture for fast feature embedding," in Proceedings of the 22nd ACM international conference on Multimedia, 2014, pp. 675–678.

[20] E. Golinko and X. Zhu, "Generalized feature embedding for supervised, unsupervised, and online learning tasks," Information Systems Frontiers, vol. 21, no. 1, 2019, pp. 125–142.

Comparison of a Supervised Trained Neural Network Classifier and a Supervised Trained Aggregation Function Classifier

Alexandre Croix, Thibault Debatty, Wim Mees

Royal Military Academy
Brussels, Belgium
Email: a.croix@cylab.be, t.debatty@cylab.be, w.mees@cylab.be

Abstract—**In this paper, we compare the efficiency of two binary classifiers. The first one uses the Weighted Ordered Weighted Averaging (WOWA) aggregation function whose coefficients are learned thanks to a genetic algorithm. The second is based on an artificial neural network trained by a backpropagation algorithm. They are trained to be used in a multi-criteria decision system. These kind of multi-criteria system are more and more common in the cyber-defence field. In this work, we compare the performance of these two classifiers by using two criteria: Area Under the Curve of a Receiver Operating Characteristics (ROC) curve and the Area Under the Curve of a Precision-Recall (P-R) curve. This second criterion is more adapted for imbalanced dataset what is often the case in the cyber-security field. We perform a complete parameter study of these classifiers to optimize their performance. The dataset used for this work is a pool of Hypertext Preprocessor (PHP) files analyzed by a multi-agent PHP webshell detector. We obtain different good results, especially for neural networks and highlights the advantage of the genetic algorithm method that allows a physical interpretation of the result.**

Keywords–Machine learning; neural network; aggregation functions; webshell.

I. INTRODUCTION

In the machine learning field, these last years, one method appears to be better than other ones: *neural network*, and particularly *deep learning*. The principle of this kind of algorithm has been known for a long time, but the usage increased these last years for two main reasons: new neural network structures were discovered, and the hardware is now powerful enough to produce good results in an acceptable time.

Sometimes, without a good analysis, a neural network is used to solve a problem. But in some cases, it is not the best choice for autonomous learning. It is often interesting to compare the performance of different learning algorithms to solve a problem. This comparison avoid to use a non-optimized algorithm for the question we are trying to answer. That can increase the performance and can produce better results.

In this paper, we focus on a specific task: the training of two classifiers whose objective is to distinguish if a PHP file, previously analyzed, is a webshell or a harmless PHP file. These two classifiers are: (i) an aggregation function in which the parameters are learned by a genetic algorithm and (ii) a neural network trained by the backpropagation algorithm. These classifiers are chosen instead of others (e.g., decision tree, Support Vector Machines (SVM), etc) to compare the performance of a classifier structure very used in practice and an classifier using an aggregation function that is not widely known.

In order to be classified, the PHP files were analyzed by a PHP multi-agent detector composed of 5 different modules. Each agent produces a score between 0 and 1 that is used as inputs for the two classifiers.

We performed a parametric study on both of the classifiers to determine the set of parameters that produces the best result. The dataset used for this work contains 23,415 PHP files where 1,833 [1] are actual PHP webshells.

In this situation, it is really interesting to study the performance of the classifiers for two mains reasons. First, the study can give some information about the efficiency of the different agents used by the detector. Then, the dataset is highly unbalanced and the obtained results can be very different from a "classical" dataset (balanced, a lot of elements).

The rest of the paper is arranged as follow: Section II explains which aggregation function is used for the classification and describes the structure of the genetic algorithm that learns parameters. Section III describes the structure of a neural network, and more specifically the neural network uses in this work. In Section IV, we present our comparison methodology and the results obtained. We conclude and we talk about some way to continue this work in Section V.

II. WOWA AGGREGATION FUNCTION AND GENETIC ALGORITHM STRUCTURE

In this section we describe the WOWA operator and its advantages, how a genetic algorithm works and why this algorithm was chosen for this problem.

A. WOWA operator

The WOWA operator, WOWA for Weighted Ordered Weighted Averaging, is an aggregation function introduced by Viçen Torra in 1996 [2]. This operator generalizes the Weighted Mean (WM) and the Ordered Weighted Averaging (OWA) and allows to merge a set of numerical data in a single result. To aggregate numerical data, WOWA uses two weighting vectors: one for the weighted mean (w) and the other for the OWA operator (p). The weighted mean, weights data in agreement with their sources and OWA gives importance to the data according to their scores.

WOWA combines the advantages of Weighted Mean and OWA operator. In the other hand, WOWA is more complex because it requires two parameters for each data source.

$$WOWA = f(a_1, a_2, ...a_n, w_1, w_2, ...w_n, p_1, p_2, ...p_n) \quad (1)$$

where

- a_i are data sources
- w_i are WM weights
- p_i are OWA weights

This operator allows good accurate results and can be tuned with more parameters than usual aggregation functions. Despite this, this operator is only rarely used in practice.

Learning aggregation operator weights from training dataset is an optimization problem[3]. The optimization algorithm minimizes (or maximizes) a cost function to try to find the global minimum (or maximum) of the solution surface. According to the literature, the algorithm selected to optimize the different weights of the aggregation function is a genetic algorithm[4].

B. Genetic Algorithm structure

A Genetic Algorithm is an evolutive process that maintains a population of chromosomes (potential solutions). Each chromosome is composed of several characteristics called "genes". In this work, a "gene" is a single weight and a "chromosome" is an element composed of two weight vectors (w and p). The weight vectors contain several "genes" whose the sum is equal to 1.

The algorithm has five main steps represented in Figure 1.

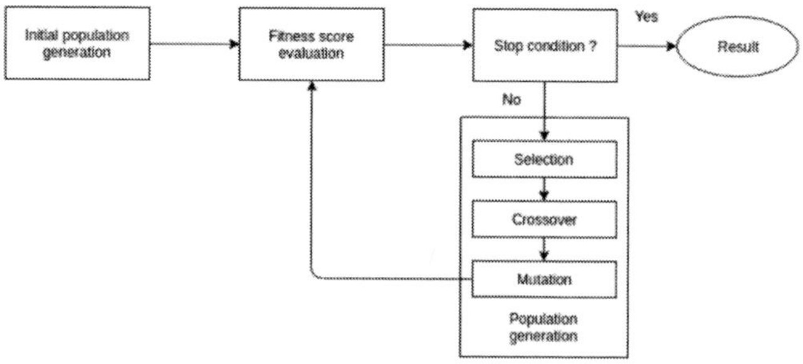

Figure 1. Structure of a Genetic Algorithm

- **Initial population generation**: a set of potential solutions is randomly generated. All "genes" (weights) are random values between 0 and 1. Then, the weights vectors are normalized.
- **Fitness score evaluation**: all population elements are evaluated by a fitness function.
- **Selection**: according to their fitness score, some elements are selected to be used in the next generation $t + 1$.
- **Crossover**: the selected elements from the previous generation are combined two-by-two to generate new *chromosomes* for the current generation. These new elements keep some characteristics from their parents.
- **Mutation**: each element in the new population has a probability to be mutated. Concretely, a random gene is selected and replaced by another random value. The mutation is very important to avoid converging too fast to a local minimum. The mutation allows to "jump" to another location in the space of solutions and can discover better results.

This process is repeated until it reaches a termination condition. That can be a sufficient accuracy, a slow convergence since some generations or a fixed number of generation. A complete description of these steps is available in [5].

III. NEURAL NETWORK STRUCTURE AND BACKPROPAGATION ALGORITHM

An artificial neural network is a computing system inspired by the biological neural networks that constitute animal brains. An Artificial Neural Network is based on a collection of connected units or nodes called artificial neurons, which loosely model the neurons in a biological brain. Each connection, like the synapses in a biological brain, can transmit a signal to other neurons. An artificial neuron receives a signal, processes it and can transmit the result to other neurons connected to it. Figure 2 represents the structure of an Artificial Neural Network. It contains three neurons as inputs, five in the hidden layer and two for the output.

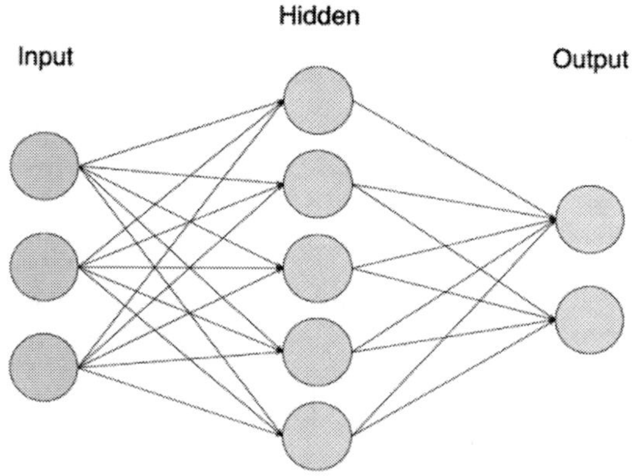

Figure 2. Structure of an Artificial Neural Network

Except for the input layer, a neuron receives several signals (usually real numbers) from the previous layer. These signals are weighted by coefficients and added. Then, the neuron produces an output signal following an activation function that it transmits to the next layer. Figure 3 represents the functioning of an artificial neuron.

In a mathematical point of view, a neuron works following:

$$y = \phi(\sum(x_1\omega_1 + x_2\omega_2 + ... + x_n\omega_n + b)) \quad (2)$$

A *deep* neural network is an artificial neural network with several hidden layers and is very efficient for image recognition or voice recognition there are some big datasets with a lot of features as input (pixels, etc.).

In our problem, it is very difficult to find real PHP webshells and we have only five inputs for each analyzed file. A classical neural network is more suitable for this kind of classification. Our neural network is made of three layers: a five neurons input layer (for the five agents in the webshell

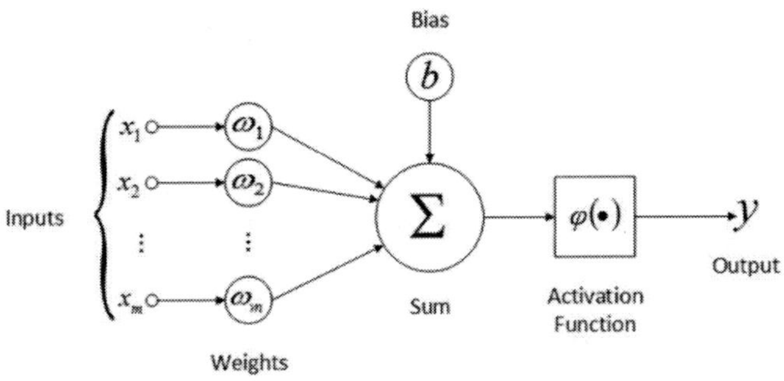

Figure 3. Representation of the functioning of an artificial neuron

detector), a hidden layer and a two neurons output layer (webshell or harmless file).

The job of the algorithm is to find a set of internal parameters (edge's weight and bias) that perform well against some performance measure. It is the cost function. The process is iterative, the convergence occurs over multiple discrete steps that improved internal parameters.

Each step involves using the model with the current set of internal parameters to make predictions on some samples, comparing the predictions to the real expected outcomes, calculating the error, and using the error to update the internal model parameters. This update procedure is the backpropagation (backward propagation) algorithm.

Backpropagation aims to minimize the cost function by modifying the network's weights. The level of adjustment is determined by the gradients of the cost function with respect to those parameters [6]. We do not describe the mathematical principle of the backpropagation algorithm, it is relatively complex and it is not the purpose of this work.

IV. Parametric Study and Evaluation

A parametric study has been performed on the classifiers in order to optimize their performances before comparison. The training dataset used for this work is composed of 23,415 PHP files and contains 1,833 PHP webshells [1].

To evaluate the performance of our classifiers, we use the $k-fold$ cross-validation[7] method (k equals to 10 is known to produce good results). It consists of separating the dataset in k folds, performing the training part on $k-1$ folds and testing on the last fold. This operation is repeated k times by changing the fold used for the evaluation. All these k intermediate results are meant to obtain a general result.

The number of PHP webshell in the dataset is small. With a random fold generation, there is a high probability to obtain very different repartitions. To avoid this issue, each fold is generated with a fixed number of webshells.

The number of webshells in a fold is quite smaller than the number of regular PHP files. To increase the penalty of not detecting a webshell, we artificially increase the number of webshells in the learning dataset. Concretely, we duplicate several times each score related to a webshell.

A. Performance evaluation methodology

To evaluate the efficiency of a binary classifier, we used two measurements: (i) the AUC of a ROC curve and (ii) the AUC of P-R curve.

1) Roc curve: The ROC curve is a classical tool to evaluate the performance of a binary classifier[8]. The ROC is a graphical plot that illustrates the diagnostic ability of a binary classifier system as its discrimination threshold is varied. It is created by plotting the true positive rate (true detection) against the false positive rate (false alarm) as shown in Figure 4

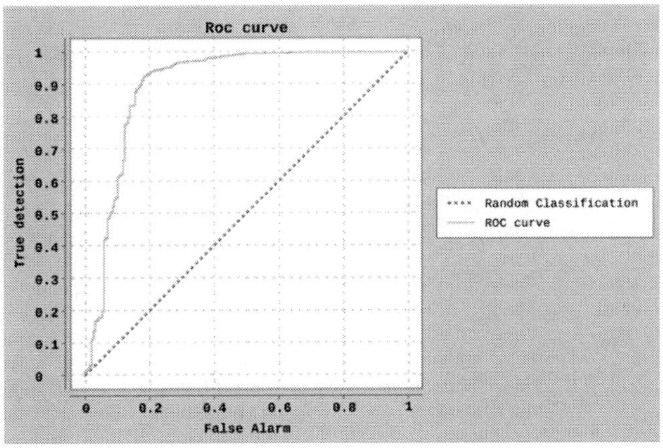

Figure 4. Example of a ROC curve

The Area Under the Curve gives a score that allows us to easily evaluate and compare the performance of several classifiers. Closer to 1 the AUC is, better is the classifier.

The dotted blue line represents the behaviour of a random classifier. If the ROC curve is under the curve, that means it is less efficient than a random classification.

2) Precision-Recall curve: A Precision-Recall curve (P-R curve) is, as the ROC curve, a graphical tool to evaluate the efficiency of a binary classifier. It is created by plotting the Recall (X-axis) against the Precision (Y-axis) as shown in Figure 5. Concretely, the precision and the recall are computed for several threshold values. This tool is more informative than the ROC curve for imbalanced dataset [9][10]. Indeed, the P-R curve focuses on the minority class, whereas the ROC curve covers both classes.

Like for the ROC curve, it is very difficult to compare visually different graphs, the AUC solves this issue and allows us an easy comparison. In our dataset, the ratio webshell-harmless file is smaller than 0.1. The evaluation of efficiency by using a P-R curve is perfectly adapted in this situation.

The dotted blue line on the graph represents the behaviour of a random classification. A P-R curve under this line is less efficient than a random classifier. The value of this line is $y = \frac{Webshell}{normal\_files}$

B. Genetic Algorithm parametric study

A genetic algorithm has several parameters that can be tuned to optimize results. In our parametric study we tested the following parameters:

- **Population size**: number of elements in each generation of the population. We varied this parameter between 40 and 200 by step of 10.
- **Crossover rate**: percentage of the population kept to set up the next generation. We varied this parameter between 5 and 95 by step of 5.

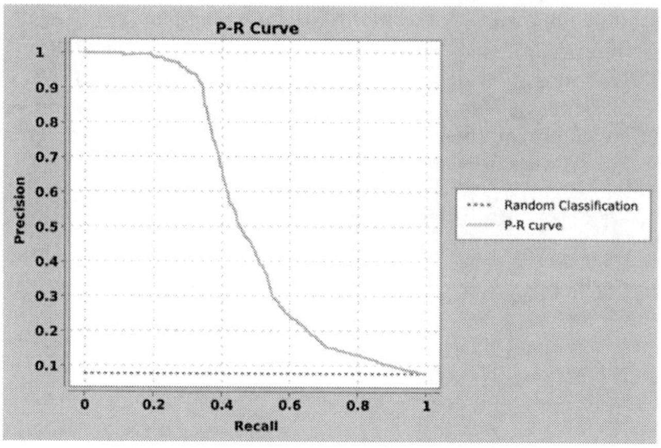

Figure 5. Example of a Precision-Recall curve

- **Mutation rate**: probability that a gene is randomly mutated. We varied this parameter between 5 and 95 by step of 5.
- **Generation number**: number of generations before stopping the algorithm. The way the algorithm is built, the best element of a generation is equal or better than the best element of the previous generation. Increasing the number of generation can only improve the performance of the classifier, but the improvement is not really significant for generation higher than 200. We fixed the generation number parameter to 200.
- **Fitness score evaluation**: method used to determine the fitness score of a chromosome. Two fitness criteria are implemented in our algorithm: (i) the distance criterion and (ii) the AUC criteria.

To determine the best parameters combination, we tested each parameter independently of the others. It is an approximation. Indeed, it is highly improbable the parameters are completely non-correlated. However, the parametric study shows the importance of the different parameters. We tested all the values of *population size*, *crossover rate* and *mutation rate* with the distance fitness score evaluation and the AUC fitness score evaluation. For each parameter, we perform a 10-folds cross-validation and kept the parameter values that produce the best AUC ROC result and the best P-R AUC value.

a) Distance fitness score: For each chromosome in the population, the WOWA function is computed on all examples of the dataset. The obtained results are substracted to the results given in the training dataset. All these differences are added to obtain a total distance that is the fitness score of the chromosome.

b) AUC fitness score: For each population element, the WOWA function is also computed on all examples of the dataset. Then, these results are used to obtain the ROC. The AUC of this curve is the fitness score of the chromosome.

1) Parametric study results: The first thing we note is the AUC fitness score produces better scores than the other fitness score for all values of all parameters. Intuitively it is logical. This criterion tries to optimize the AUC of a ROC curve that is also a performance criterion of the classifier.

Table I shows, for each parameter, the value that produces the best ROC AUC and the result associated with it. All these parameter values will be used in combination as a new model in the next section.

TABLE I. GENETIC ALGORITHM PARAMETER VALUES THAT PRODUCE THE BEST RESULTS IN THE PARAMETRIC STUDY FOR THE ROC CRITERION

Parameter name	Parameter value	ROC result
Population size	75	0.88114
Crossover rate	40	0.88117
Mutation rate	20	0.88125
Fitness function	AUC	0.88125

TABLE II. GENETIC ALGORITHM PARAMETER VALUES THAT PRODUCE THE BEST RESULTS IN THE PARAMETRIC STUDY FOR THE P-R CRITERION

Parameter name	Parameter value	P-R result
Population size	130	0.73502
Crossover rate	30	0.73612
Mutation rate	5	0.73401
Fitness function	AUC	0.73612

Table II shows, for each parameter, the value that produces the best P-R AUC and the result associated with it. All these parameter values will be used in combination as a new model in the next section.

C. Neural Network parametric study

As for the genetic algorithm, neural networks can be tuned by modifying some parameters. It is a very difficult point to design correctly a network with the right parameters. The set of basic network parameters are called *Hyperparameters*. In this work, we tuned the most common ones:

- **Activation function**: function used by neurons for the activation. The activation function manages the value of the neuron output. The signals of the previous layer are weighted by the internal parameters, added together and this result is used as input for the activation function. In this work, we used the most common activation functions: tanh, ReLu, sigmoid. Figure 6 represents these three functions.
- **Neurons number**: number of neurons in the hidden layer. Intuitively, we can guess that more neurons are in the hidden layer, more accurate will be the classification. In practice, it is more complicated. Too many neurons can produce an overfitting phenomenon. We varied the number of neurons between 5 and 50 for each activation function.
- **Learning rate**: parameter that controls how much the model change in response to the estimated error each time the model weights are updated. Choosing the learning rate is challenging as a value too small may result in a long training process that could get stuck, whereas a value too large may result in learning a sub-optimal set of weights too fast or an unstable training process. We varied this parameter between 0.1 and 0.95 by step of 0.05, between 0.01 and 0.009 by step of 0.01 and between 0.001 and 0.009 by step of 0.01 for each of the three activation functions.
- **Batch size**: size of the batch. During the training, the dataset elements passed through the network one after

one. The batch size is the number of elements that pass through the network before tuning the weights of the network. We varied the batch size between 1000 and 2000 by step of 200 for each of the three activation functions. It was not possible to use a batch size smaller than 1000 in Google Colaboratory.

- **Epoch number**: number of time the entire dataset is passed through the network. A high value of this parameter usually increases the efficiency of the learning but also the time needed. We varied this parameter between 100 and 350 by step of 50. As for the batch size, it was not possible to use epochs number bigger than 350 in Google Colaboratory

As explained in Section I, the learning of an Artificial Neural Network is clearly faster with GPU. To train our model in a reasonable time, we used the Jupyter Notebook on Google Colaboratory platform. Unfortunately, this platform has some time restriction and does not provide a sufficient infrastructure and to test the whole range of parameters we wanted to test.

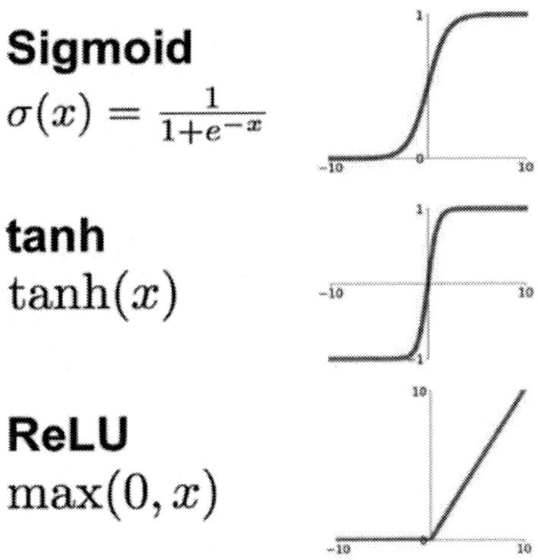

Figure 6. Equations and curves of activation functions

1) Parameters study results: As for the Genetic Algorithm classifier and the fitness function, the activation function in the neural network classifier that produces the best results for all values of all parameters is the ReLu function. Table III and IV show the values of the parameters that produce the best results for the two evaluation criteria.

TABLE III. NEURAL NETWORK PARAMETER VALUES THAT PRODUCE THE BEST RESULTS IN THE PARAMETRIC STUDY FOR THE ROC CRITERION

Parameter name	Parameter value	ROC result
Neurons number	38	0.93761
Learning rate	0.04	0.93979
Batch size	2000	0.92746
Epochs number	350	0.94989
Activation function	ReLu	0.94989

Table III shows, for each parameter, the value that produces the best ROC AUC and the result associated with it. All these neural network parameter values will be used in combination as a new model in the next section.

TABLE IV. NEURAL NETWORK PARAMETER VALUES THAT PRODUCE THE BEST RESULTS IN THE PARAMETRIC STUDY FOR THE P-R CRITERION

Parameter name	Parameter value	P-R result
Neurons number	38	0.80854
Learning rate	0.05	0.81336
Batch size	2000	0.78883
Epochs number	350	0.83951
Activation function	ReLu	0.83951

Table IV shows, for each parameter, the value that produces the best P-R AUC and the result associated with it. All these neural network parameter values will be used in combination as a new model in the next section.

D. Comparison of the classifiers

For each classifier (genetic algorithm or neural network), we selected the set of parameters that produces the best ROC AUC and the best P-R AUC. With these four models, we ran 10 times a 10-folds cross-validation and we meant the results to minimize the variance.

Table V shows the results for all the 4 classifiers with the corespondent evaluation criterion.

TABLE V. RESULTS OF A 10-10-CROSS VALIDATION OF THE CLASSIFIERS

Classifier	ROC	P-R
Genetic Algorithm	0.900598	0.745871
Neural Network	0.946812	0.812567

The parameter values of these four models are given in the Tables I, II, III and IV in Section IV.

Figures 7, 8 and 9 represent some example curves obtained during the 10-folds cross-validation.

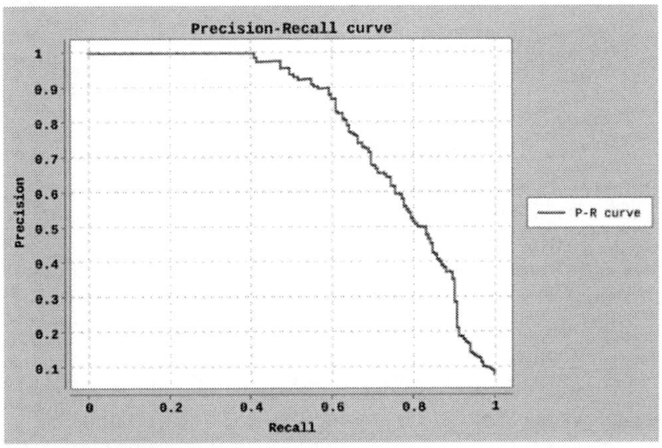

Figure 7. Representation of a Precision-Recall curve for a Neural Network. Parameters: Neurons Number: 46 - Learning Rate: 0.01 - Batch Size: 2000 - Epochs Number: 100 - Activation Function: ReLu

V. CONCLUSIONS AND FUTURE WORKS

In this work, we show that a classification based on an artificial neural network trained by the backpropagation algorithm gives better results than a classification using an aggregation function trained by a genetic algorithm.

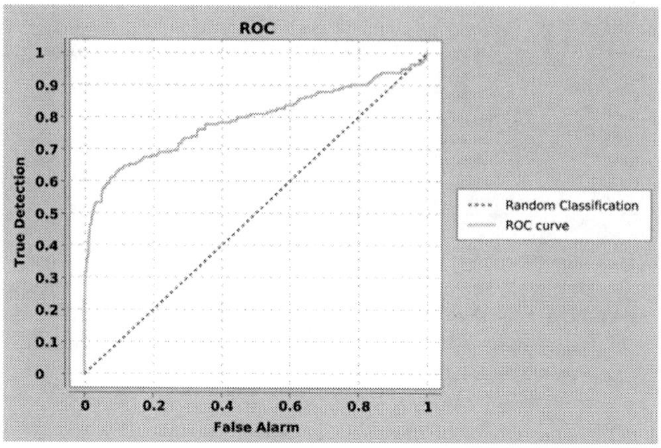

Figure 8. Representation of a Roc curve for a Genetic Algorithm. Parameters: Population Size: 125 - Crossover Rate: 60 - Mutation Rate: 25 - Fitness score: AUC

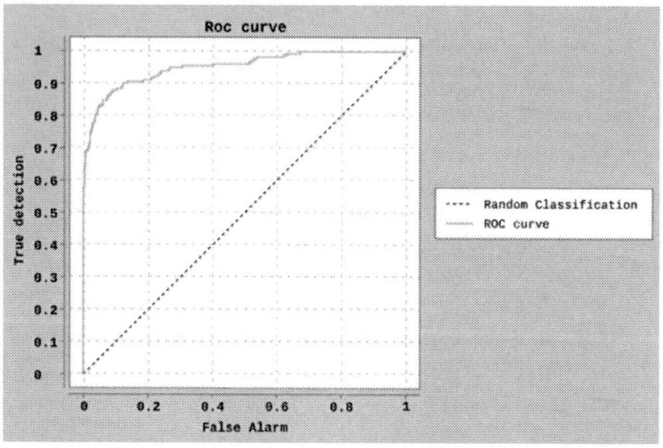

Figure 9. Representation of a Roc curve for a Neural Network. Parameters: Neuron number : 40 - Learning Rate : 0.06 - Batch Size : 2000 - Epoch number : 350 - Activation function : ReLu

The neural network is more efficient on the two performance criteria used in this work: ROC AUC and P-R AUC. Moreover, because of the restrictions applied to Google Colaboratory, we were not able to test a significant amount of values for the *batch size* and *epochs number* parameters. It is logical to assume that the results would be even better with a much larger *number of epochs*.

However, it is important to note that the training of a neural network is very slow on CPUs. To obtain results in a reasonable time, it is essential to equip yourself with GPU which is expensive.

We noted that for the genetic algorithm, the *AUC* criteria produces always better results than the *distance* criteria. On the neural network, we noted the activation function that gives the best results, is always the *ReLu* function.

During our work, we noted that the parameters of the genetic algorithm have only a very small influence on the result. It may depend on the dataset used, however, a parametric study seems to be much less important for the genetic algorithm than to train a neural network.

Another important point is about the interpretation of the internal parameters after the training. On an artificial neural network, it is difficult to interpret the meaning of the network parameters (weight, bias, etc). A neural networks is often used as a "black-box". The trained aggregation function, on the other hand, gives interesting information about the modules that are aggregated. It highlights the modules with high importance and, mostly, the less important. This could point out that a module is inefficient and improve it in priority.

For example, a typical w weights vector obtained by the genetic algorithm with the dataset used in this work is $w = [0.4407, 0.532, 0.0204, 0.0027, 0.0042]$. We note easily that the most important agent is the second one: the webshell signature analyzer. On the other side, the least effective agent is the obfuscation detector in the fourth position.

This work could be improved in several points. In the first time, it should be interesting to perform a bigger parametric study on the neural network classifier. We think it is possible to increase the efficiency of the results obtained with a better infrastructure to train the model.

It seems interesting to determine the correlation between the different parameters of the algorithms. Indeed, we performed our parametric study by tuning independently each parameters. If we knew the correlations between the different parameters, we would probably be able to determine a better parameters combination.

The algorithms designed for these works are made to be easily used in another project. It could be interesting to test these classifiers on different types of data to determine if the parameters are independent of the dataset or not.

References

[1] Z.-H. Lv, H.-B. Yan, and R. Mei, "Automatic and accurate detection of webshell based on convolutional neural network," in Cyber Security, X. Yun, W. Wen, B. Lang, H. Yan, L. Ding, J. Li, and Y. Zhou, Eds. Singapore: Springer Singapore, 2019, pp. 73–85.

[2] V. Torra, "Weighted owa operators for synthesis of information," vol. 2, 10 1996, pp. 966 – 971 vol.2.

[3] V. Torra, "On the learning of weights in some aggregation operators: the weigthed mean and owa operators," 1999, URL: http://digital.csic.es/handle/10261/2244 [accessed: 2020-08-19].

[4] D. Nettleton and V. Torra, "A comparison of active set method and genetic algorithm approaches for learning weighting vectors in some aggregation operators," International Journal of Intelligent Systems, vol. 16, 09 2001, pp. 1069–1083.

[5] A. Croix, T. Debatty, and W. Mees, "Training a multi-criteria decision system and application to the detection of php webshells," in 2019 International Conference on Military Communications and Information Systems (ICMCIS), May 2019, pp. 1–8.

[6] M. Nielsen, "Neural networks and deep learning - chap 2 : How the backpropagation algorithm works," 12 2019, URL: http://neuralnetworksanddeeplearning.com/chap2.html [accessed: 2020-08-19].

[7] I. Witten and E. Frank, Data Mining Practical Machine Learning Tools And Techniques, 01 2005, vol. 11.

[8] T. Fawcett, "Roc graphs: Notes and practical considerations for researchers," Machine Learning, vol. 31, 01 2004, pp. 1–38.

[9] T. Saito and M. Rehmsmeier, "The precision-recall plot is more informative than the roc plot when evaluating binary classifiers on imbalanced datasets," PLOS ONE, vol. 10, no. 3, 03 2015, pp. 1–21, URL: https://doi.org/10.1371/journal.pone.0118432 [accessed: 2020-08-19].

[10] J. Keilwagen, I. Grosse, and J. Grau, "Area under precision-recall curves for weighted and unweighted data," PLOS ONE, vol. 9, no. 3, 03 2014, pp. 1–13, URL: https://doi.org/10.1371/journal.pone.0092209 [accessed: 2020-08-19].

Why Multipath TCP Degrades Throughput Under Insufficient Send Socket Buffer and Differently Delayed Paths

Toshihiko Kato, Adhikari Diwakar, Ryo Yamamoto, and Satoshi Ohzahata
Graduate School of Informatics and Engineering
University of Electro-Communications
Tokyo, Japan
e-mail: kato@net.lab.uec.ac.jp, diwakaradh@net.lab.uec.ac.jp, ryo-yamamoto@uec.ac.jp, ohzahata@uec.ac.jp

Abstract— **Recently, the Multipath Transmission Control Protocol (MPTCP) comes to be used widely. It allows more than one TCP connections via different paths to compose one Multipath TCP communication. Our previous papers pointed out that insufficient send socket buffer makes the throughput worse than that of single path TCP, when the subflows have different transmission delays. Although our previous papers gave the detailed analysis on the throughput degradation focusing on the relationship between the send socket buffer size and the delay, they did not clarify the reason of the throughput degradation. This paper investigates the Linux MPTCP software and the MPTCP communication details, and clarifies why the insufficient socket buffer degrades the MPTCP throughput.**

Keywords- multipath TCP; send socket buffer; head-of-line blocking.

I. Introduction

Recently, mobile terminals with multiple interfaces have come to be widely used. For example, most smart phones are installed with interfaces for 4G Long Term Evolution (LTE) and Wireless LAN (WLAN). In order for applications to use multiple interfaces effectively, Multipath TCP (MPTCP) is being introduced in several operating systems, such as Linux, Apple OS/iOS and Android. MPTCP is defined in three RFC documents by Internet Engineering Task Force. RFC 6182 [1] outlines the architecture guidelines for developing MPTCP protocols. It defines the ideas of *MPTCP connection* and *suflows* (TCP connections associated with an MPTCP connection). RFC 6824 [2] presents the details of extensions to the traditional TCP to support multipath operation. It defines the MPTCP control information realized as new TCP options, and the MPTCP protocol procedures. RFC 6356 [3] presents a congestion control algorithm that couples those running on different subflows.

MPTCP has some problems when subflows are established over heterogeneous paths with different delay, such as an LTE network and a WLAN. TCP ACKnowledgment (ACK) segments from a path with longer delay return later than those from a shorter delay path. This causes a *Head-of-Line* (*HoL*) *blocking*, in which TCP data segments over a longer delay subflow block the window sliding while waiting for their ACKs [4]. In order to avoid this problem, the selection of the appropriate subflow is required. The function to select a subflow for transferring a data segment is called a *scheduler*, and several scheduler algorithms have been proposed so far. Originally, MPTCP implementation adopted the lowest Round-Trip Time (RTT) first and the round-robin schedulers [5]. However, both of them suffer from the HoL blocking. The opportunistic Retransmission and Penalization mechanism (*RP mechanism*) [6] [7] is used in the current MPTCP implementation as a default. When a data sender detects that new data cannot be sent out due to an HoL blocking over a specific subflow, it retransmits the oldest unacknowledged data through a subflow with the lowest RTT (opportunistic retransmission). At the same time, the subflow that occurred this HoL blocking is punished by halving its congestion window (penalization).

The Delay Aware Packet Scheduling (DAPS) [8] and the Out-of-order Transmission for In-order Arrival Scheduling (OTIAS) [9] take account of subflow delays and schedule data segment sending for in-order receiving. The BLocking EStimation scheduler (BLEST) [10] estimates whether a subflow will cause an HoL blocking and dynamically adapts scheduling to prevent blocking.

Those schedulers improve the MPTCP performance compared with the original scheduler algorithm, and several studies report the results of MPTCP performance evaluation through heterogeneous paths [11]-[15]. However, those proposals of schedulers and the performance evaluation reports are focusing only on the receive socket buffer. While insufficient receive socket buffer invokes HoL blocking, the send socket buffer also gives some impacts on the TCP throughput.

In our previous papers [16] [17], we pointed out that an insufficient size of send socket buffer provokes more serious throughput degradation than insufficient receive socket buffer. Although our previous papers analyzed the detailed behaviors of MPTCP by investigating the MPTCP and TCP level sequence numbers and windows, they did not discuss why such performance degradation happens. In this paper, we clarify the reason by investigating the Linux MPTCP software and the communication traces.

The rest of paper consists of the following sections. Section 2 shows the details of MPTCP data transfer procedure and the related work on the MPTCP scheduler. Section 3 gives the results of performance evaluation in the case that an MPTCP connection provides poor throughput than a single TCP connection due to the insufficient send socket buffer. Section 4 shows the behavior of Linux MPTCP software in the case of limited send buffer, and discusses the reason of the performance degradation. Section 5 concludes this paper.

II. Related Work

This section describes the related work of our work.

A. MPTCP Data Transfer Procedures

As described in Figure 1, the MPTCP module is located on top of TCP. MPTCP is designed so that the conventional applications do not need to care about the existence of MPTCP. MPTCP establishes an MPTCP connection that is associated with two or more regular TCP connections called subflows. The management and data transfer over an MPTCP connection is done by the TCP options newly introduced for MPTCP operation. In the beginning, one subflow and an MPTCP connection are established through the TCP three way handshake using a Multipath Capable (MP_CAPABLE) TCP option. Next, another subflow is established and associated with the existing MPTCP connection by use of a Join Connection (MP_JOIN) option. This option contains the identification of the MPTCP connection to be joined.

After establishing multiple subflows, MPTCP takes one input data stream from a sender-side application, splits it into subflows, and reassembles the split data streams at the receiver side. The MPTCP connection level maintains the data sequence number independent of the subflow level sequence numbers. The data and ACK segments used in a subflow may contain a Data Sequence Signal (DSS) option depicted in Figure 2. The number is assigned on a byte-by-byte basis similarly with the TCP sequence number. The value of data sequence number is the number assigned to the first byte conveyed in that TCP segment. The data sequence number, subflow sequence number (relative value) and data-level length define the mapping between the MPTCP connection level and the subflow level. The data ACK is analogous to the behavior of the standard TCP cumulative ACK, and specifies the next data sequence number a receiver expects.

We need to say that there is no window size field in the DSS option. Instead, the window size contained in the TCP header is used for the flow control in MPTCP. That is, the

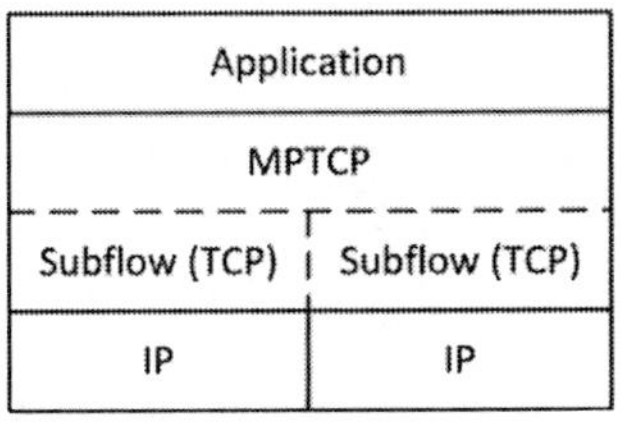

Figure 1. MPTCP layer structure.

Kind (= 30)	Length	Subtype (= 2)	Flags
Data ACK (4 or 8 octets, depending on flags)			
Data sequence number (4 or 8 octets, depending on flags)			
Subflow sequence number (4 octets)			
Data-level length (2 octets)		Checksum (2 octets)	

Figure 2. Data sequence signal option.

flow control is performed for the data sequence number at the MPTCP connection level as well as the subflow level. The control for the data sequence number is done in a way that the data sequence number is not more than the data ACK plus the window size. It is also required that the upper window edge in the MPTCP connection level (the data ACK plus the window size) does not shrink. In order to fully utilize the capacity of all subflows, a receiver needs to provide the following buffer space so that a sender can keep all subflows fully utilized [2].

$$\text{Buffer size} = \sum_{i=1}^{n} bw_i \times RTT_{max} \times 2. \quad (1)$$

Here, n is the number of subflows, bw_i is the bandwidth of subflow i, and RTT_{max} is the highest RTT among all subflows. This equation means that an MPTCP connection can send data segments at full speed during the highest RTT, even if a loss event occurs.

B. Related Work on MPTCP Scheduler

As stated in the previous section, the mechanism to assign data to multiple subflows is called a scheduler. The MPTCP implementation for Linux operating system supports the default scheduler, the lowest RTT first with RP mechanism, which is called *minRTT*. The minRTT scheduler first sends data over one subflow with the lowest RTT until its window is full. Then, it starts transmitting over the next subflow. When it detects an HoL blocking, it retransmits the oldest data as a new data segment over the lowest RTT subflow, and halves the congestion window of the subflow that caused this blocking.

The other schedulers mentioned in the previous section can be summarized as follows. DAPS aims for in-order arrival at the receiver to prevent its buffer from blocking [8]. It sends data segments in inverse proportion to the delay of individual subflows with the strategy that the younger numbered data segments are transferred through the path with shorter delay. OTIAS provides the out-of-order transmission at the sender for the in-order arrival at the receiver [9]. One of the difference between DAPS and OTIAS is that DAPS focuses on the scheduling of multiple packets, but OTIAS tries to determine the scheduling of only one packet. BLEST, on the other hand, takes a proactive stand towards minimizing HoL blocking [10]. Rather than penalizing the slow subflows, it estimates whether a path will cause HoL blocking and dymamically adapts scheduling to prevent it.

Several publications discussed the performance evaluation [6] [7] [11][-15]. The early stage papers [6] [7] [11] [12] focus mainly on measuring MPTCP throughput with changing the receive socket buffer size. Kim et al. [13] proposes a scheduler using the buffer blocking prediction based on receive buffer size and RTT. It gives the time variations of throughput as a performance evaluation. Zhou et al. [14] shows the MPTCP performance evaluation over the real Internet by changing socket buffer size under the assumption that the sizes of send and receive socket buffers are the same. Dong et al. [15] compares the performance of several schedules including DAPS, OTIAS, and BLEST. In the performance evaluation, it measured the file transfer completion time by changing RTT ratio, receive socket buffer size, and transferred file size.

Those papers have two problems. First, all of them use only macroscopic performance metrics, such as the average throughput and the completion time for a file transfer. They do not discuss the detailed performance analysis taking account of the MPTCP parameters, such as data sequence number and data ack number. Secondly, they mainly focus on the receive socket buffer. However, the send socket buffer also gives some impacts on the TCP throughput.

In contrast, we took a microscopic approach that analyzes the detailed MPTCP internal behaviors in the performance evaluation, and focused on send socket buffer size as well as receive buffer size. In [16], we evaluated the MPTCP performance by changing receive and send socket buffer sizes independently, and clarified that an insufficient send socket buffer provokes more serious throughput degradation than insufficient receive socket buffer. Kato et al. [17] provided more detailed analysis of the MPTCP communicatison under insufficient send socket buffer through dissimilarly delayed subflows.

III. THROUGHPUT DEGRADATION DUE TO INSUFFICIENT SEND SOCKET BUFFER

As for the case that send socket buffer is insufficient, our previous papers showed the following results when MPTCP communication is done by two subflows whose transmission delay is different; fast subflow and slow subflow. In the case that the send socket buffer size is small, the communication is done through only the fast subflow. As the send socket buffer size increases, the communication is done through two subflows, but the MPTCP connection level throughput is lower than the single path TCP communication whose delay is equal to the fast subflow. When the send socket buffer size becomes bigger, two subflows are used in the MPTCP communication and its throughput is larger than the bandwidth of one subflow.

In this section, we show the detailed MPTCP behaviors when the MPTCP connection level throughput is lower than a single path TCP throughput.

A. Experimental Settings

In the experiment, we use the network configuration of shown in Figure 3. Two hosts running the Linux operating system (Ubunts 16.04 LTS), data sender and receiver, are connected together through two 1Gbps Ethernet links. The private IP addresses are assigned as shown in the figure. In one Ethernet link, a network emulator is inserted in order to provide delay. Although the physical data rate is 1Gbps, the frame transmission speed is limited to 100 Mbps using Linux traffic control (*tc*) command. We establish one MPTCP connection between two hosts with two subflows, one between 192.168.0.1 and 192.168.0.2 (called *fast subflow*) and the other between 192.168.1.1 and 192.168.1.2 (called

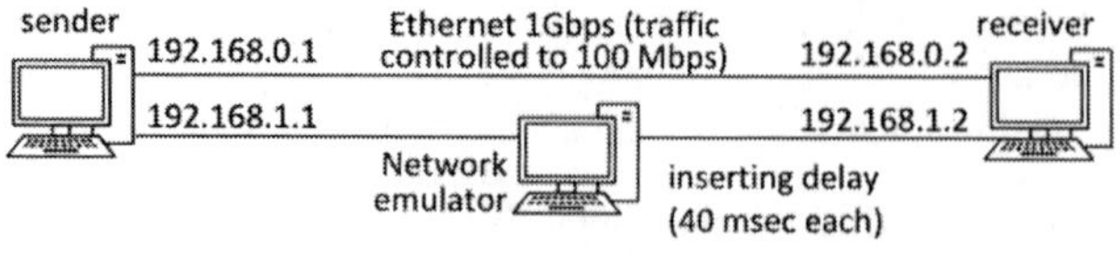

Figure 3. Network configuration for evaluation.

slow subflow). The scheduler is the default one, minRTT. By consulting the results in our previous papers, the delay inserted at the network emulator is set to 40 msec for one direction, i.e., 80 msec in round-trip. The send socket buffer size is set to 1,048,576 bytes (1 Gibibytes) for the minimum, default, and maximum sizes, using the `sysctl -w net.ipv4.tcp_wmem` command. The receive socket buffer at the receiver uses the default value, which is 4,096, 87380, and 6,291,456 bytes for the minimum, default, and maximum sizes, respectively.

In the performance evaluation, *iperf* is used in both hosts and bulk data transfer is executed for 10 seconds. During the bulk data transfer, packet traces are collected at the sender side by use of *tcpdump*. Those traces are examined in detail with *Wireshark*, a network protocol analyzer whose version is 3.2.4. We also execute *tcpprobe* in the sender side in order to collect TCP related information like congestion window size during data transfer.

B. Results and Analysis

We executed five experiment runs under the conditions described above. The throughput measured at the receiver side ranges from 42.4 Mbps to 49.8 Mbps. The average is 46.8 Mbps and the standard deviation is 3.54 Mbps. Since the link bandwidth of the fast subflow is 100 Mbps, the MPTCP connection level throughput is lower than the subflow bandwidth.

Hereafter, we pick up the forth experiment run whose throughput is 48.6 Mbps. Figure 4 shows the time variation

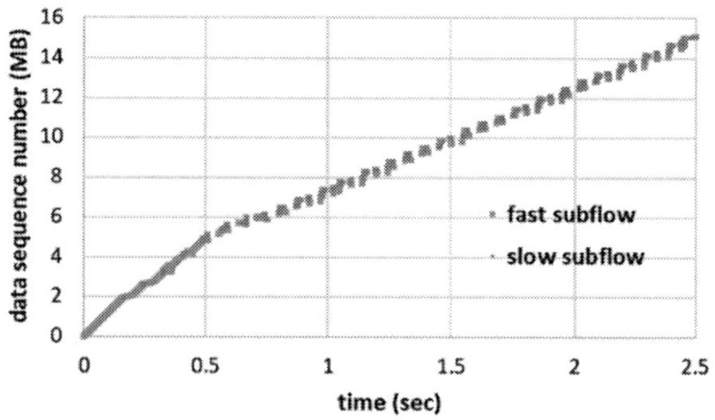

(a) from 0 sec to 2.5 sec.

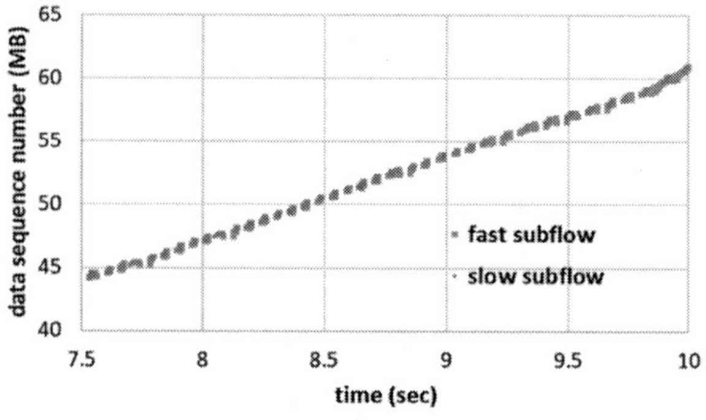

(b) from 7.5 sec to 10 sec.

Figure 4. Time variation of data sequence number.

of the data sequence number sent over the fast and slow subflows. In this figure, we show the graph focusing on the results during the first and the last 2.5 secs. The two graphs show similar tendencies. The data sequence number is increasing in both fast and slow subflows. The increase itself is intermittent, that is, the data transmission in this case repeats sending and stopping. This behavior is considered to be the reason for low throughput.

Figure 5 shows the time variation of the MPTCP data sequence number and the TCP sequence number focused on the period between 7.5 sec and 8.1 sec. By zooming in the change of the data sequence number, we can find that there are several retransmissions in the fast subflow, e.g., at 7.55 sec, 7.74 sec, 7.78 sec, some of which are explicitly indicated in the figure. Figure 5(b) shows the increase of TCP sequence numbers in the fast and slow subflows, and there are no retransmissions in both of them. This result means that the retransmissions shown in Figure 5(a) are the opportunistic retransmissions installed in the minRTT scheduler.

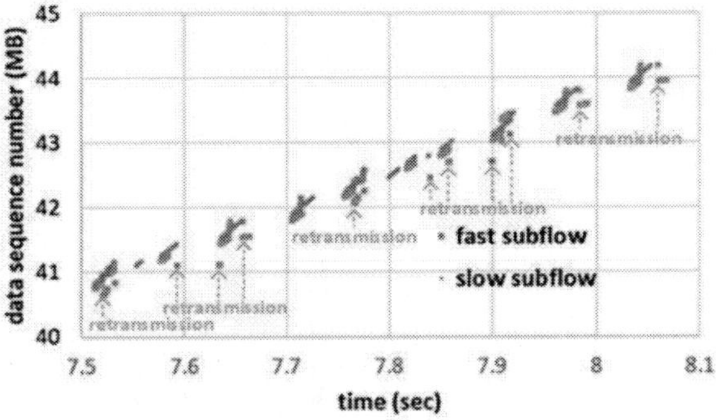

(a) data sequence number

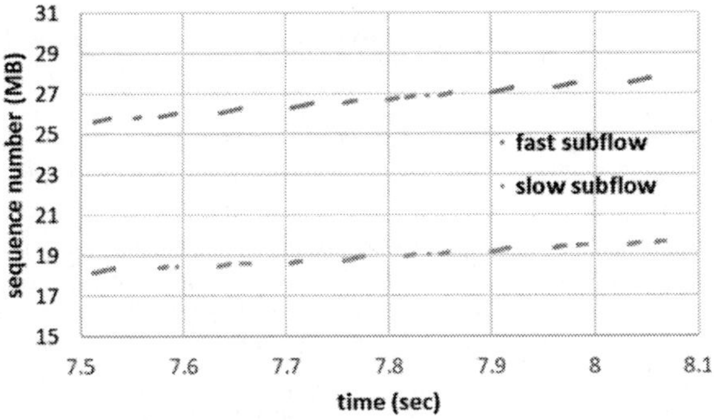

(b) TCP sequence number

Figure 5. Detailed behavior between 7.5 sec and 8.1sec.

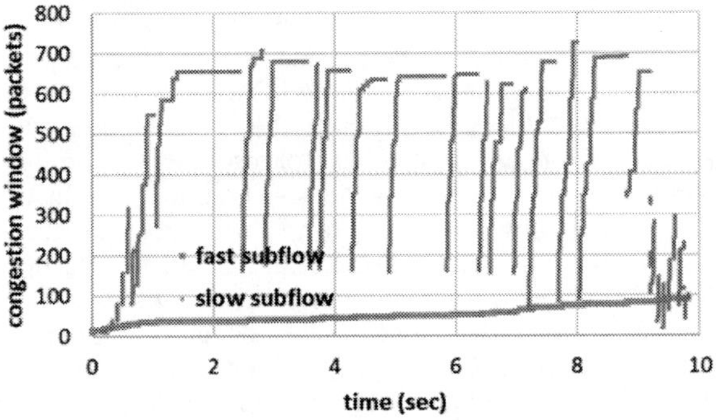

Figure 6. Time variation of congestion window size.

We also measured the values of the congestion window size of the fast and slow subflows, at the timing of sender receiving ACK segments by use of the tcpprobe module. Figure 6 shows the time variation of congestion window size in the fast and slow subflows. The congestion window size of the slow subflow increases up to around 700 packets and undergoes drops more than 20 times. We confirmed that there were no packet losses in the TCP level, and so these drops are caused by the penalization implemented in the minRTT scheduler. The congestion window size in the fast subflow, on the other hand, experienced no drops. The reason that the window is kept in a relatively low value is that the congestion window validation [18] was effective due to small RTT in the fast subflow.

IV. Analysis of Linux MPTCP Software

This section shows the detail of Linux MPTCP software and discusses why the performance degradation happens.

A. *Internals of Linux MPTCP Software*

When an application sends a data using MPTCP, function `tcp_sendmsg_locked()` processes this request. Figure 7 shows its outline. The main part of this function is a while loop for handling data given by an application. In the loop, the buffer status is checked at first. If there is no send socket buffer space, checked by `sk_stream_memory_free()`, or if the socket buffer for a data segment cannot be allocated, done by `sk_stream_alloc_sk()`, then the control is jumped to `wait_for_snnbuf`. Here, this module will wait for some period by `sk_stream_wait_memory()`. On the other hand, if the send socket buffer has enough space, the data is copied to the allocated buffer (`skb_add_data_nocache()`) and transmitted (`__tcp_push_pending_frames()` or

```
tcp_sendmsg_locked(struct sock *sk, msg, size)
    // msg: data to send, size: data size
{
  while(msg_left(msg)) { //loop while msg is left
    if(new_segment) {
      if(!sk_stream_memory_free(sk)) //if no sock buf
        goto wait_for_sndbuf;        //jump
      skb = sk_stream_allock_skb(sk) //allocate buffer
      if(!skb)                       //if allocation failed
        goto wait_for_sndbuf; //jump
    }
    skb_add_data_nocache(sk, skb, msg, size);
        //copy data to socket buffer
    if(forced_push(sk)) {
      __tcp_push_pending_frames(sk);
                            //call mptcp_write_xmit()
    } else if(skb == tcp_send_head(sk))
      tcp_push_one(sk);       //call mptcp_write_xmit()
    continue; //go to while for next segment
wait_for_sndbuf:
    sk_stream_wait_memory(sk, timer);
  }
  return sent_data_size;
}
```

Figure 7. Outline of tcp_sendmsg_locked().

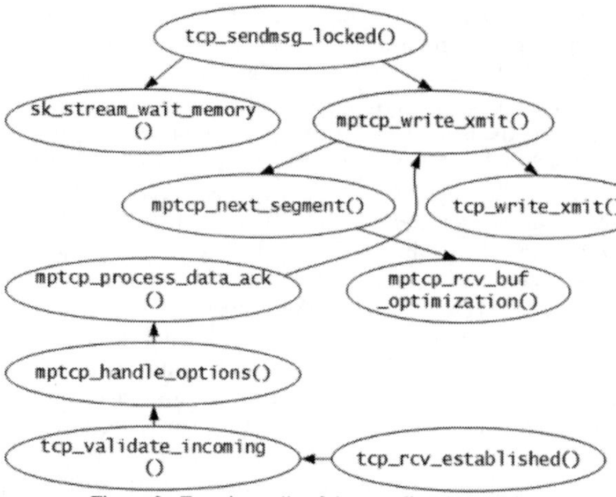

Figure 8. Function calls of data sending and receiving.

tcp_push_one()). The latter two functions will eventually call mptcp_write_xmit() to perform actual sending out. This program structure tells that the waiting on the send socket buffer shortage follows a different processing path from the sending data segment.

Figure 8 shows the relationship of function calls in the data sending and receiving. As described above, the data sending is handled in mptcp_write_xmit(), which calls mptcp_next_segment() for obtaining the data segment being sent next, and tcp_write_xmit(), which sends the data segment out to the IP module. Within the mptcp_next_segment() function, mptcp_rcv_buf_optimization() is called to check whether to perform the RP mechanism. When the RP mechanism is performed actually this function returns the buffer addresses that contains the data segment to be transmitted.

This figure also describes the function calls when receiving a data or ACK segment. When the TCP module receives a segment in the ESTABLISHED state, tcp_rcv_eshtablished() is called. In this function, the segment itself and its parameters are checked in tcp_validate_incoming(), which calls mptcp_handle_options() for processing a DSS option. In this function, mptcp_process_data_ack() is called for a data ACK parameter, and then this function calls mptcp_write_xmit() eventually. In this function, the RP mechanism is performed when it is necessary.

The following two points need to be mentioned. First, the waiting for buffer release in sk_stream_wait_memory() and the other processing are completely independent. Especially, the behavior of sending data requested from the upper layer stops completely during this waiting, because tcp_sendmsg_locked() is the only function to handle the data send request from the upper layer and it is blocked in this waiting function. The other is that the RP mechanism is applied to the subflows other than the one invoked the mptcp_rcv_buf_optimization() function.

B. Behaviors of Linux MPTCP Software

Figure 9 shows the time variation of congestion window sizes in the fast and slow subflows from 7.5 sec to 8.1 sec.

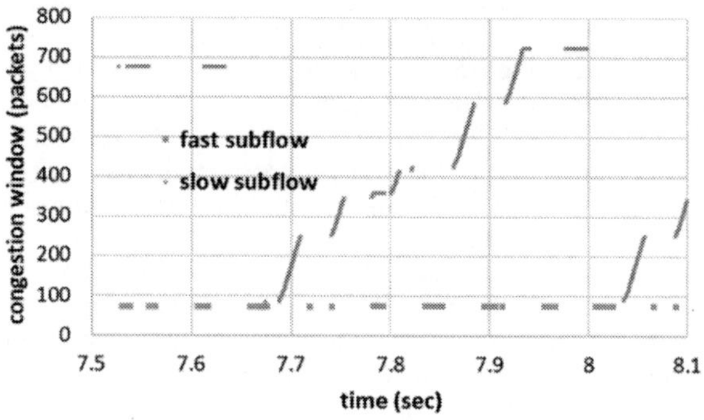

Figure 9. Time variation of congestion window size between 7.5 sec and 8.1 sec.

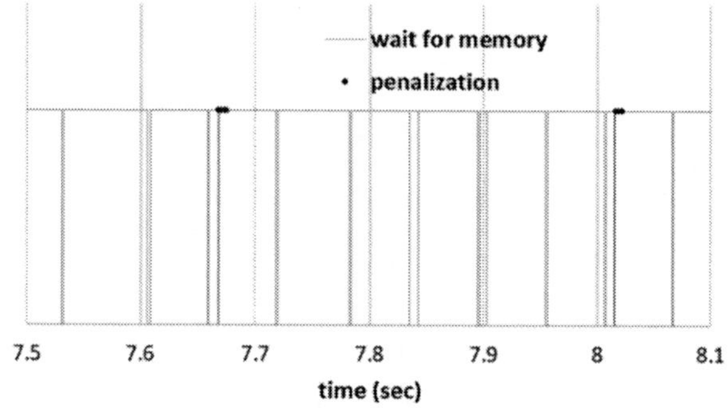

Figure 10. Behavior of wait for memory and penalization.

During this period, the window of the slow subflow is reduced twice, between 7.6 sec and 7.7 sec, and between 8.0 sec and 8.1 sec.

In order to analyze the MPTCP software behavior in Linux, we modified the Linux kernel to generate the timestamps of the entry and exit of sk_stream_wait_memory(), and those of the penalization in mptcp_rcv_buf_optimization(). Figure 10 shows those results between 7.5 sec and 8.1 sec. In this figure, the blue line is the situation of the processing of wait-for-memory timer. The upper side in the graph means the timer is on, i.e., the function is blocked by waiting for memory release. The lower side indicates the function is not blocked but working. The black points indicate that the penalizations are invoked.

This figure suggests the followings. First, the tcp_sendmsg_locked() function blocks very often in order to wait for the send buffer release, and the blocking keeps long and so the tcp_sendmsg_locked() function seems to be almost always blocked. During the blocked periods, the function cannot perform anything for resolving the throughput degradation. The other is that the penalization that reduces the congestion window size of the slow subflow does not occur so many times as the send socket buffer starvation. During the 0.6 sec shown in the figure, only two sets of penalization occur. It should be noted that, at each set of penalization, the actual window reduction occurs multiple times. In the case of this figure, three reductions happened at each penalization. Throughout a 10 sec data transfer analyzed here, the buffer starvation happened 278 times. On the other hand, the penalization occurred 28 times, each of which included one to three window reductions.

Based on those considerations, we can summarize the reason of the throughput degradation is the followings. First, the handling of send socket buffer starvation is done in the very beginning of TCP data send processing, and the way is just to block the control for some period. During this waiting period, no mechanisms to recover degraded throughput, such as the RP mechanism, can be invoked. Second, these mechanisms may be invoked when an MPTCP sender receives ACK segments, but the frequency of these invocations are much less than that of buffer starvations.

V. CONCLUSIONS

In this paper, we pointed up the MPTCP performance degradation in the situation that subflows have different transmission delays and the send socket buffer size is insufficient. We showed this situation by the experiments using the in-house network and discussed the details of the MPTCP parameters during the degradation. We also showed the internal structure of Linux MPTCP software focusing on the buffer starvation and the MPTCP scheduler. In the end, we showed a possible reason why the performance degradation occurs. We are going to propose a new scheduler function to resolve this degradation caused by the insufficient send socket buffer size.

REFERENCES

[1] A. Ford, C. Raiciu, M. Handley, S. Barre, and J. Iyengar, "Architectural Guidelines for Multipath TCP Development," IETF RFC 6182, Mar. 2011.

[2] A. Ford, C. Raiciu, M. Handley, and O. Bonaventure, "TCP Extensions for Multipath Operation with Multiple Addresses," IETF RFC 6824, Jan. 2013.

[3] C. Raiciu, M. Handley, and D. Wischik, "Coupled Congestion Control for Multipath Transport Protocols," IETF RFC 6356, Oct. 2011.

[4] M. Scharf and S. Kiesel, "Head-of-Line Blocking in TCP and SCTP: Analysis and Measurements," IEEE GLOBECOM '06, pp.1-5, Nov. 2006.

[5] Icteam, "MultiPath TCP – Linux Kernel implementation, Users:: Confiugre MPTCP," https://multipath-tcp.org/pmwiki.php/Users/ConfigureMPTCP.

[6] C. Raiciu, et al., "How Hard Can It Be? Designing and Implementing a Deployable Multipath TCP," 9th USENIX Symposium on Networked Systems Design and Implementation (NSDI '12), pp.1-14, Apr. 2012.

[7] O. Paasch, S. Ferlin, O. Alay, and O. Bonaventure, "Experimental Evaluation of Multipath TCP Schedulers," 2014 SIGCOMM Workshop on Capacity Sharing Workshop (CSWS '14), pp.27-32, Aug. 2014.

[8] N. Kuhn, et al., "DAPS: Intelligent delay-aware packet scheduling for multipath transport," IEEE ICC 2014, pp. 1222-1227, Jun. 2014

[9] F. Yand, Q. Wang, and P. D. Amer, "Out-of-oder Transmission for In-order Arrival Scheduling for Multipath TCP," 28th International Conference on Advanced Information Networking and Aplications Workshops, pp. 749-752, May 2014.

[10] S. Ferlin, O. Alay, O. Mehani, and R. Boreli, "BLEST: Blocking Estimation-based MPTCP Scheduler for Heterogeneous Networks," IFIP Networking 2016, pp. 431-439, May 2016.

[11] C. Paasch, R, Khalili, and O. Bonaventure, "On the Benefits of Applying Experimental Design to Improve Multipath TCP," 9th ACM Conference on Emerging Networking Experiments and Technologies (CoNEXT '13), pp.393-398, Dec. 2013.

[12] B. Arzani, A. Gurney, S. Cheng, R. Guerin, and B. T. Loo, "Impact of Path Characteristics and Scheduling Policies on MPTCP Performance," 28th International Conference on Advanced Information Networking and Applications Workshops, pp.743-748, May 2014.

[13] J. Kim, B. Oh, and J. Lee, "Receive Buffer based Path Management for MPTCP in Heterogeneous Networks," 2017 IFIP/IEEE Symposium on Integrated Network and service Management (IM), pp.648-651, May 2017.

[14] F. Zhou, et al., "The Performance Impact of Buffer Sizes for Multi-Path TCP in InternetSetups. In: 2017 IEEE 31st International Conference on Advanced Information Networking and Applications (AINA), pp.9-16, Mar. 2017.

[15] P. Dong, et al., "Performance Evaluation of Multipath TCP Scheduling Algorithms," IEEE Access, Vol. 7, pp. 29818-29825, Feb. 2019.

[16] T. Kato, M. Tenjin, R. Yamamoto, S. Ohzahata, and H. Shinbo, "Microscopic Approach for Experimental Analysis of Multipath TCP Throughput under Insufficient Send/Receive Socket Buffers.," 15th International Conference WWW/Internet 2016, pp.191-199, Oct. 2016.

[17] T. Kato, A. Diwakar, R. Yamamoto, S. Ohzahata, and N. Suzuki, "How Insufficient Send Socket Buffer Affects MPTCP Performance over Paths with Different Delay," 6th World Conference on Information Systems and Technologies (WorldCIST 18), pp. 614-624, Mar. 2018.

[18] N. Handley, J. Padhye, and S. Floyd, "TCP Congestion Window Validation," IETF RFC 2861, Jun. 2000.

Location Privacy Preservation of Vehicle Data in Internet of Vehicles

Ying Ying Liu
Department of Computer Science
University of Manitoba
Winnipeg, Canada
Email: umliu369@myumanitoba.ca

Austin Cooke
Online Business Systems
Winnipeg, Canada
Email: austin.cooke12@gmail.com

Parimala Thulasiraman
Department of Computer Science
University of Manitoba
Winnipeg, Canada
Email: thulasir@cs.umanitoba.ca

***Abstract*—Internet of Things (IoT) has attracted a recent spark in research on Internet of Vehicles (IoV). In this paper, we focus on one research area in IoV: preserving location privacy of vehicle data. We discuss existing location privacy preserving techniques and provide a scheme for evaluating these techniques under IoV traffic condition. We propose a different strategy in applying Differential Privacy using k-d tree data structure to preserve location privacy and experiment on real world Gowalla data set. We show that our strategy produces differentially private data, good preservation of utility by achieving similar regression accuracy to the original dataset on an Long Term Short Term Memory (LSTM) neural network traffic predictor.**

Keywords–Internet of Things; Internet of Vehicles; Location Privacy; Differential Privacy; Privacy Preservation Scheme.

I. Introduction

In recent years, a new networking concept has emerged. From the growing number of devices that are connected to each other by various means, researchers have coined a term for this network: the Internet of Things. The Internet of Things (IoT) has exploded in the last decade, facilitating the arrival of other novel ideas such as "Big Data", and many derivatives have spawned from IoT's core philosophy which involves a globally connected society. One of these derivatives involves facilitating the arrival of automated vehicles. This network specifically deals with vehicles communicating with each other, their infrastructure and other connected devices to form a cohesive, safe environment for automated vehicles to thrive in. This derivative is appropriately named the Internet of Vehicles (IoV). IoV is an evolution of traditional Vehicular Ad Hoc Networks (VANETs) with new enabling technologies such as Cloud and 5G [1]. Of course, in order to provide the necessary support for a network of automated vehicles, some data needs to be exchanged. Such data may include the location of a vehicle, an ID, and a timestamp. Unfortunately, however, the integrity of the data could be threatened by malicious individuals or companies.

In this paper, we focus on protecting the identity of individuals being revealed from sharing location data in IoV applications. There are several reasons why location privacy is challenging in IoT and IoV:

- Compared to relational data, location data imposes additional challenges in adding privacy protection with a balance between privacy and utility. For example, location data from wearable sensors that record an individual's trajectory has an uneven geometric distribution. Downtown areas may have dense trajectory, whereas, suburbs may have sparse trajectory. Applying state-of-the-art privacy protection, such as differential privacy protection to each single point will greatly affect data utility because the sparsely distributed location data will be overwhelmed with noise. This challenge remains true in IoV, where certain areas have heavier traffic and certain areas have lighter traffic.
- The utility of location data is very important for many IoT applications. For example, in location-based social networks, the preservation of location patterns (combinations of locations) are important for the analysis of protected data. In IoV, traceability poses an even higher standard on the utility of location data.
- Due to the high velocity and volume of location data from sensors, it is very challenging to design an efficient data structure to represent location data in both IoT and IoV.

II. Related Work

In the traditional location privacy research in VANETs, a large amount of work have concentrated on the use of pseudonyms to achieve anonymity and trace-ability at the same time. Raya and Hubaux [2] propose a Privacy-Preserving Authentication (PPA) scheme based on traditional Public Key Infrastructure (PKI) that uses traditional digital signature techniques to authenticate messages. However, this scheme is not scalable as it adds both a huge storage burden to the vehicles for preloading the digital certificates and a burden to communication bandwidth by including the digital certificates in the message. Wang et al. [3] introduce a Two-Factor LIghtweight Privacy-preserving (2FLIP) authentication scheme by using Message-Authentication-Code (MAC) and hash operations. 2FLIP is the first authentication scheme that achieves both strong privacy preservation and DoS resilience, however, it relies on the assumption of additional available devices. Each vehicle is bonded to a telematics device with biometric technology to verify the identities of multiple drivers and to provide evidence to trace each driver. A Tamper-Proof Device (TPD) is embedded in an On-Board-Unit (OBU) to store the system key and to sign and verify messages. Zhong et al. [4] propose a privacy-preserving scheme using a certificate-less aggregate signature to achieve secure Vehicle to Infrastructure (V2I) communications. The authors use a Trace Authority (TRA) to generate pseudonyms and track the real identity during the communication to achieve trace-ability. The computation cost is reduced through pre-calculation at the Road Side Unit (RSU).

With regards to location data in IoT, Bates et al. [5] explore some ideas regarding privacy protection in a fitness tracking social network using location fuzzing to introduce "geo-indistinguishability". However, this only protects large locations and not the single location scenario that we consider here. In a recent paper [6], the authors propose an algorithm LPT-DP-k for location privacy protection of location access count data. The algorithm first constructs a Location Privacy Tree (LPT) to preserve relationships among location patterns (i.e., trajectories of locations). It then selects k location patterns with probabilities based on access frequency for data sampling. In the last step, Laplace mechanism for differential privacy protection is applied to the selected sample patterns. The authors show that their algorithm achieves high utility and effectiveness of protecting location access data. However, there are a few drawbacks of this work, which we will address in this paper. First, the protection of frequent accessed location patterns does not protect individual privacy at less popular locations in ID based IoV data. Second, the LPT data structure grows exponentially when the number of locations grow, making the algorithm impractical for large amount of data.

Throughout our research, we find that almost every researcher has had different ideas about what location privacy should be and how to protect it. Despite efforts in exploring different techniques in achieving location privacy of IoT data, there is a lack of consensus on the definition of location privacy. Furthermore, there are few holistic views of location privacy breaches and mitigation at different stages of an IoV application.

The contributions of this paper are as follows:

1) We examine potential attacks of location privacy for IoV traffic condition service.
2) We provide a novel birds eye view of existing location privacy preserving techniques and provide a scheme of evaluating these techniques for IoV traffic condition service.
3) We investigate a different strategy of applying Differential Privacy (DP) to the real world Gowalla dataset than the one proposed by [6]. We show that instead of locations that are accessed frequently, the locations with less *unique visitors* are extremely sensitive. Instead of applying DP to frequencies of location patterns, we apply DP to aggregated location groups based on their geometric positions. We use a k-d tree data structure which is a natural choice for generalizing the locations so that differential privacy can be more appropriately applied to protect sensitive locations. We show that our strategy produces for differentially private data, good preservation of utility by achieving similar regression accuracy to the original dataset on an Long Term Short Term Memory (LSTM) neural network traffic predictor the location groups.

The paper is organized as follows: Section III and Section IV discuss the necessary motivation, problem and background knowledge to understand the concepts discussed in this paper. Section V includes the bird's eye view of the location privacy preservation scheme and an overview of the metrics by which we evaluate each method. Section VI and section VII include explanation of our experiment in Differential Privacy and analysis of the results. Finally, we conclude with section VIII where our contributions are summarized and we propose some future work for this topic.

III. MOTIVATION

The phrase "data is the new oil" refers to the priceless value that data has. We have been experiencing the early stages of the "information age" since the wide adoption of the world wide web. Only in recent years has the general public slowly realized the value of the data that they generate when interacting with internet capable devices. It has become common to hear about data privacy breaches in various companies. Facebook, Mariott, and even United States Postal Service have all been victims of data privacy breaches in the millions of records within the past year [7]–[9]. These companies all stored their records in plain text. However, if these companies had employed some privacy preserving techniques within their data, this would have prevented attackers from being able to derive any value from the data. This is one of the reasons privacy preservation in general is important.

A general IoV model involves communication between vehicles, infrastructure and a number of other entities. The data stored in or exchanged between any of these entities may contain all sorts of sensitive data. Even though it would be unwise to store a direct universal identifier (e.g., license plate number for an ID), these systems will need some way to identify each of the vehicles that are on the network. It has been shown that even by storing seemingly harmless qualities of vehicles or individuals, or using weak privacy protection techniques, it is trivial to re-identify an individual. Qualities such as age, salary, and geographic location can all lead to re-identification through a background information attack [10]. These qualities are referred to as "Quasi-identifiers", and can be surprisingly elusive if one is not aware of general privacy attacks and techniques.

A. Model Setting and Problem Statement

For the purposes of this paper, we are concerned with vehicle's data, specifically the storage of this data in the IoV Cloud. Each data record includes some ID, a Timestamp, and Location. The Cloud stores such information to perform operations on it in order to provide services to automated vehicles such as traffic condition services which we will focus on here. Traffic condition services are a classification of services that provide solutions to the problem of avoiding traffic related issues or gaining traffic related information. The Traffic condition service model consists of three main stages.

- The first stage is concerned with vehicles updating the Cloud with its ID, location, and timestamp. This is essential for being able to support basic traffic related services as it provides information about where vehicles are at a particular time.
- The second stage regards the vehicle querying the Cloud about traffic information around a particular location. An example query may look like: "How many vehicles are at location X?" The Cloud will compute the query and return the answer to the vehicle that queried the Cloud via the third stage of this model. It is clear that the data about a vehicle or group of vehicles contain extremely sensitive information, and

should be stored with the utmost privacy in the data storage unit (the Cloud in this case).

- Although the data are stored in the Cloud, they may be requested for a number of reasons that do not fall under the use case of providing the traffic condition service. The data may be published to allow for the research community to experiment ideas on real data sets in order to fine tune, improve and innovate new services. Additionally, and unique to traffic data, the data here may be audited by an insurance company in the event of a vehicle insurance claim. The data may also be requested by a police department or other law enforcement agency to aid in the investigation or search for a criminal. These requirements alone cast a wide and complicated net when considering how best to store the data so that it maintains realistic utility, and preserves the privacy of the individuals using the services.

In our paper, we analyze location privacy preservation in the three stages of data handling for IoV traffic condition service. We take this opportunity to outline some of the potential attacks that can be carried out on this model. We assume for the first two following attacks menitoned below, the Cloud uses some ID for each user, that the adversary does not initially know. However, the Cloud does not utilize any other privacy protection techniques. In the last attack, we assume that the Cloud is the adversary and would like to track a user through the user's queries.

B. Attack 1: Simple UserID background attack

The first attack involves an adversary querying the Cloud to gain an individual's location based on their user ID. The adversary does not know the user's ID in the Cloud. However, with a small amount of background information, the adversary can easily obtain this ID as we will demonstrate. Assume our victim is Officer Tom. Each day Tom checks in at a military base that only he has access to. Therefore he is the only person that is ever at this location. The adversary happens to know this, as well as the location of the military base. The adversary decides they would like to find out Tom's user ID but cannot query this directly. So the clever adversary decides to query the Cloud with the following instead: "SELECT * FROM DB WHERE UserID = (SELECT UserID FROM DB WHERE location = X)", where X is the location of the military base. Since Officer Tom is the only person ever at this base, the Cloud will return a single row from the database that contains Tom's UserID. Now the adversary can learn the location of Officer Tom even when he is not at the military base.

C. Attack 2: Dynamic UserID background attack

This attack is similar to Attack 1, however in this case, the Cloud employs the use of dynamic UserIDs, where the ID for any user is mapped to a unique list of values that change from time to time, so that even if an adversary obtains one of their UserIDs, they cannot successfully track the location of that particular user. However, we show that this approach is still not effective to ensure location privacy. Consider the situation from Attack 1, where Officer Tom is still the only resident at a military base that the adversary knows the location of. The adversary can determine whether Officer Tom is there at a given time or not. Suppose the adversary runs the query: "SELECT count(*) FROM DB WHERE location = X", again where X is the location of Officer Tom's military base. The Cloud will return a value, 0 or 1 indicating whether Officer Tom is there or not at the current time.

D. Attack 3: Untrusted Cloud attack

For this final attack, the Cloud is untrusted and is the adversary. We assume that the users are innocent and trusted. The Cloud contains traffic conditions of various locations that a user may be interested in but does not have this particular user's location. The Cloud would like to find the location of the user, say user Tom. If Tom queries the Cloud regarding a particular location, then the Cloud can infer that Tom may be interested in this location and may either be heading there at some time in the future, or Tom may already be in that location. If the Cloud's method for identifying individual users are unclear, the Cloud can still determine which locations are popular and which are not based on the number of queries about a particular location. Although, this attack is less likely to happen in practice, it is important to be considered.

In the following section, we describe work that has been conducted on data privacy in general that is relevant to the techniques we explore in this paper.

IV. Background: Privacy Techniques

This section details the core concepts of the privacy techniques that we have chosen to consider in our paper, as well as some pros and cons of these techniques as a whole.

A. Differential Privacy

Differential Privacy is first presented in 2006 by Dwork [11]. Differential privacy is a technique used in long-term data storage or data publishing. The core idea here is to eliminate the risk of an individual joining a statistical data set [12] (i.e., the risk is the same as if you had not joined the set). Differential Privacy involves comparing two databases that differ by at most one row [11]. Differential Privacy is achieved if the probability of selecting any two rows from the databases is the same or worse than a coin flip [12]. This effectively removes the possibility of a background knowledge attack since the likelihood of picking any two rows is the same, regardless of what an individual knows about the data set. Specifically, we explore ϵ-differential privacy. To achieve ϵ-differential privacy, noise is added among the rows of a database using a Laplace distribution, according to the value of ϵ [12]. As ϵ is increased, the utility of the data is increased and privacy is decreased. As ϵ is reduced, the opposite happens and we achieve better privacy at the cost of losing utility [12]. Generally, Differential Privacy is superior to many other data privacy techniques such as k-anonymity [10], t-closeness [13], l-diversity [14] and their variants since Differential Privacy provides privacy and removes the possibility of a background knowledge attack, which all of these other techniques are susceptible to [15]. ϵ-Differential Privacy can also be extended to group privacy or individuals that contribute more than one row to the data set. Although Differential Privacy is a valuable concept and an admirable goal, it is not perfectly private. To be perfectly private would mean not releasing any data at all, ever. However in order to be productive, as a society we need to agree that the benefits of sharing some data outweigh the risks [12].

B. Private Information Retrieval

Private Information Retrieval (PIR) is a concept that is proposed in 1997 by Chor et al. [16]. The authors of this original paper realize that although there are many techniques developed to protect the privacy of data stored in a database, there are no techniques to protect the users that query the database. For example, if a user queried the database about some points of interest at some location, this implies that the user has some interest and may be heading to this location, or is already at this location. The authors achieved this private information retrieval by encrypting the user's query and giving the database the encrypted query. Then, the database will run some computation on the encrypted query and return an encrypted result. Here the database has no idea what has been queried or returned. A recent improvement on PIR for vehicles is known as PIR in Vehicle Location-Based Services (VLBS) proposed by Tan et al. [17] in 2018. This technique is designed to work well in the vehicular setting and is much faster than standard PIR. PIR in VLBS allows the user to filter the queried data set such that privacy is maintained. This is achieved by partitioning the queryable area into segments and assigning Points of Interest (POI) to certain areas based on their distance from a road segment. The size of the groups of POI are always the same, and since the query and response are encrypted, there is no way for the adversary to know what data have been requested or returned.

C. Garbled Circuit

Garbled Circuits are a relatively old concept presented by Yao in 1986 [18]. This concept provides an environment for secure (and therefore private) computation between two parties, where the receiving party (evaluator) is only able to perform computation on the encrypted result of the sending party's (garbler's) message. In circuit logic, a set of gates can be mapped to a simple truth table, where the gates represent logical operations. In a garbled circuit however, the mapping to the truth table is rearranged by the garbler. The garbler will take input values to a gate and encrypt them, so that the other communicating party does not know the input. The garbler will perform the gate operation on the input values prior to encryption to obtain the output value. Then, each encrypted input is paired with the corresponding output and the value is stored together in the re-arranged truth table. Figure 1 follows from [19], here W_X^Y is mapped from $X = Y$, so $W_G^0 = (g = 0)$:

g	e	output $g \wedge e$		garbled output		permuted garbled output
0	0	0		$\mathsf{Enc}(H(W_G^0, W_E^0), 0)$		$\mathsf{Enc}(H(W_G^0, W_E^1), 0)$
0	1	0	$\Rightarrow$	$\mathsf{Enc}(H(W_G^0, W_E^1), 0)$	$\Rightarrow$	$\mathsf{Enc}(H(W_G^1, W_E^1), 1)$
1	0	0		$\mathsf{Enc}(H(W_G^1, W_E^0), 0)$		$\mathsf{Enc}(H(W_G^0, W_E^0), 0)$
1	1	1		$\mathsf{Enc}(H(W_G^1, W_E^1), 1)$		$\mathsf{Enc}(H(W_G^1, W_E^0), 0)$

Figure 1. The garbling of an AND gate [19]

Now the evaluator would like to decrypt exactly one ciphertext from the garbled truth table, to revel the values of g and e that correspond to W_G^g and W_E^e that the garbler has sent [19]. The evaluator also receives the garbled gate from the garbler. But there are some restrictions on this decryption. The evaluator cannot be sent both W_E^0 and W_E^1 because then the evaluator can decrypt two ciphertexts [19]. The evaluator can not ask for which specific value they want either since they do not want the garbler to know which specific value they are after. This is called oblivious transfer and allows the evaluator to find out only W_E^e without revealing e to the garbler. The evaluator also needs to know when decryption succeeds and when it does not in order for this technique to succeed [19].

The next section will describe techniques that we consider will achieve vehicle location privacy, as well as some attacks and mitigation that can be imposed on these techniques.

V. Overview of Privacy Techniques and Proposed Attacks, with Solutions

We evaluate the techniques using three metrics. As shown in Table I, each metric is concerned with location privacy at a different stage in our model. The three metrics are: location privacy at traffic update, location privacy at traffic storage (or trajectory privacy) and location privacy at traffic query. The number of ticks represents the effectiveness of a technique for a particular privacy concern. Table II shows that each technique uses a slightly different model in terms of which communicating party is identified as the adversary. In certain techniques, the Cloud is the adversary, and the vehicle is an innocent user. In other techniques, the Cloud is trusted and the vehicle is not trusted.Some models may also involve a trusted third party, in addition to the Cloud and the vehicle. This third party is commonly referred to as a Trusted Authority (TA) in IoV literature.

TABLE I. Location Privacy Metrics in IoV for Traffic Condition Service

Privacy Concerns	*Dynamic Pseudonym*	*Differential Privacy*	*Private Information Retrival*	*Trusted Agency + Garbled Circuit*
Location Privacy at Traffic Update	✓			✓
Location Privacy at Traffic Storage	✓	✓✓		✓✓
Location Privacy at Traffic Query	✓		✓✓	✓✓

TABLE II. Location Privacy Parties in IoV for Traffic Condition Service

Parties	*Dynamic Pseudonym*	*Differential Privacy*	*Private Information Retrival*	*Trusted Agency + Garbled Circuit*
Third Party Agency	Trusted	N/A	N/A	Trusted
Cloud	Not Trusted	Trusted	Not Trusted	Not Trusted
Vehicle	Trusted	Not Trusted	Trusted	Trusted

A. Dynamic Pseudonyms

The first technique we examine involves the use of pseudonyms. The Cloud is the adversary and the vehicle and TA are trusted. This technique is centered around the idea of protecting a user's location by mapping their real identifier to a constant pseudonym that is generated by the TA. Here, the TA is used as an intermediary between the vehicle and the Cloud. However, this technique is susceptible to Attack 1. So location privacy is not adequately preserved here.

An alternative pseudonym technique that is also considered is the dynamic pseudonym, where, a user's real identifier is mapped to a list of pseudonyms that change at a predetermined time, and therefore appear different to the Cloud. Only the

TA is able to determine the real identity of the mapped pseudonyms. This technique is, however, susceptible to Attack 2. Therefore the pseudonym approach does not achieve location privacy for an individual.

B. Differential Privacy

The second technique we consider involves adding Differential Privacy to the Cloud that stores our data. In this model, we have only the Cloud and the vehicle involved in communications, where the Cloud is trusted however the vehicle/ user is not. Here the user will attempt to gain information about other users using seemingly harmless queries. As is standard in Differential Privacy, noise is added to the database rows to add privacy. However if an adversarial user queries the Cloud regarding traffic information in various locations they may be able to obtain a picture of what the general traffic concentration appears to be. Another weakness of this technique is the fact that vehicles are constantly checking in their locations to the Cloud with updates. This breaks Differential Privacy if the Cloud is not dynamically updating its records. Making an attack similar to Attack 1 or Attack 2 viable.

C. Private Information Retrieval

For our third technique, we explore a special case of Private Information Retrieval. PIR in VLBS can be utilized to provide privacy at query time. Here the Cloud is the adversary and the vehicle is trusted. Since the queries to the Cloud are encrypted, the Cloud has no way of knowing what the vehicle's are querying. However, the Cloud attempts to figure this out based on which rows are returned after a query. But according to PIR, a group of the same number of rows are returned each time a query is asked making it impossible to pin point exactly what the vehicle was querying about. However, if a vehicle chooses to update the Cloud at any point, its exact location will be revealed to the adversary. As a consequence of this, the vehicle's location privacy at storage is not maintained since the vehicle checks in to update its location over time.

D. Garbled Circuit

Finally, our fourth technique involves using a garbled circuit in conjunction with a TA. This technique attempts to satisfy each metric that we are evaluating with. In this model, the Cloud is our adversary and is untrusted once again, and the vehicle/ user is trusted, along with the TA. Consider the situation where the vehicle updates the Cloud with its location. The Cloud only receives encrypted data to store and cannot directly decrypt this without some assistance from the TA, which does not expose the location of the vehicle without the vehicle's permission. On this same note, location privacy of a vehicle is preserved over the long term as the data stored is encrypted. On a query about traffic related to a certain location, the Cloud is not aware of the value that is being requested for. Therefore location privacy is preserved once again. This technique seems to be the most private, however it is also the most complex.

VI. EXPERIMENT

As shown in section 2, row based location data is susceptible to attacks that may personalize sensitive location data. In our experiment section, we investigate Differential Privacy to centrally stored location data in the same real dataset used by Yin et al. [6]. The location check in data Gowalla was a location-based social network that was active between 2007 and 2012. The dataset includes a total of 6,442,890 check-ins of these users over the period of Feb 2009 and Oct 2010. Figure 2 shows a snapshot of the Gowalla dataset. Although

Userid	time stamp	lat	long	location id
0	2010-10-19T23:55:27Z	30.2359091	-97.79514	22847
0	2010-10-18T22:17:43Z	30.269103	-97.749395	420315
0	2010-10-17T23:42:03Z	30.255731	-97.763386	316637
0	2010-10-17T19:26:05Z	30.2634181	-97.757597	16516
0	2010-10-16T18:50:42Z	30.2742919	-97.740523	5535878
0	2010-10-12T23:58:03Z	30.2615994	-97.758581	15372
0	2010-10-12T22:02:11Z	30.2679096	-97.749312	21714

Figure 2. Snapshot of Gowalla Dataset

the dataset is not strictly IoV data, it shares similairty with IoV data by having location, timestamp, and ID in each row. It should be mentioned that since this dataset is not strictly traffic data and does not necessarily have continuous timestamps for each user by minutes or hours, this issue can be rectified by generalizing timestamps to dates and then building a contingency table with missing dates, as we will discuss in a later subsection.

We generalize individual locations to location groups by splitting the geometric plane using $k-d$ tree such that each group has roughly the same amount of locations. Each row of the aggregated data includes timestamp, location group, and unique count of users. We then apply Laplace noise to the user count to achieve $\epsilon-$Differential Privacy for the location data. The programs are written in Python, and the experiments are run on a MacBook Pro with 2.3 GHz Intel Core i5 and 8 GB 2133 MHz LPDDR3.

A. Data Cleaning

After plotting the normalized Gowalla locations, we notice some outliers that affect the generalization of geometric distribution. As shown in Figure 3, a few outliers at the topright corner greatly affects the performance of $k-d$ tree.

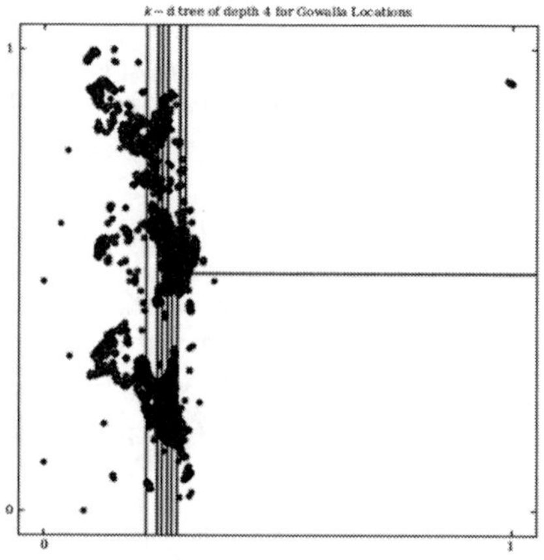

Figure 3. Gowalla Locations With Outliers

We remove these outliers by removing 37 locations with large z scores, a statistical metric of a value relative to the sample mean and standard deviation. Figure 4 shows the plot of normalized Gowalla locations after the outliers are removed.

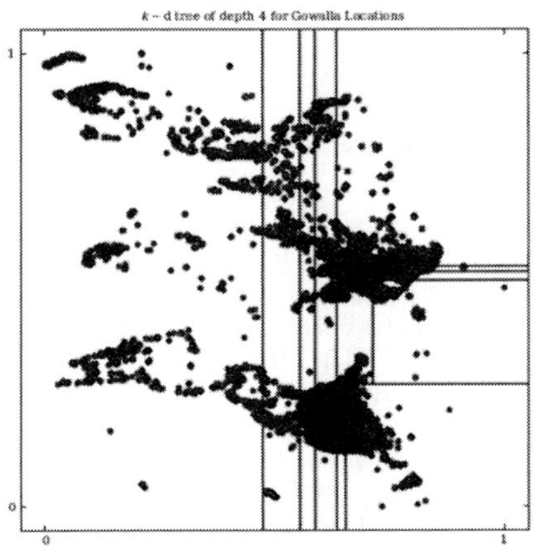

Figure 4. Normalized Gowalla Locations Without Outliers

B. Building Contingency Table

In order to prepare a differentially private dataset for sharing and publishing, it is important to make sure a contingency table is built on top of the original generalized data and before Differential Privacy is applied [20]. For our data, building a contingency table means to create continuous dates for each location group and unique user combination. To do this, we calculate the minimum and maximum dates in the dataset, and add missing dates to all location groups with user count set to 0. Note that the original dataset has timestamps based on hours and minutes, however it is less common for a user to visit a location on an hourly basis and more common for the user to visit the location at different times of different dates. Therefore, we generalize the timestamp to dates to avoid excessive numbers of rows being added to the contingency table, which affects the data utility.

C. Generalization

We experimented different depths of 4, 5, 6 of the $k - d$ tree for the generalization of locations. Through evaluation we determine that depth 6 is proper for the group generalization as it provides more granularity. After each location is assigned a group ID, the original dataset is aggregated to a dataset with dates, location groups, and count of unique users at the date/location group combination. The data cleaning and generalization shrinks 6,442,890 checkins to 40,128 aggregated records. Figure 5 shows the generalized location data of the Gowalla dataset.

D. Differential Privacy

For each generalized data point, Lap($1/\epsilon$) is added to the user counts. In our experiments, we tried $\epsilon = 0.1, 0.5, 1.0$. Figure 6 shows $0.1-$differentially private Gowalla dataset. From the first glance, this dataset shares similar distributions as the original dataset. At a closer look, we can notice the noise added to each location group.

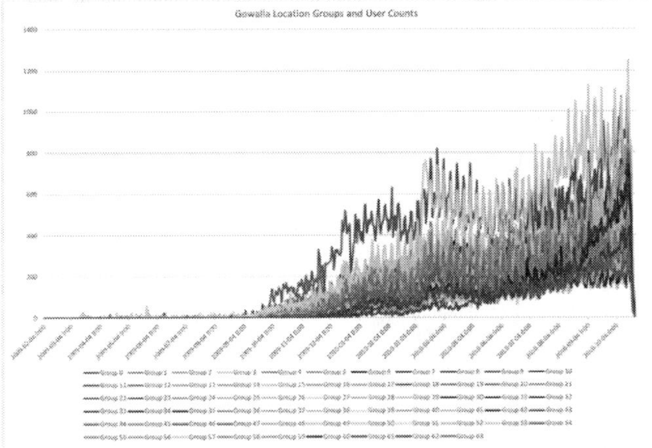

Figure 5. Gowalla Location Groups and User Counts ($k - d$ tree depth = 6)

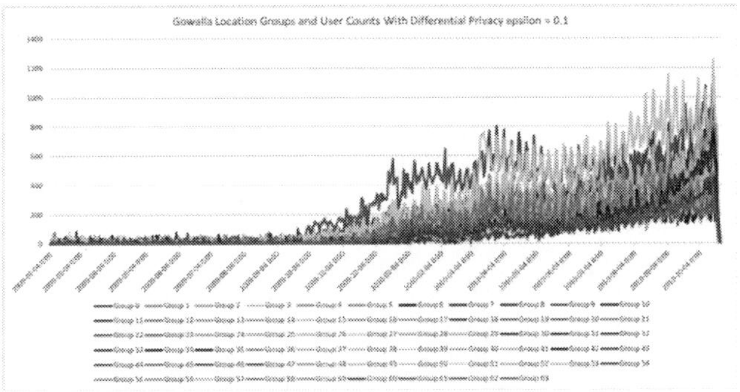

Figure 6. Gowalla Location Groups and User Counts with Differential Privacy ($k - d$ tree depth = 6)

VII. Evaluation and Analysis of Results

A. Data Quality

In order to quantify the utility of our differentially private dataset, we measure and compare the regression accuracy of a traffic predictor when it is trained by the original dataset and the differentially private dataset. This approach is similar to the evaluation of classification quality in Mohammed et al. [20]. We use an LSTM traffic predictor utilized in Fu et al. [21] and train two models using 2009-02-04 to 2010-08-31 of the original and differentially private datasets as training data respectively, and then we use the 2010-09-01 to 2010-10-23 of the original dataset as test data. The model is trained with a sliding window of 7 (representing one week) and iteration of 600. After successfully training our predictors, we measure

TABLE III. Location Group 63 Prediction Comparison of Different Training Models

Measurement	*Orig model*	*DP* ϵ = 0.1	*DP* ϵ = 0.5	*DP* ϵ = 1.0
Explained variance score	**0.713**	**0.670**	0.390	0.469
RMSE (root mean squared error)	**45.676**	**48.893**	56.583	50.343
R2 score	**0.513**	**0.442**	0.253	0.409

the regression accuracy of the predictors in terms of explained variance score, Root Mean Squared Error (RMSE) and R2 score using the metrics package of Python scikit-learn [22].

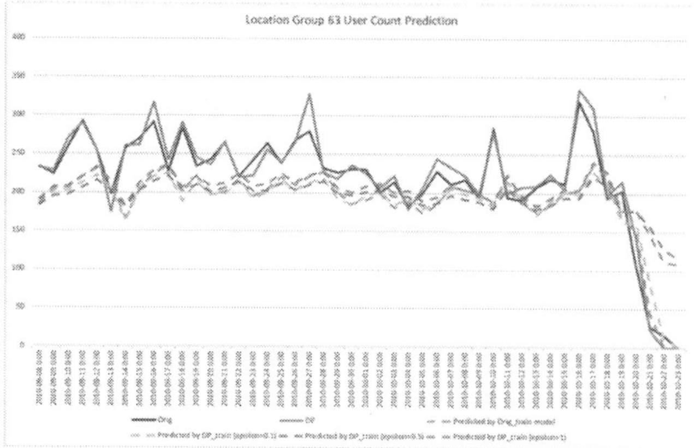

Figure 7. Location Group 63 Real Data vs. Prediction

Table III shows the comparison of predictions made by models trained by different versions of location data for Gowalla location group 63. We observe that the predictor trained with 0.1−differentially private data has very close accuracy to the model trained with original data. Figure 7 shows that in general, the predicted data by all DP-data-trained models are reasonable compared to the real data.

VIII. Conclusion and Future Work

In this paper, we conduct a thorough study of location privacy in IoV traffic condition service through investigation of potential attacks and mitigations. Based on this knowledge, we develop a novel overview of location privacy preservation scheme. Lastly, we develop a Differential Privacy strategy to centrally store location data and demonstrate the preservation of data utility quantitatively.

There is a lot of potential for future work. Section V leaves many avenues open for pursuing research on the techniques we have proposed here. Private Information Retrieval can be studied much more extensively to determine its overall effectiveness and to examine whether there is another variant of PIR or some existing technique coupled with PIR to satisfy location privacy using the three metrics designed in this section. Conducting some experiments on the TA and Garbled Circuit technique could also be an important step to implement a robust location privacy preserving technique as it provides the most utility and the most privacy of all models observed in this paper.

References

[1] E. Borcoci, From Vehicular Ad-hoc Networks to Internet of Vehicles, 2017, URL: https://www.iaria.org/conferences2017/ [accessed: 2020-06-01].

[2] M. Raya and J.-P. Hubaux, "Securing vehicular ad hoc networks," Journal of computer security, vol. 15, no. 1, 2007, pp. 39–68.

[3] F. Wang, Y. Xu, H. Zhang, Y. Zhang, and L. Zhu, "2flip: a two-factor lightweight privacy-preserving authentication scheme for vanet," IEEE Transactions on Vehicular Technology, vol. 65, no. 2, 2016, pp. 896–911.

[4] H. Zhong, S. Han, J. Cui, J. Zhang, and Y. Xu, "Privacy-preserving authentication scheme with full aggregation in vanet," Information Sciences, vol. 476, 2019, pp. 211–221.

[5] W. U. Hassan, S. Hussain, and A. Bates, "Analysis of privacy protections in fitness tracking social networks -or- you can run, but can you hide?" in Proceedings of the 27th USENIX Security Symposium. USENIX, 2018, pp. 497–512.

[6] C. Yin, J. Xi, R. Sun, and J. Wang, "Location privacy protection based on differential privacy strategy for big data in industrial internet of things," IEEE Transactions on Industrial Informatics, vol. 14, no. 8, 2018, pp. 3628–3636.

[7] "Zuckerberg says facebook working with fbi to investigate security breach," URL: https://www.cnbc.com/video/2018/09/28/zuckerberg-says-facebook-working-with-fbi-to-investigate-security-breach.html [accessed: 2020-06-01].

[8] "Marriott data breach is traced to chinese hackers as u.s. readies crackdown on beijing," URL: https://www.nytimes.com/2018/12/11/us/politics/trump-china-trade.html [accessed: 2020-06-01].

[9] "Usps site exposed data on 60 million users," URL: https://krebsonsecurity.com/2018/11/usps-site-exposed-data-on-60-million-users [accessed: 2020-06-01].

[10] L. Sweeney, "k-anonymity: A model for protecting privacy," International Journal of Uncertainty, Fuzziness and Knowledge-Based Systems, vol. 10, no. 05, 2002, pp. 557–570.

[11] C. Dwork, "Differential privacy," Automata, languages and programming, 2006, pp. 1–12.

[12] ——, "Differential privacy: A survey of results," in International conference on theory and applications of models of computation. Springer, 2008, pp. 1–19.

[13] N. Li, T. Li, and S. Venkatasubramanian, "t-closeness: Privacy beyond k-anonymity and l-diversity," in 2007 IEEE 23rd International Conference on Data Engineering. IEEE, 2007, pp. 106–115.

[14] A. Machanavajjhala, J. Gehrke, D. Kifer, and M. Venkitasubramaniam, "l-diversity: Privacy beyond k-anonymity," in 22nd International Conference on Data Engineering (ICDE'06). IEEE, 2006, pp. 24–24.

[15] D. Kifer, "Attacks on privacy and definetti's theorem," in Proceedings of the 2009 ACM SIGMOD International Conference on Management of data. ACM, 2009, pp. 127–138.

[16] B. Chor, O. Goldreich, E. Kushilevitz, and S. Madhu, "Private information retrieval," 1997, pp. 0–20.

[17] Z. Tan, C. Wang, M. Zhou, and L. Zhang, "Private information retrieval in vehicular location-based services," IEEE, 2018, pp. 56–61.

[18] A. C.-C. Yao, "How to generate and exchange secrets," in 27th Annual Symposium on Foundations of Computer Science (sfcs 1986). IEEE, 1986, pp. 162–167.

[19] S. Yakoubov, "A gentle introduction to yao's garbled circuits," 2017, pp. 1–12, URL: http://web.mit.edu/sonka89/www/papers/2017ygc.pdf [accessed: 2020-06-01].

[20] N. Mohammed, R. Chen, B. Fung, and P. S. Yu, "Differentially private data release for data mining," in Proceedings of the 17th ACM SIGKDD international conference on Knowledge discovery and data mining. ACM, 2011, pp. 493–501.

[21] R. Fu, Z. Zhang, and L. Li, "Using lstm and gru neural network methods for traffic flow prediction," in 2016 31st Youth Academic Annual Conference of Chinese Association of Automation (YAC). IEEE, 2016, pp. 324–328.

[22] "scikit-learn metrics," URL: https://scikit-learn.org/stable/modules/model_evaluation.html#regression-metrics [accessed: 2020-06-01].

Evaluation of a Multi-agent Anomaly-based Advanced Persistent Threat Detection Framework

Georgi Nikolov
Royal Military Academy
Brussels, Belgium
Email: g.nikolov@cylab.be

Thibault Debatty
Royal Military Academy
Brussels, Belgium
Email: t.debatty@cylab.be

Wim Mees
Royal Military Academy
Brussels, Belgium
Email : w.mees@cylab.be

Abstract—**Cyber attacks have become a major factor in the world today and their effect can be devastating. Protecting corporate and government networks has become an increasingly difficult challenge, when new persistent malware infections can remain undetected for long periods of time. In this paper, we introduce the Multi-agent ranking framework (MARK), a novel approach to Advanced Persistent Threat detection through the use of behavioral-analysis and pattern recognition. Such behavior-based mechanisms for discovering and eliminating new sophisticated threats are lacking in current detection systems, but research in this domain is gaining more importance and traction. Our goal is to take a on-hands approach in the detection by actively hunting for the threats, instead of passively waiting for events and alerts to signal abnormal behavior. We devise a framework that can be easily deployed as a stand-alone multi-agent system or to compliment many Security Information and Event Management systems. The MARK framework incorporates known and new beyond state-of-the-art detection techniques, in addition to facilitating incorporation of new data sources and detection agent modules through plug-ins. Throughout our testing and evaluation, impressive true detection rates and acceptable false positive rates were obtained, which proves the usefulness of the framework.**

Keywords–anomaly-based analysis; command & control channel; advanced persistent threat; aggregation.

I. Introduction

Corporate, government and military networks have often been prime targets for malicious actors and the current security solutions have proven not to be sufficient any longer. In recent years, these types of attacks have become more frequent and more sophisticated; using zero-day vulnerabilities and social engineering, the attackers can set a foothold in a network and work unnoticed for long periods of time. A recent example of a cyber-attack on a major scale is the one orchestrated on computer systems from Ukraine to the United States in 2017 [1]. The attack hijacked a tax accountant package widely used in Ukraine and distributed the malware via its update mechanism, targeting the supply-chain, a common Advanced Persistent Threat (APT) attack technique.

Currently major networks are protected via Security Information and Event Management (SIEM) systems, collecting log events and alerts and then correlating them; Splunk [2] or IBM QRadar [3] are some prominent examples of such systems. Useful as they may be, these detection solutions often focus on the initial attack and less on the possible persistency of a threat as they lack understanding of (1) the complex behavior of Advanced Persistent Threats (APT) and (2) the precision needed to correlate prolonged malicious activity that may take place over multiple hosts over prolonged periods of time. Our paper introduces the MARK framework, with the goal to detect APTs once they have established a foothold in a network. Contrary to the majority of currently established Intrusion Detection Systems (IDS) and their use of signature-based detection, focused on passive detection through the correlation of events and alerts, our system takes a more active approach by automating the data-driven threat hunting process. This type of detection approach has become more and more relevant, a lot of new research has been invested in new threat hunting methods [4]. The MARK framework accomplishes this by analysing data from multiple sources and searching for abnormal or suspicious behavior, through pattern recognition.

The rest of the paper is arranged as follows: Section II describes the design and methodology used for the implementation of the MARK framework. The detection agents that are used for the analysis are presented together with the aggregation and scoring system set in place. Section III presents the different steps in the evaluation of our framework and the results produced. Finally we conclude in Section IV and offer possible future avenues to advance our framework in Section V.

II. The Multi-Agent Ranking Framework

In this section, an overview of the Multi-Agent Ranking Framework is provided. The general goal and design of the framework is discussed, together with an explanation of the methodology used for the different agents and the score aggregation mechanism.

A. Goal

The MARK framework uses multiple agents to detect possible APTs, using behavioral analysis instead of the common knowledge-based approach, focused on signature analysis. Research into the subject of creating a modular behavior-based analysis has been conducted, such as the one proposed by [5] and [6]. In our project we combine domain knowledge with information collected from multiple agents about the behavior of possible threats and apply fuzzy logic to determine the possibility of malicious intent. We designed the framework as a multi-agent system that can be deployed on a centralized server, collecting raw data from multiple sources and correlating the findings.

Our framework is developed with the goal to be deployed as a stand-alone detection system, or complement currently available off-the-shelf SIEM systems, working in parallel with other detection tools, providing exponential benefits over an extended period of time. The implementation and integration of the MARK framework are shown in Figure 1.

The solid red arrow represents how the malicious actor can set-up the instructions which should be relayed to the infected machine inside the compromised network via a Command & Control (CnC) channel, represented by the dashed red arrow. This channel can be used by a malicious actor to send commands to the infected machine and receive responses, for example network reconnaissance information or exfiltrated data. In the majority of protected networks, the outbound traffic is restricted to only layer 7 channels, such as HTTP(S), SMTP or DNS. This means that any CnC channel must pass through the proxy choke point, denoted in blue. This is an important reason why our system focuses primarily on analysis of HTTP and SMTP proxy logs, as those are the most likely means to detect the CnC channel communication with the malicious server. The MARK framework continuously collects data from the proxy, alongside netflow data and end-point data, shown in green. All this information is fed to the MARK framework, analyzed, aggregated and then, using visualisation techniques, displayed to the domain expert for analysis. For a more in-depth look at how the system is developed, the code for the MARK framework is available at [7]. The agents, described

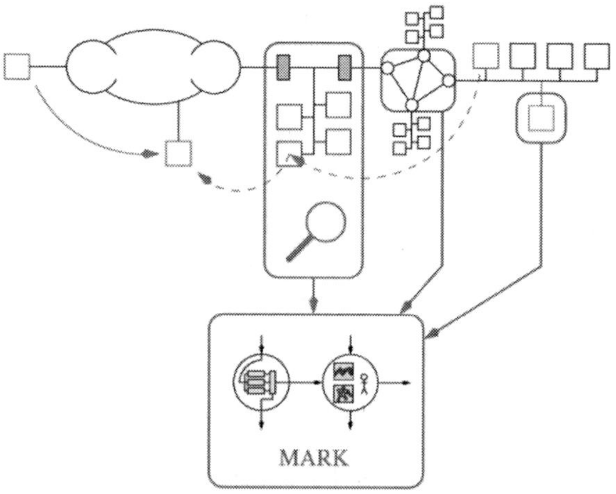

Figure 1. MARK framework diagram

in Section II-B, work independently from each other and their results are aggregated. Afterwards a ranking of the possible threats is created, as shown in Section II-C. Our goal is to observe the behavior of the different clients in the monitored network and based on a list of characteristics, the framework will decide the degree of suspiciousness a given connection has. The MARK framework is not intended to classify by itself what is a threat and what is benign, but to combine the detection system with the knowledge of a domain expert in analysing and filtering the results to come to these conclusions. This is enabled through:

- new agents can be configured for different precision through parameterization and new ones can be added as plug-ins
- using "detection through visualization" implementing Visual Analytics techniques [8]
- a whitelisting option is present so the analyst can eliminate known harmless domains that may have been flagged as false positives

B. Agents

The MARK framework is designed to be data agnostic; different data sources can be added with minimal difficulty, and the analysis capabilities can be extended, via a plug-in system, with new detection techniques. In our current implementation, we have multiple detection agents for analysis of HTTP logs and SMTP data. These agents are not meant to run on the client machines, but act as independent modules, that focus on specific behavioral characteristics of an APT. Through the analysis of these different characteristics, the agent's findings are aggregated so significant patterns can be discovered. Each agent can also be adapted through the use of parameters, specific for each detection technique. The characteristics that we focus on are the following:

- number of unique domains per IP and visa versa
- frequency and periodicity of the connection
- geo-positioning of connection's server
- upload size and POST count
- "lonely" single connections and time anomalies that signify abnormal behavior
- unreachable server connections

C. Scoring and Aggregation

In the area of intrusion detection, aggregation can be applied for a number of reasons. A first motivation can be to obtain a condensed view of the outputs from a number of IDS sensors located at different positions in the network [9]. Another motivation can be to reduce the false alarm rate by modeling attacks and correlating observed events with known attack scenarios or intrusion objectives [10]. In our APT detection system however, potential evidence about a single event needs to be accumulated, evidence that is produced by a number of independent agents, each verifying some a priori defined hypothesis. Such a malware behavior hypothesis expresses a specific part of the domain knowledge of a human network security expert, who will typically use vague natural language terms when expressing his knowledge. For that reason the knowledge is represented in the form of fuzzy sets and fuzzy expert system rules. The fuzzy set is defined as a pair *(U,m)* with membership function:

$$m : U \rightarrow [0, 1] \quad (1)$$

For each evidence score produced, the suspiciousness of the evidence x is defined by:

$$0 < m(x) < 1 \quad (2)$$

In order to combine the fuzzy evidence, produced by the different agents, we use the Ordered Weighted Averaging (OWA) operator, introduced by Yager [11], that has been used successfully for a number of evidence aggregation problems in the area of network security [12]. The OWA operator is defined by the function:

$$F(a_1, ..., a_n) = \sum_{j=1}^{n} w_j b_j \quad (3)$$

for a collection of weights $W = [w_1, ..., w_n]$ and where b_j is the largest j^{th} of the scores a_n.

At the end of the aggregation, a ranked list of possible threats is compiled, where false positives are ranked lower and the true positives are elevated.

III. EVALUATION THROUGH SIMULATED SCENARIOS

To determine the detection capabilities of the MARK framework, three scenarios were developed and simulated log files were generated to be analyzed by the system. This section discusses how we simulate scenarios using real world data and documented APTs, that are modeled and injected into the real world log files. The flow of the aggregation and evaluation is shown in Figure 2.

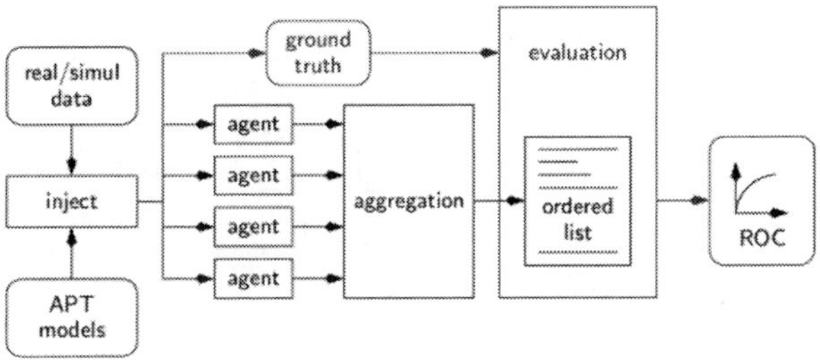

Figure 2. MARK evaluation diagram

A. Scenario configuration file

We test and validate the MARK framework through the use of simulated scenarios and each scenario is defined through a configuration file with the following parameters:

- predetermined duration of the scenario
- predetermined number of clients and respective IPs
- real world data used to generate the logs to be analyzed
- set number of attacks, which have:
  - predetermined victim (internal IP that is considered infected)
  - type of attack
  - characteristics of the attack

When each scenario is generated, a "ground truth" file is also created that holds information about the attacks that have been injected. This "ground truth" file is used during the evaluation to determine if the attacks have been successfully detected and placed high in the ranked list.

1) Dataset used: Recent real world log files, provided by various agencies, are used to simulate our scenarios and keep them as close as possible to real world situations. Each log file, originally in JSON proxy format, consists of all the HTTP connections from a single day. The proxy logs are transformed from JSON format to SQUID format, but other formats can easily be supported by the framework. The specifications of the real world datasets used for evaluation, are shown in "Table I". The scenario configuration file is read to determine the start date, end date and the IP addresses of the network. A mapping is done between the real world IP addresses from the proxy logs and the IP addresses to be used in the scenario.

TABLE I. REAL WORLD DATASET SPECIFICATIONS

Original Format	real world proxy logs
Transformed Format	Squid logs
Number of Log Files	106
Size	336.3 GB

2) Whitelisting: While running the scenarios, whitelisting is used to remove known no-threat servers from the results. This is done for two reasons:

1) Known servers such as facebook/google/etc. have services that constantly send requests to their servers in a periodic manner, which can cause false detection (ex. facebook groups, google analytics, windows live)
2) Known adwares have similar behaviors to APTs, where periodic connection is established to the ad-server, which can also be regarded as a false positive detection.

For the preliminary analysis we use two whitelists:

- **Whitelist.txt** - holds a regex of known non-threat domains which have produced an evidence. After analysis they have been considered harmless
- **1Hosts_Pro_Domains.txt** - a compilation of 217.530 known adware domains [13]

B. Simulated Scenarios

A number of attacks are simulated and injected in the real world log files to act as our simulated network activity. These logs serve to simulate the background traffic that occurs daily in any given network and is used by malicious actors to obfuscate their actions. The injected attacks range from basic periodic attacks to high complexity real world APTs such as the Trojan Nap APT [14], the Regin APT [15] and Careto APT [16]. These APTs are used as baseline and modified to generate synthetic APTs with variable behavior through parameterization, where a variable density of attacks is defined for each scenario. In such a manner the framework's detection capabilities can be tested with varying degrees of difficulty.

For the sake of brevity we will showcase the characteristics of one of the scenarios used.

1) Scenario 1: The first scenario consists of multiple hosts inside a network that have been infected and a static, periodic CnC channel has been established between them and an outside server.

2) Scenario 2: The second scenario uses state models that simulate real world APTs, with high density through the use of outbound connections with high periodicity.

3) Scenario 3: In the third generated scenario, the duration is doubled and a larger number of clients are used. State models of real world APTs are used, but lower APT density is defined through lower and varying periodicity. The characteristics of Scenario 3 are shown in "Table II" and the generated scenario variations are shown in "Table III".

TABLE II. SCENARIO 3 SPECIFICATIONS

File Format	text file
Logline Format	Squid logs
Subnet	10.0.0.1 - 10.0.0.249
Number of Attacks	10
Average Running Time	90 hours

TABLE III. SCENARIO 3 GENERATED LOGFILES

Name	Lines	Unique Client-Server pairs
scenario3.1	2302306	97230
scenario3.2	2208271	91528
scenario3.3	2619919	93360
scenario3.4	2867952	98962
scenario3.5	2590393	96000
scenario3.6	2994435	106286
scenario3.7	2453249	89857
scenario3.8	2697416	102319

C. Iterative Evaluation

To evaluate our findings, each scenario is run multiple times, where each time we run a different variant of the scenario with different modeled attacks and varying parameters. The evaluation happens in multiple:

1) review the results generated by the individual agents
2) evaluation of the precision of the OWA operator weights
3) generate the Receiver Operand Characteristics (ROC) and Area Under the Curve (AUC) for each scenario variation using the produced ranked list
4) compute the amount of data a domain specialist has to manually analyze to discover all true threats

1) Agent Evaluation: Each agent is responsible for a specific characteristic analysis and presents different paradigms. We can evaluate the results generated by comparing them to the already known behavior of the generated APTs and further analyze other highly ranked connections that might be of importance. To showcase how the different agents are evaluated, the output of the Frequency Agent is presented.

Frequency Agent: As with other agents, a set of specific parameters exists that can be adapted to fine-tune the detection rate of the agent. The Frequency agent is defined through the following parameters:

- time window of analysis, by default set to 24 hours
- sampling interval, set to 2 seconds
- minimum coverage by the peaks detected, modeled using fuzzy logic parameters set to $[0.1, 0.5, 0, 1]$
- peak threshold, set to 1.3
- suspiciousness score, modeled using fuzzy logic parameters set to $[1.3, 2, 0, 1]$

First the periodicity is determined through the computation of a Frequency Spectrum using a Fast Fourier Transformation (FTT) and further removing unnecessary noise data as shown in Figure 3. Through this type of visualization, it is clear that a periodic frequency is present. Any peaks under the threshold (blue line) are considered noise and disregarded. As with all detection agents, the threshold selected is adapted manually for the highest performance. A Time Sequence is also generated as shown in Figure 4, to better visualise if a periodicity is present. Comparing the results to the "ground truth" can show if adjustment of the parameters is needed for better precision.

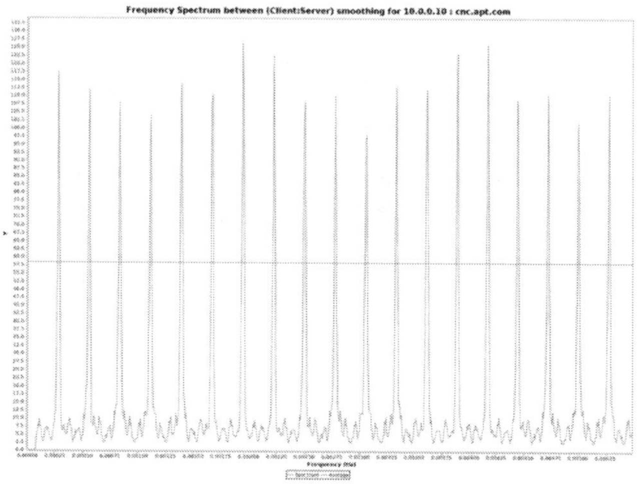

Figure 3. Frequency Spectrum between (Client:Server) smoothing for 10.0.0.10 : cnc.apt.com

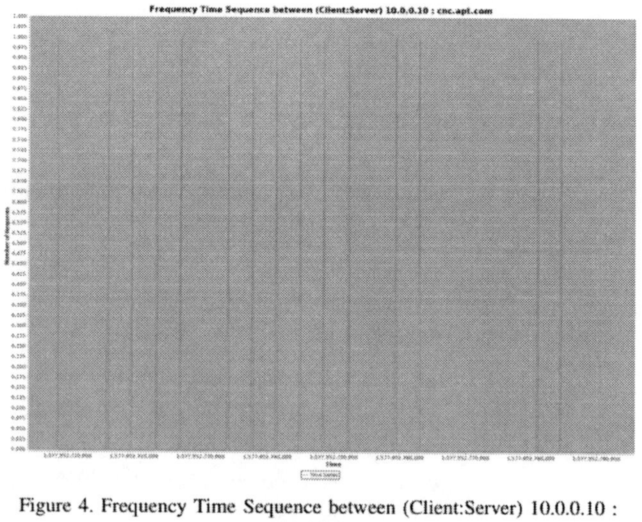

Figure 4. Frequency Time Sequence between (Client:Server) 10.0.0.10 : cnc.apt.com

2) Scatterplot Evaluation: By plotting the highest and the second highest scores for each tuple client-server, using a scatterplot, we can evaluate if the weights used in our OWA aggregation are precise or if they need to be adjusted. A scatterplot generated for one simulated scenarios is shown in Figure

5. The weights used for the evaluation are $[0.2, 0.4, 0.3, 0.1]$, where the highest produced score is assigned a lower score to prevent agents that are more active and produce a large amount of evidence to generate high quantities of false positives. The

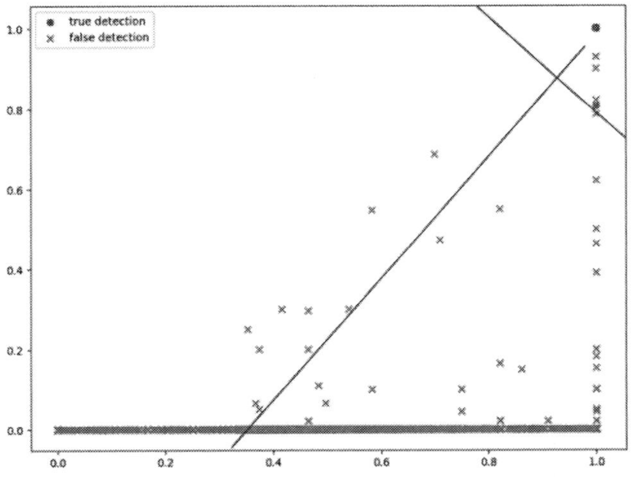

Figure 5. Example Scatterplot Scenario 2.6

true detection scores are all situated in the top right corner of the graph, signifying that both the highest and the second highest scores given by the detection agents were high. The majority of false detection are placed on the bottom, as a score for them has been generated only by one of the agents, where the other one didn't qualify them as suspicious.

The goal is to find a separation line and its slope in such a way that all true detection is above the line and as many possible false detection are situated under the line. To do that, we first need to calculate the blue line and rotate it 90° to get the function describing the black line and its slope. A number of false positives will always be included above the separation line, but that number can be minimized.

3) Boxplot and ROC: To evaluate our ranked list and the precision of our detection, we compute ROC and calculate the AUC. The ROC is a graphical representation that illustrates the diagnostic capabilities of a detection system. It is created by plotting the true positive rate (true detection) against the false positive rate (false alarm). The goal is to have a ROC that climbs as fast as possible, which would signify that the true positives are encountered earlier in the list, ideally at the top of the ranked list.

The Area Under the Curve gives a score that allows us to easily evaluate and compare the performance of the framework across multiple scenarios. The closer to 1 the AUC is, the better is the performance. All the calculated ROC and AUC for Scenario 3, described in Section III-B3, are shown in Figure 6. Sub-figure (a) shows the results when no whitelisting was used. For comparison, in sub-figure (b) the results when whitelisting has been applied to the generated ranked lists are shown. It is important to note that the results become better as we embody the role of the domain expert and analyze the entries of the ranked list.

In the Boxplots presented in Figure 7, the distribution of the AUC values calculated for our scenarios is presented. The results show a high detection rate, though the results are not tightly grouped. By applying whitelisting the resulting median is higher and lower variation in results is present. This signifies that our results become more homogeneous and even though in each scenario and its variations the attacks were parameterized differently, generally all attacks were ranked high and close together.

4) Manual analysis of the generated data: The final step is to consider the amount of entries a domain expert has to go through manually, to be able to detect all possible infections. As we see in the results presented in Table IV, with some exceptions, 100% of all attacks have been ranked in the top 20. This means that an analyst would need to analyze 20 entries, to be sure to go through all possible attacks in these particular scenarios. T his is highly important as our framework is designed to work hand in hand with a real world domain expert through the use of Visual Analytics and domain knowledge. It is imperative to minimize the time spent by the analyst on reviewing insignificant data and instead focus on information that is of greater importance.

TABLE IV. SCENARIO 3 NUMBER OF ENTRIES TO ANALYZE FOR 100% TRUE DETECTION

# List Entries	PD score Scenario 3 variants							
	3.1	**3.2**	**3.3**	**3.4**	**3.5**	**3.6**	**3.7**	**3.8**
10	0.4	0.9	0.9	0.9	0.6	0.4	0.9	0.9
20	0.9	1.0	1.0	1.0	1.0	0.9	1.0	1.0
30	1.0	1.0	1.0	1.0	1.0	1.0	1.0	1.0
40	1.0	1.0	1.0	1.0	1.0	1.0	1.0	1.0
50	1.0	1.0	1.0	1.0	1.0	1.0	1.0	1.0

IV. Conclusion

Throughout the research and development of the MARK framework, it became evident that the need for a robust system for APT detection is apparent. The system we developed offers a novel solution for the detection of attacks that typically offer greater challenge to detect, because of their unique nature.

During the evaluation we discovered the importance of setting the OWA operator weights correctly greatly benefices the correct ranking of the threats. Furthermore, by judiciously choosing the assigned weights, the amount of false positives can be lowered drastically.

The efficiency of the framework is demonstrated via the ROC and AUC computed for the different generated scenarios. It can be observed that the AUC is close to 1, signifying that all malicious connections have been discovered and placed at the top of the ranking list. This also leads to better visibility for the domain expert and significantly less time spent on analysis of large amounts of data.

V. Future Work

There are multiple avenues that can be examined for the future development of the MARK framework. First we will research and implement new detection techniques such as the use of graph theory for APT detection, as showcased in [17].

The aggregation of our evidences can be fine-tuned by incorporating the Weighted Ordered Weighted Averaging (WOWA) operator [18] and combine it with Machine Learning algorithms to augment the multi-criteria decision system [19].

Using WOWA we are not limited to assigning weights to the different scores produced by the agents, but also to the agents themselves.

Different network infrastructures have different specifications. As a future work we intend to implement Machine Learning algorithms and semi-supervised learning techniques [20], that will help configure the parameters used by the different detection agents depending on the environment wherein the MARK framework is deployed.

REFERENCES

[1] "Cyberattack hits ukraine then spreads internationally," https://www.nytimes.com/2017/06/27/technology/ransomware-hackers.html, retrieved: January, 2020.

[2] SPLUNK, "Siem, it operations, security, devops," https://www.splunk.com/, retrieved: January, 2020.

[3] IBM, "Ibm qradar siem," https://www.ibm.com/products/qradar-siem, retrieved: January, 2020.

[4] E. C. Thompson, "Threat hunting," in Designing a HIPAA-Compliant Security Operations Center. Springer, 2020, pp. 205–212.

[5] W. Mees, "Multi-agent anomaly-based apt detection," in Proceedings of Information Systems Technology Panel Symposium, 2012, pp. 1–10.

[6] P. Panero, L. Vlsan, V. Brillault, and I. C. Schuszter, "Building a large scale intrusion detection system using big data technologies," PoS, 2018, p. 014.

[7] RUCD. Mark framework. [Online]. Available: https://gitlab.cylab.be/cylab/mark

[8] R. F. Erbacher, "Intrusion behavior detection through visualization," in SMC'03 Conference Proceedings. 2003 IEEE International Conference on Systems, Man and Cybernetics. Conference Theme-System Security and Assurance (Cat. No. 03CH37483), vol. 3. IEEE, 2003, pp. 2507–2513.

[9] H. Debar and A. Wespi, "Aggregation and correlation of intrusion-detection alerts," in International Workshop on Recent Advances in Intrusion Detection. Springer, 2001, pp. 85–103.

[10] F. Cuppens, F. Autrel, A. Miege, and S. Benferhat, "Correlation in an intrusion detection process," in Internet Security Communication Workshop, 2002, pp. 153–172.

[11] R. R. Yager, "On ordered weighted averaging aggregation operators in multicriteria decisionmaking," IEEE Transactions on systems, Man, and Cybernetics, vol. 18, no. 1, 1988, pp. 183–190.

[12] O. Thonnard, W. Mees, and M. Dacier, "Addressing the attack attribution problem using knowledge discovery and multi-criteria fuzzy decision-making," in Proceedings of the ACM SIGKDD workshop on CyberSecurity and intelligence informatics, 2009, pp. 11–21.

[13] C. M. Barrett. Filterlists is the independent, comprehensive directory of filter and host lists for advertisements, trackers, malware, and annoyances. [Online]. Available: https://filterlists.com/

[14] M. Parkour. Trojan Nap aka kelihos/hlux - feb. 2013 status update. [Online]. Available: http://www.deependresearch.org/2013/02/trojan-nap-aka-kelihoshlux-feb-2013.html (2013)

[15] C. . I. S. Agency. Regin malware. [Online]. Available: https://us-cert.cisa.gov/ncas/alerts/TA14-329A (2014)

[16] K. Lab. Unveiling "Careto"-The Masked APT. [Online]. Available: https://d2538mqrb7brka.cloudfront.net/wp-content/uploads/sites/43/2018/03/20133638/unveilingthemask_v1.0.pdf (2014)

[17] T. Debatty, W. Mees, and T. Gilon, "Graph-based apt detection," in 2018 International Conference on Military Communications and Information Systems (ICMCIS). IEEE, 2018, pp. 1–8.

[18] V. Torra, "The wowa operator: a review," in Recent developments in the ordered weighted averaging operators: theory and practice. Springer, 2011, pp. 17–28.

[19] A. Croix, T. Debatty, and W. Mees, "Training a multi-criteria decision system and application to the detection of php webshells," in 2019 International Conference on Military Communications and Information Systems (ICMCIS). IEEE, 2019, pp. 1–8.

[20] R. A. R. Ashfaq, X.-Z. Wang, J. Z. Huang, H. Abbas, and Y.-L. He, "Fuzziness based semi-supervised learning approach for intrusion detection system," Information Sciences, vol. 378, 2017, pp. 484–497.

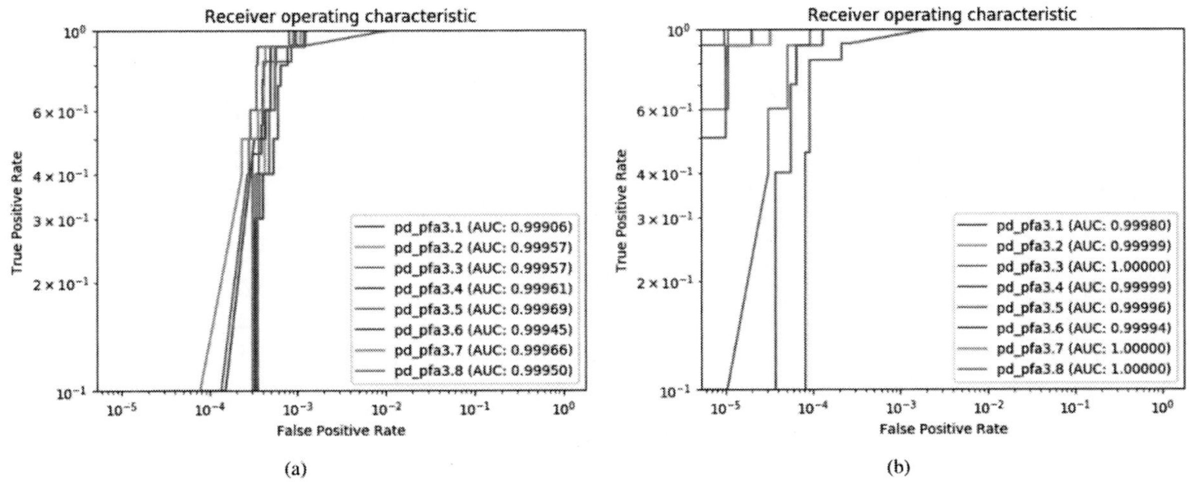

Figure 6. (a) Scenario 3 no whitelisting (b) Scenario 3 with whitelisting

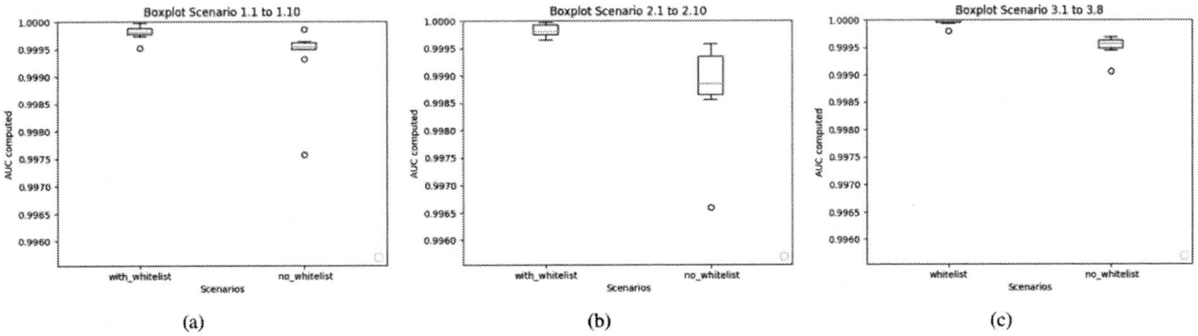

Figure 7. Boxplots for the computed AUC, without and with the use of whitelisting, for Scenario 1, Scenario 2 and Scenario 3